Religion Exposed:

Corruption, Deceit, & the Evil Spirits

Responsible

D1785425

By Alexander J. King

Contents

"Religion" is not the belief in a divine Creator or the spiritual engagement of a people to the supernatural. It is a man-made system of socio-political control and especially, it is a system deliberately designed for misuse. That misused institution of social and political power is religion, and it must be condemned.

PREFACE

The first thing I should tell you is that I am African, and that at the time of this book's completion, I am 22 years old. I wrote more than half of this book at around 18, and very ill, but more serious illnesses prevented me from continuing until after I turned 22 and managed to deal with some of the sicknesses myself. Still very ill, I pushed through to write what you are about to read, because I knew that the forces responsible for my sicknesses, intended for me to die before I could do great harm (to them) with the knowledge I possess. I typed away somewhat frantically, to reveal as many things as I could, and to present everything as clearly as possible, for I did not want the things I knew to die with me. At the time of publication this book will probably not be complete, but I know I would have written plenty. Deep down, I was very well aware that the architect of my fate would never allow for me to die by the hands of evil, but still, it is better to be safe than sorry.

As you will soon find out, this book is the **only one** of its kind, and many of the things you will learn from it are things you will not learn anywhere else. I did not write it to tell you what you wanted to hear, I wrote this book to impart crucial revelations to you. I have seen the dragon's face, and beyond that, I have seen its wings. I have seen the nations over which they span, and I have seen the egg from which the dragon has hatched. What I am about to share with you are delicate things of which certain people would rather have you live your life in complete ignorance. They are things which various forces have been fighting to keep hidden from you for many decades. Some of it common-sense to the wise and experienced, but most of it belonging to a sense not so common, even to the wise.

I will expose the lies to you, uncover the truths for you, and wake many of you from your stupors. I will show you how God and religion are on opposite ends of the fence, why God and science are inseparable, why religion is nonsense, and why atheism is a delusion.

I am a Christian worshiper of God the Creator, but I get along very well with people who identify themselves as atheists. Far better in fact, than I get along with religious people. Before I give you an overview of who I am, let me give you some very small background information:

I have been through an unusual and rather disturbing lot in my life. Being very different from most people, I have had a strong spiritual connection to the world from an early age. As a consequence, I am sensitised to spirits and their activity. I have had to endure the misfortune, and the fortune, of encountering spirits of many different kinds for a long time. I have seen ghosts, I have seen angels, and I have seen demons.

I have spoken to spirits of different kinds, but I have also had to fight spirits of different kinds. My encounters with evil spirits are due primarily to the fact that I have many enemies who think that an evil spirit can do to me what they fail to do on their own.

I have travelled in the spirit to places which truly opened my eyes, and to this day God continues to show me things I have struggled to accept at times. So surprising many of them have been, that I cannot share them here, simply because most people are not yet ready to understand them.

With this book I will inform you about what lurks behind the cloaked intentions of the people who are homing their skills in the art of deception against you. I will blow away dust and cobwebs to unveil truths behind the excess of amorphous information you are being given by television, by priests, the government, and the pseudo-science being pumped into the brains of the people around you.

If you would appreciate being host to a plethora of intellectually stimulating thoughts, then it is in your best interest to keep reading. If you desire knowledge which you will very rarely ever come across, then keep reading. Should you happen to call yourself an agnostic, a Muslim, a Hindu, an atheist, or anything else that you feel defines your perspective on theism, then indeed, you should keep reading.

If you are Christian, and have several doubts about the information you are being given in this life, or especially if you think you know it all, then you should keep reading, because I can guarantee that more than a few surprises await you. Remember: the intention of this book is never to shock or scare you, but only to help shine light onto the path of truth for you.

So allow me to introduce you to our confused world. Or at least, to reinforce any legitimate concerns you are sure to already be having about it. I will begin by discussing religious Christian people, but I can assure you that atheists, agnostics, Muslims, and every other type of person, will benefit equally (if not much more) from these texts, because I have a lot to say to each and every single one of you.

I will sometimes go off topic to explain some essential concepts, and at times, the things I reveal may scare you, but please understand that my motive is to inform, not to frighten. If I have scared you more than I have helped you find the truth, then it is probable that you did not read this book properly.

Everything I discuss in this book is interlinked and related. If something does not quite make sense to you at first, it soon will. Even if it requires a bit of investigation on your part (something for which I have supplied a very rich bibliography). Initially, I will take things easy with you (at least, relatively), but from the third chapter things will start getting much deeper, and I will go into the real issues. So let us begin:

Chapter One: INTRODUCTION

About Me

As a kid, I was very "unusual" (I still am). I was always that one boy who stood out as different from every other boy most people had ever met, and I was very much notorious for non-conformist (what some people would call "bad") behaviour throughout primary school. I remember making one teacher so angry, that she tried to throw me out the window of the three-story building our classroom was situated in. In retrospect, she was probably under the influence of an evil spirit.

I was such a "naughty" boy, that I had to skip through five years of school, and finished early. You see: Each and every time I was about to be expelled from one school, I would leave, and skip a grade or two before entering the next. My parents would then present papers to the new school claiming that I had just arrived from a foreign country, and needed a school to attend.

This was to circumvent the usual practice of schools calling a child's previous school to enquire about whether or not he/she was a trouble-maker, and whether or not it is advised that the new school enrol him/her. It was the only way to get a new school to accept me. I was the kind to never do any homework and I certainly would not bother to do any sort of studying, but I would pass all my subjects just fine, and that was working for me. I had no reason to change, and I still do not.

I was/am a pragmatic individual, and immensely resistant to the society's impressions. I was a high-energy, and troublesome boy right until I arrived in my final year of high school. Once there, I turned into what I will only describe as a partial introvert, due primarily to an unrelenting plague of spiritual problems.

Soon after hitting my 15th year of life, I was struck with a very unpleasant, and unsurprisingly wrong, diagnosis of bipolar disorder, along with what "healthcare professionals" claimed were the assorted symptoms. I was always very different from the other children my age, but it was after all the nonsense about my mental health that my inability, and unwillingness, to act and think like most people, became more apparent to me.

Since then, I have been thrust into a diverse assortment of anomalous circumstances. Of course I never did have bipolar disorder, and neither do most people who are given such a diagnosis, but it is far too easy for someone to say, "He is very different from everyone else, and behaves quite peculiarly, so he must be bipolar".

Like A.D.D. (attention deficit disorder) and A.D.H.D. (attention deficit hyperactivity disorder), bipolar disorder is a term so frequently abused by poorly qualified psychiatrists and psychologists, that in some places it is a much a common diagnosis as the flu virus. Unsurprisingly, being diagnosed with A.D.D. is the story of any child not predisposed to behaving like a quiet little sheep.

Children with active brains and inquisitive minds, are told to "Sit still", and "be quiet" in order to keep them from becoming individuals who authorities cannot control. This is no conspiracy by teachers to impede the growth of children (although there are in fact people in high places who conspire to that end), but the nullification of a child's creativity, individuality, and confidence, is typically the inevitable consequence of a traditional school system, and the ignorance of people who call themselves medical practitioners.

My parents were told that I had A.D.H.D. as well as Bipolar Disorder, and the people who told them that, attributed those mental disorders to my unwillingness to sit at any one place and read a text book or concentrate on boring repetitive things. The thought of being idle and staring at a page of uninteresting, and in my opinion, poorly conceived information, is something I just would not tolerate.

To this day, I have come across only 2 books which I deemed worthy of some of my time. Owing to this, is the fact that in my life, I have never (ever) read more than 10% of any book. Not once. Not even the two books I thought were worth my time. I prefer films (the very few which are decent) and videogames, because books in general, and in my opinion, are an inefficient avenue of information. For the record, so is the traditional school system. But you need not reveal to me the irony in the fact that here I am, typing away at a book of my very own, and expecting other people to read it.

Indeed, I have never been (and never will be) one to fit into what our world is readily forcing on us as people, and I have always been that one kid in every few thousand people who disagreed with a generally accepted notion or who displayed an entirely different approach to things. I can vividly recall the events of one such occasion:

I was in the second grade, seated on the floor with over 7000 other children in the school hall. We sang a song praising God as we did every Monday (as this was a Christian school), and subsequently were entertained by a few of the teachers' grievances about our bad behaviour on school grounds, as usual.

After everything else was said and done, one of the teachers (the one who would later try to throw me out of her classroom window) picked up a Bible and lectured us about the many creations God has brought into existence.

She pointed to a lizard and asked: "Who made that?"

We all shouted: "God!"

Then she pointed to a tree outside and asked "Who made that?"

We again shouted "God!"

She also pointed at all of us and asked "Who made you?"

We all shouted "God!"

Then, she pointed to her Bible and asked "Who made that?"

They unanimously shouted "God!"

I however, shouted "Man!" —A distinct sound they all picked up on and rapidly reacted in shock at. A universal gasp engulfed the atmosphere, and they looked in my direction as the teacher lifted her head slightly to observe and thereafter question, my assertion.

My explained reasoning was that mankind had written that book and printed it. However true its scriptures may or may not be, God did not actually make the Bible. The teacher then said to me that the Bible comprised of God's words, and so in effect was made by Him.

I of course still disagreed with her, but responded with a child's "Ok", lest there be dissension. Already I was quite well known by the entire school for my naughtiness, so being labelled a "heathen" in addition was not something I looked forward to.

My entire primary school life was in fact jam-packed with detentions, angry teachers, and quite a few children made to cry by the results of my mischievous pranks. I have even set records for the highest number of accumulated demerits at two of the primary schools I attended, which I have recently been informed, still stand today as unbroken records (Merits and demerits were a system of points given as punishment and reward).

It was never my intention to acquire infamy, but I got it anyway. Detention was my home, eccentricity was a prime characteristic of mine, and deceptively cold but extremely hot chili sauce was my staple food, as refrigerated chili sauce was cruelly put into our mouths at the aftercare centre I belonged to, whenever we were naughty.

My behaviour was so disconcerting to the authoritarian minds at the school I attended, that I was made to visit several psychologists, one of whom complained that I only liked doing "the easy puzzles". The other, prescribed some psychiatric medication for me, which was meant to sway me from my highly inquisitive and energetic disposition. And another one of them told my parents that my mind was "far too advanced" for someone my age, and recommended to my school, that I be placed in a "special class" (as per the school's facilities) because the current grade I was in could not "contain my mind".

Fortunately, my father was a highly knowledgeable pharmacist who knew better than to allow his son to take the snake-oil psychiatric drugs being given to school children, so he was quite pleased to see me throw the "medication" away. In the stead of psychiatric treatment, my parents opted for me to be placed in a special class, and in the second grade, that is where I went. A small group of other youngsters joined me. To my recollection the small class comprised of the following children, who arrived about a week apart from one another:

- The first child I can remember, was a very shy, slim, and timid little Asian boy who never, ever, uttered a single word. Not even to the teachers. He would convey his intentions and emotions by facial expression or gesticulation, on the rare occasions that he bothered to communicate at all. He was always alone, but really did not seem to mind it. On one occasion however, he very softly whispered "stop it" to me after I had been bothering him for some time to see if I could actually make him say something. Baffled at the fact that he had just said something to me, and equally proud of my achievement, I indeed did stop.

- The second child was a European boy with a very rare skin condition. He was allergic to almost everything. Really. One could not even touch him without subjecting him to a purgatory of painful rashes. His skin therefore looked very spotted and bumpy, with patches of rash everywhere. I always felt squeamish of him, but nevertheless, I appreciated him for his personality.

Luckily, he had at his disposal, a special ointment with which he curbed the effects of his allergies. Drastically reducing the severity of his violent skin reactions upon contact with even something as common as tap water.

- The third child was a small African boy with whom I became good friends. He was a bit of a bookworm, participated in spelling bees, was a good boy in class, and had a severe stammering problem. Because he was quite the good kid and I was quite the naughty one, we complimented each other quite well. In fact, I suspected that secretly, he wanted to be just like me.

Now though, in his teens (at the time of writing this), I hear he is almost half as naughty as I was. He does seem to do his best to give teachers a hard time. He is still a great kid.

- The fourth child was myself. I was well known for my hyperactivity, a tendency to "fiddle with everything", and a unique methodology for making fun of people. Oftentimes I would find myself being sacked from the classroom, or given "time outs", but I was continuously grateful for such 'punishments', for they allowed me to sit and think about the many things in this world that interested me. The classrooms were very boring places, and that is partly why whenever the opportunity arose, I spiced things up by making people cry or by making them laugh. Whichever they chose to do.

- The fifth student was a little Caucasian girl who in all mannerisms and likelihood, was absolutely normal. I still do not quite know why exactly she was put there, because aside from her fascination with the overrated "Harry Potter" series of books, she seemed to be your average, every-day little girl who liked pink dresses.

- The sixth child, was a European boy almost as notoriously devious and stubborn as myself. Amassing quite the collection of misdeeds against his name, he was sent to the special class most definitely because the normal classes could not tame nor tolerate him. He and I got along quite well.

The class may have had one or two more students, but I cannot recall further. I spent the whole year in that class before moving to the next grade the following year. The adventures that ensued would make for some interesting tales, but they are best left to a few real-world conversations, and perhaps (though unlikely) even another book. Some very funny material in there, now that I look back. Life was very much an adventure for me.

The Meaning of Life

Now, it is crucial that the following extract: The Meaning of Life, be understood by you, for the purpose of this book and optimally, for the benefit of your overall understanding of the nature of life.

The body of text to follow, is an excerpt of something I wrote when I was 17. The meaning of life made itself known to me as I was stirring a batch of chemicals (non-narcotic, FYI) in the kitchen. As it turns out: the link between chemistry and the meaning of life is not quite as non-existent as it may seem. Before reading the body of the text, there is prerequisite terminology you are required to comprehend fully.

Existence: To be, is to exist. Stating that "something is" (in any circumstance), is to state that it exists (in that circumstance). It is a widely disseminated misconception that something can only be said to be in existence, once it is so in objectivity.

Reality: Reality, or an entity within it, is correctly defined as being in the context of that which is perceived. The word (reality) is usually spoken in an objective sense, however it is not exclusively so.

Objectivity: When something is said to be objective, it is understood that peoples' perceptions (which are inherently and absolutely subjective) share a general commonality about it.

Purpose: The function performed, or the reason for said function (only when attributing to a cognizant causative).

The Meaning of life, is "purpose". This is not merely a subjective philosophical statement or inference. It is derived from a computational analysis in metaphysics.

Exposition

Purpose alludes to a defined functionality, while existence, objectively or not, is a state absolutely in accordance with it. As I am about to explain, purpose applies to both the inanimate and the cognitively active, but the latter is usually interpreted in a philosophical sense about it.

For example: A pebble, immediately has purpose the instant it is recognised and/or realized by an individual. That very purpose, for the fraction of time in reference, and in (but not limited to) the context of the perceiver's frame of reference, is 'realization' itself. It performs a function within the thought processes of said observer. The moment something imposes itself upon our perception, and consequently our reality, it has done so with an inherent characteristic of functionality (a purpose), and through that, it exists for the perceiver, regardless of its tangibility, shape, or form.

Relative to a cognizant entity or confined space, something will not exist until the effect of this something is recognised. For example: If John is a boy who lives in Scotland, and Peter is a boy who lives in England, relative to Peter's reality, John will not exist. Not unless Peter becomes aware of John, and/or the sphere of John's influence is large enough to impose itself upon Peter's reality, and inevitably then, effect John a purpose relative to Peter.

Further evidence lies in the nature of causality. You see: Everything has a cause, and everything has an effect. This effect will be its purpose in all circumstances because cause, effect, and purpose are mutually inclusive. Life, existence, and purpose, with "life" subject to elimination, are to each other, dependencies, and without purpose there can be no existence nor can there be life.

Everything we are, do, know, have, and see, is what constitutes life, and these variables have purposes attached to them. Even from a conclusion as simplistic as "you live to fulfil a purpose", this can be easily understood. To claim that the meaning of life is anything other than purpose is to only name that which purpose subsumes, in a hierarchy of significance.

For example, if one says that the meaning of life is "happiness", then happiness would become the assigned purpose. To ever say or even think, that "the meaning of life is..." you would be stating that which will fall under a purpose. Life cannot be devoid of meaning. It would be semantically incorrect to ever make the statement that it is, and no methodology of circumvention can ever refute this fact without becoming illogical. As I have shown, "purpose" is therefore the meaning of life.

Now, "The Purpose of Life" is a supplementary question with a similar solution: The purpose of life is to have meaning. There is no higher end to being. Life facilitates a meaning, and that meaning is a purpose: merely an operation. Simply put: the meaning of life is to have meaning, which is purpose. And the purpose of life is to facilitate that meaning.

We are all here for a purpose, and for the most part that purpose is ours to decide. Whether we strive for a life of great accomplishments or for one of mediocrity is irrelevant to the fact that our existence is purposeful.

The Conventional "Christian Way"

"What is the purpose of Christianity"? Now that is a good question. Another good question is: "How is a Christian meant to live his/her life"? The average Christian might answer: "To bring people closer to God", and "Like Christ lived His" respectively, but the unpleasant reality is that most Christians are really quite detached from God (although I am sure many will disagree, given that they are incredibly naïve), and the history of Christianity is one of division, religious indoctrination, and authoritarian control.

Nowadays, Christianity is something about which most Christians do not know that much. They do not know its history, and they do not really know what the Bible says. They know some of what it says, yes, but not most of it. Most Christians today are quite neutral about Christianity, and go to church because they feel they have to.

They attend church gatherings, don their guise of pretentious holiness for an average of 2 to 4 hours a week, and dissemble. After their obligations as church goers have been fulfilled, they revert to whatever lifestyle they kept prior to the church gathering. If you are Christian, it is likely that you know many of these kinds of people. They lead rather "unclean" lives, but go to church on a regular basis.

Keep in mind that I did not say "imperfect lives", I said "unclean lives". Perfection and cleanliness are two very different things. The former, is something we can never ascertain, and anyone who asserts otherwise (that you be "perfect", or "mimic Christ" because He was perfect) is not to be paid any attention. Such a person is either naïve, or trying to trick you.

Attempting to openly mimic Christ or be perfect will only have you join a long and growing list of holier-than-thou hypocrites. You will succumb to the perceived obligation to uphold a fake persona of holiness that you will have to present before people. I assure you that you do not want that to happen to you, or anyone else that you may know.

Holier-than-though hypocrisy is inflicting itself upon almost every pastor on television, almost every person who has written a book about his/her experiences as a Christian, and almost every church goer assigned a position of authority within a church.

These people are pressured into appearing "holy" and "pure" for the sake of their public image, and as a result, they often live stressful double lives. They also do not do God any justice by pretending to be holy, as they are trying to please people. They are not trying to please God. They are squandering their efforts to be seen as perfect. They are hypocrites wanting to be seen by people as "clean before the Lord".

If this in any way whatsoever describes you, then please, cease this nonsensical behaviour immediately. I am every bit as human as you are, pastors are every bit as human as you are, and the men who wrote the Bible were every bit as human as you are. Relax, be a good person, and enjoy life. Being connected to God is about **you** and **God**. Your relationship with God is no one else's business. God knows your heart. There is no need to portray yourself in any specific light in conformity to other peoples' sensibilities. Just be you.

Speaking of 'just being you': Do you know that there is a small village in Austria called "Fucking"? Yes it is spelled and pronounced that way, and is no expletive to the people there. In fact, they are shocked when English-speaking people reveal to them what the name of their town means in English. However, they are not about to change its name just because it offends a few English-speaking people, and they are not going to go to hell for the mere fact that the name of their town is as hilarious as it might be offensive.

My point is: what is in your heart is all that matters. It is a religious lie that saying the "f word", "s word", etc. is sinful/evil/whatever. It does not matter what comes out of your mouth if your heart is filthy. Make sure your spirit and soul are clean, before you ever start looking to please other people with pretentious cleanliness. The devil does not usually use "swearwords" or come in a satanic demeanour when he intends to deceive people. Rather, he utters niceties and presents himself pleasantly. The same is true of most serial killers and rapists. They are full of beautiful words and attractive demeanours, yet are internally diseased.

What offends other people is irrelevant to the truth, and simply having "non-offensive" things to say really does not mean much at all. It is a useless metric for the sanctity of one's self. In fact, the majority of the men and women who claim not to speak "swearwords", are hypocrites who are more concerned with what other people think of them than they are about actually being decent human beings.

I do not make use of any "bad words" in my book because there is no reason to. It is a matter of maintaining decorum, not a matter of maintaining pretence. There is a difference, and one needs to learn the distinction between the two. In life and in conversation it is not uncommon for me to use "offensive" terms, because it is funny and usually results in much joy and laughter for those with whom I am conversing. Expletives mean nothing to me.

If you utter "curse words" only when negativity is associated with them, then you need to deal with that negativity which plagues you. Once you do, you will either stop saying those words, or they will not mean anything to you any longer. Enjoy life, live life, and be happy. Your enemies may wish that you were God's exception, but He brought us all to this life so that we may enjoy it, and contribute positively to the system within which His creations dwell. I will speak more about this as we move onward but for now, forgive my digression.

Now I was saying: that as a Christian, you probably know quite a few dishonest, church-going people. In fact, you may even be one yourself. You know the kind of people I am talking about: Folks who cannot live up to the standard they preach in church gatherings, and who probably like the "No one is perfect. We are all sinners" excuse.

"Who are you to judge me?", many Christians are quick to say, once you have pointed any hypocrisy out to them. Note though, that I am not casting judgment of damnation upon anyone. I just tell it like it is. A spade is a spade, and a hypocritical Christian, is a hypocritical Christian.

Ironically, religious Christians are some of the most judgmental and insincere individuals I have ever known. Often expressing distaste at those who do not go to church or read the Bible, while it is usually in their very churches that evil runs most rampant with pretenders and with liars. I have seen the true nature of many church goers, and from what I have seen, I can confirm that demons go to church as well.

Couple this with the many false teachings embroiling the Christian religion, and we have a serious problem. "What false teachings?" you may ask. Well, there are many, and an entire book could be written about them. Although a section of this book will be dedicated to addressing them, you will see that I have far more important things to share with you.

For example: I have observed that most religious church-goers, tend to exhibit a strong aversion to the truth. They do not like things which do not speak in favour of their desires. Due to this fact, many pastors resort to the practice of giving their congregations what their congregations want. Not what they need. Modern pastors have to do one of two things (or a clever combination of both):

- Tell people things which will only serve to please them.

OR

- Keep people in the confines of servitude by threatening them with Bible doctrine.

Neither of which will be to any useful outcome to anyone other than the pastor. Most pastors eagerly seek to be loved by their sheep however, so the former is most commonly found to be their choice of operation.

After reading enough of this book, tune in to a Christian-dedicated channel, sit back, and observe my point in action. If you, being a pastor, should happen to look your people in the eyes and tell them that the behaviour they exhibit outside of the churches is disgusting and contradictory, you seem to oppose their very beings, and so will probably notice a drastic reduction in the number of people attending your church.

This is why charismatic churches are filled to every corner with ignorant, self-pleasing people, while the places where true wisdom lies (as few as they are), with priests/people who actually possess God-ordained power, have but only a small number of attendees. "Even when you hardly have money in your pocket, give it to the lord, and you will be blessed with more money!" is the kind of nonsense many people in charismatic churches enjoy listening to.

I was recently surprised by this when a while ago, I made the decision to attend a certain church with a friend of mine. An unusual event, as I typically never go to churches, but the incentive was the prospect of connecting with some attractive women there. Were it not for that, I would never have gone.

So I went to that church, and upon arrival I saw a hoard of people. There was a sense of party-going about the church and that church day, as everyone was very much excited to be there. Strangely excited, for a group of church-goers, I thought. I was told that "this is how excited the people are every Sunday", so there must have been a good reason for it.

I was prepared to join in on this excitement myself, but as soon as the church service began, a band came onto the stage, and started to play loud music. The crowd loved it, and began going crazy. Dancing everywhere and shouting. The performers were singing "We love you God", "We are here for you God", etc. Some in the crowd shouted "Jesus!" in celebration, and there was a lot of energy overall about these people and their activities.

To the uninformed mind this might all seem to be great stuff. "Just what God wants. People are happy, and are singing for Him". However, none of what I witnessed on that day, is what God would have wanted. It was very much what the people wanted, yes. But not what God would want. There is nothing wrong with being excited, but only as long as you are excited for the right reasons. You see, these people had gone there to please themselves above all else. They did not really care about assembling to talk about God. This church was a club, a party, and place of foolishness. Nothing more than that.

Its attendees were there only to dance and to be told silly stories by unscrupulous pastors, and I could see that the performers were only there to perform, and get people jumping up and down. It was written all over their facial expressions, all over their actions, and signed on every one of their Western, Hip-Hop dance moves. I did not need my spirit to tell me that this was all some contemporary pop-culture garbage trying to pass itself off as a reputable establishment of Jesus Christ's, but my spirit told me anyway. This specific church was called Hillsong, and was founded by a highly charismatic Australian pastor.

So charismatic in fact, that he managed to get the people cheering for him and his word. **His word**, not God's. I heard the girl I had gone to church with that day, say: "Oh my gosh, the word today (word of God) was amazing!" But what she in fact meant to say was: "The pastor's words and charisma blew me away! He told me everything I wanted and thought I needed, to hear!"

When on stage, this pastor spoke with a silly grin on his face about how he could see things in the spirit realm, and how God wants people to see things in the spirit realm because it is cool, and can make them become successful. He did not literally say it was "cool" to see in the spirit realm, but he did his very best to covey such a message.

After his little performance, he displayed a list of ailments and afflictions via a big-screen projector, and told the audience to pray for those who had those problems. Sicknesses such as AIDS, ear pain, neck pain, head pain, etc. were all up there, and the people lifted their hands and each prayed in silence. At least, it would seem they were each praying.

I felt quite bothered by the fact that these were simply lists of illnesses. They did not even have names of people attached to them. How can you pray against suffering when you do not even know who you are praying for? You see, the Hillsong church is just another church of scam artists, and it uses music to lure naive and self-pleasing people to it.

If that church wanted to help anybody, they might have asked people in the crowed to air their grievances, and request from one another to aid in prayer. But of course, that would be a far more time-consuming thing to do, so why not just display irrelevant and useless information on a big screen for people to senselessly pray to instead?

The pastor's co-pastor then went on stage to start spinning a web of lies about how we put our money in the places we care about. He said: "God loves it when we give. A big part of being Christian is giving, and a key area in our lives where we give is in our finances... I want us to think about that as we give today (give to the church)". He actually said that load of trash, and somehow the people lapped it up with very little, if any, concern at all.

People who happily attend such charismatic churches only want hope, and to be happy. Even if this means avoiding the truth at all cost, because they are too mentally weak to choose the straight and narrow path of truth. What distinguishes a seeker of truth from an ignorant and naïve sheep is his/her undying thirst for facts.

Naive sheep, flock towards what they wish was true. They tend to believe only what they want to, and seek salvation from happiness. The reality is that salvation brings happiness, it is not the other way around. Those who are strong, and those whom God has usually chosen, move in the opposite direction to what the general masses march towards, because those whom God has chosen or who have found their way to Him do not need lies to make them feel comfortable.

Truth-seekers understand that whether or not it tastes nice, if it is of the truth, they will swallow the pill. The medicine of truth, is a stepping-stone to victory. Palatable or not, you cannot change whatever is wrong, with the sweetener of lies.

As Mathew Chapter 7, and Verse 25 states: "If you build your foundation upon the sand, the rain will wash it away, and your house will crumble".

Use solid rock. Support your beliefs with facts, and you will see that the truth really does set you free. A false hope, like a house built on sand, will keep you happy for now, but in the long run, a false hope will not only have disappointed you, it will have robbed you of the desire to change your life for the better, at a time when you could have easily done so.

As a naïve religious person, when you finally realise this, if ever you do, you could find yourself feeling the greatest of regrets, because you will not just lose a house. You will lose everything that you stored inside of it. Thinking them secure because there were walls around them, when they never were secure, because the ground beneath them was weak.

"If I give money to the church, I will be blessed". Such selfishness is at the core of almost every single person who pays their tithe, and in the hearts of almost all those who attend charismatic churches. It mildly shocks, and greatly annoys me, that I regularly come across a considerable number of people who hold the mistaken belief that you are without a doubt to be blessed when you give 10% of your income to the church, and that you have sinned once you have not done so. But then again, all these people lack the insight and thoughtfulness that is required of them to discern the contrary truth for themselves.

If you belief God needs your money, let me ask you: Can God not make his own? If by some remarkable stroke of redundancy, He actually did require your money, do you think the money you are giving to churches would hold any validity to God when it does not come from your heart? When you are simply giving because you have been told to do so, in the expectation that you will get something from Him? Do you think that the $100 given to a church because you feel it is required of you, will please God more than being driven by empathy to give just ten cents to the starving street child nearby when you see that he/she is suffering? No, no, no, and no. In fact, paying a tithe to thieving pastors will only displease Him. Starving child or not, God does not need your money.

Now, let me state in their favour that churches need to pay for utility bills, and/or rent, etc. They do in fact need money in order to sustain their operations, but there is no shame in them merely stating that. Rather, it would seem that they attempt to extort funds from the church goers by inducing guilt in them, or praying on their selfish desire for blessings. Having them think that all they need to do is give their hard earned money "to God", so that blessings shall rain upon them in plenty.

You can give money to churches, but be an intelligent human being about doing so, and educate yourself about the reasons as to why your church needs your money. Specific people in the Bible might have had a valid reason for requesting 10% of certain people's toil, but not nearly as valid a reason as modern Christians seem to think, and certainly also, not nearly as applicable to modern Christians.

Chapter Two: THE BOOK

A book famed and notorious in equal measure for its scriptures, the Bible is the most influential book in human history. This book has helped free many a person from a sinful life, helped heal countless others, and even today, can be an effective tool against unkind spirits, demons, and the like (more on evil spirits later).

Unfortunately the Bible is also responsible for the misbeliefs of many men and women, for the mere fact that it is a book which contains in it a variety of different messages which can be used for a variety of different purposes. In developing countries especially, the Bible is highly responsible for the cultural ideologies of societies, and people who read it in earnest believe its every word to be God's very own words jotted down on paper and brought to them by the Western world.

What is ironic is that the West is now losing interest in Christianity and adopting atheism. The irony is augmented when you consider that the Bible, being a book of peace and love (mostly), was brought to Africa and several other places by people who enslaved and tortured its inhabitants. You might wonder: "Did they not read this Bible of theirs before coming here?!"

In actual fact they did, and they used it to justify their evils. Colonialists and their missionaries who invaded people's lands and force-fed Christian doctrine to them after having them enslaved, allowed Christianity to spread down generations, resulting in a very large number of people today who are devout Christians. Many of them now only as devout as they think other people would care to see.

This wide-spectrum religious brainwashing by invaders from the West was very important for them, as it was hard to colonize people who thought for themselves and were independent. You see, autonomy by a people is the greatest enemy to authoritarianism, and to fight the coming-together of people, one must either set them against one another or subdue them to your cause. Colonialists did both. Ask any credible historian, and he/she will tell you how.

Even today, governments around the world are employing tactics of division to prevent the masses from acting as a coherent whole. There is strength in numbers, but not when the numbers are too occupied by internal conflicts or trivial matters on television to pose a threat. "Democrats", "Republicans", "liberals", "conservatives", "rich", and "poor". All fighting each other for purposes irrelevant to the real issues that lie before them.

This is why colonialists brought their slave-nations a book which was used to soil minds with much religious doctrine and to turn their slaves into narrow-minded sheep. They have done it so well that the term "sheep" is now something many Christians are proud to be called. Take the time to observe an actual sheep in action however, and you will be graced only by the great magnitude of mediocrity that is, that foolish animal. To the sheep herder, sheep are good for two things: consumption and exploitation.

Quite a few years ago, I had a rather old Christian woman say to me "...yes! I am a sheep, and I am proud". The Oxford dictionary defines a sheep to be: "**a bashful, defenceless, or easily-led person**", and indeed that old woman was one. Being a sheep is by definition, a bad idea, but still, Christians accept the term. You see, the Bible has several types of readers:

- Those (very, very few) who read it intelligently and for the purpose of verifiable knowledge.

- Those who understand the dynamics of spiritualism enough to read it, and make effective use of its scriptures.

- Those who read it for the sake of their academic courses, or to have something to argue about.

- Those who read it more than anyone else, so that they may quote all its scripture to you, yet are the most foul of demon-inhabited witches.

- Those who whole-heartedly accept its scriptures and are as a result, overly insistent Bible thumpers.

- Those who whole-heartedly accept its scriptures and are as a result, feeble people who arguably could be blown over by your sneeze.

With regards to the feeble ones, you cannot really blame them. After centuries of slavery and indoctrination by other people, the words "...do not lean on your own understanding", do take their toll on a society.

I have been to places most affected by this kind of debilitating indoctrination, and from my observations, not only has it prevented people from developing both spiritually and intellectually, it has also destroyed lives. It is a message which spirals down from peoples' ancestors all the way through to our current generation, which unsurprisingly, due to several factors, is now slowly rebelling against it. Not only because it does not make any sense, but because people seem to use it in whichever way they wish.

A Man's Own Religion

As a child, the various church meetings and sermons of which I was a reluctant audience member, had taught me very little other than the fact that most people have not any legitimate basis for the things they choose to believe from the Bible. My encounters of all these so-called "chapters" and "verses" being read at me with no apparent end to them, would leave me thinking: "But what's the point?" and "How on Earth is that useful information?" I struggled to contain my ever-present boredom, and to me, church was just another useless formality of the human experience.

You see, a typical Sunday (or school morning) church session involves the reading of a few passages specifically chosen for the speaker to convey a message of his own construction through the interpolation of Biblical text and inferences from it. This selective reading of the Bible is the reason Christians will ignore the Bible's call to kill homosexuals, the Bible's condemnation of the wearing of clothes which are made of "wool and linen", the Bible's prohibition of a woman to wear men's clothing, etc. yet Christians will talk about paying tithes.

This, despite the fact that the only time Jesus Christ is documented to have ever mentioned the tithe, is the moment he insulted the clergy for their greed. Mathew Chapter 23, and Verse 23: "Woe to you, scribes and Pharisees, hypocrites! For you tithe mint and dill and cumin, and have neglected the weightier matters of the law: justice and mercy and faithfulness. These you ought to have done, without neglecting the others. You blind guides, straining out a gnat and swallowing a camel".

"The Bible is the word of God, and we must do as God says. So give me your money". A laughable notion, but that is essentially what many pastors are saying to people. Pastors are at liberty to say such things because they know mainstream Christianity is more about the Bible than it is about God. As any atheist will confirm: "Because the Bible says so" is an irritatingly recurring theme with religious Christians. You know, I once tuned in to a dedicated Christian channel (the Rhema Network or TBN) and witnessed yet another atrocity being committed by yet another pastor of that network. He was telling people that after paying the initial 10% of their income to the church, they should progress to increasing the percentage periodically. This pastor said that the more they paid, the more blessings would befall them. I wondered how a man could have no shame telling people lies of such magnitude.

The number one problem with Christianity today is this: Christians practice Christianity in whichever way they like, and the religious among them will quote what the Bible says when they need it, and ignore what it says when they do not need it. For example: They will toss aside the notion that human ghosts roam the Earth "…because the Bible does not say anything about human spirits wondering the Earth", and they will say there is no such thing as an alien being "…because the Bible does not mention aliens". Yet these same religious people will condemn the practice of human slavery, even though the Bible condones it. The Bible most certainly does not say slavery is wrong. In fact the Bible portrays Jesus Christ Himself as condoning slavery. In Luke Chapter 12, and Verses 42 to 48 Jesus talks about having slaves and how the slave owner can beat them: "Who then is the faithful and wise manager, whom his master will set over his household, to give them their portion of food at the proper time? Blessed is that servant whom his master will find so doing when he comes. Truly, I say to you, he will set him over all his possessions. But if that servant says to himself, 'My master is delayed in coming,' and begins to beat the male and female servants, and to eat and drink and get drunk, the master of that servant will come on a day when he does not expect him and at an hour he does not know, and will cut him in pieces and put him with the unfaithful. And that servant who knew his master's will but did not get ready or act according to his will, will receive a severe beating. But the one who did not know, and did what deserved a beating, will receive a light beating". Note, that in his adulteration of the Bible, King James' and others' translations of the above Bible verses, substituted the word "slave" with "servant", but Jesus is not talking about mere servants here. He is talking about slaves. Not that it would be OK to beat your servants either.

"The Bible is God's word, so we must do as it says". That is, unless whatever it says is quite obviously immoral. Religious Christians of today have common sense enough to know that slavery is wrong, whether the Bible says so or not, but most of them will throw common sense away when the Bible presents them with things that do not confront them as being improper, deviant from reality, or poorly justified. It is because of the glaring issues with quite a few of the Bible's proclamations, that people take from the Bible what they wish to take from it, and glaze over that which they know would not be of much fruitful application in their lives.

You see, the Bible itself has necessitated the highly selective manner in which people decide to quote from it. It has been written by many different authors, and in such a way that although there is a central theme the Bible coherently adheres to, there are many contradictions. For example, in Matthew Chapter 10, and Verses 34 to 36 Jesus says: "Do not think that I have come to bring peace to the earth. I have not come to bring peace, but a sword. For I have come to set a man against his father, and a daughter against her mother, and a daughter-in-law against her mother-in-law. And a person's enemies will be those of his own household". Yet in Mark Chapter 9, and verse 50, Jesus tells people to: "be at peace with one another". No decent human being desires to be at war with his/her family, so of course only the latter of the afore-quoted Bible texts will be of any use to a good Christian.

It is not just an issue of people's morals compelling them to ignore certain Bible passages, it is an issue of logic as well. For example, the Bible is quite clear on matters of independence and strength. That is: according to quite a few Biblical passages, you have no independence or strength. You are entirely reliant on God, and he is to fight all your battles for you. The Bible for the most part claims you need not worry about thinking for yourself or helping yourself, because God will help you.

Bible passages like Proverbs Chapter 3, and Verse 5: "Trust in the Lord with all your heart, and do not lean on your own understanding", would lead to the detriment of anyone who took them seriously, and passages like Luke Chapter 6, and Verses 27 to 31, would do far more harm: "But I say to you who hear, Love your enemies, do good to those who hate you, bless those who curse you, pray for those who abuse you. To one who strikes you on the cheek, offer the other also, and from one who takes away your cloak do not withhold your tunic either. Give to everyone who begs from you, and from one who takes away your goods do not demand them back. And as you wish that others would do to you, do so to them. "If you love those who love you, what benefit is that to you? For even sinners love those who love them. And if you do good to those who do good to you, what benefit is that to you? For even sinners do the same. And if you lend to those from whom you expect to receive, what credit is that to you? Even sinners lend to sinners, to get back the same amount. But love your enemies, and do good, and lend, expecting nothing in return, and your reward will be great, and you will be sons of the Most High, for he is kind to the ungrateful and the evil. Be merciful, even as your Father is merciful".

It is fair to say that anybody who takes the above verses literally, and obeys them to the letter, is a fool, and the fruits of his/her life will reflect that of a fool who other people will surely trample upon. People know this, and it is because they know this, that they do not read many Bible passages literally. Instead they will have to reinterpret much of the Bible so that it can make sense to them, or they will focus only on certain aspects of scripture so as to attain something meaningful from it.

Asking for you to be good to others, charitable, and kind, makes perfect sense. Asking you to let people steal from you, abuse you, and beat you however, makes no sense. No sense at all. I guarantee that God does not want for you to be mistreated and abused. The notion that there is virtue in being abused as one of "God's people", and that you should allow abuse until God decides to intervene (whenever that may be), is a satanic notion. It must be ignored completely.

The Bible surely was not written or inspired by satan, but it is being used by satan to commit atrocities against mankind, to lead people astray, and to make them weak for the devil's domination. For example: It is rather fantastical for one to imagine the following from Romans Chapter 12, and Verse 20: "if your enemy is hungry, feed him; if he is thirsty, give him something to drink; for by so doing you will heap burning coals on his head", but is it practical? Aside from the verse's highly contradictory conclusion, does it in fact make sense to abide by Romans Chapter 12, and Verse 20?

I mean: If you were being threatened with death by a known serial killer and he suddenly demanded food from you, would you give it to him? Let me be more specific… If said serial killer was several meters away, clenching a knife as well as his stomach in hunger, and demanded your sandwich, would you walk over there and give it to him? Surely, Jesus of the Bible might have done that, but would it be sensible for you to do that? Of course not. You would keep as far from him as you could, call the police, or perhaps pull out your gun if you had one. Romans Chapter 12, and Verse 20 would be far removed from your mind because Romans Chapter 12, and Verse 20, is rather quite useless in any time of trouble.

Let us also look at what Romans Chapter 13, and Verse 1 to 7 says: "Let every person be subject to the governing authorities. For there is no authority except from God, and those that exist have been instituted by God. Therefore whoever resists the authorities resists what God has appointed, and those who resist will incur judgment. For rulers are not a terror to good conduct, but to bad. Would you have no fear of the one who is in authority? Then do what is good, and you will receive his approval, for he is God's servant for your good. But if you do wrong, be afraid, for he does not bear the sword in vain. For he is the servant of God, an avenger who carries out God's wrath on the wrongdoer. Therefore one must be in subjection, not only to avoid God's wrath but also for the sake of conscience. For because of this you also pay taxes, for the authorities are ministers of God, attending to this very thing. Pay to all what is owed to them: taxes to whom taxes are owed, revenue to whom revenue is owed, respect to whom respect is owed, honour to whom honour is owed".

Is the above text true? Is it true that every authority which exists has been instituted by God? Is it true that rulers are not a terror to good conduct? Is it true that every ruler is God's servant for the good of the people, and that they are ministers of God? No, no, no, and no. These things are not true.

Throughout history, many rulers have tortured, oppressed, subjugated, and killed innocent people for the sake of wicked ideologies, and yet the Bible says you must be in subjection to rulers. It is therefore apparent that Romans Chapter 13 was only written for the benefit of people in power. In fact, it is because of messages like that which is written in Romans Chapter 13, that Adolf Hitler wrote in his book (**Mein Kampf**), the following: "*...I believe that I am acting in accordance with the will of the Almighty Creator: by defending myself against the Jew, I am fighting for the work of the Lord.* (Page 60 [English Translation]". Even in this day and age, rulers are committing atrocious acts of evil, and the most evil among them are the United States, and British governments, along with the globalists who secretly control them.

Bible passages like the ones I have just quoted are read to people to make them feeble-minded, weak, and foolish. They are read to African children when one intends to rob the children's continent of resources and sing the children to sleep as he/she does so. They are read to poverty-stricken and illiterate citizens of Rome when one intends to rule tyrannically over them and deceive them with the selling of indulgences. Bible passages like the ones I have just quoted, are used to promote evil and to make people unintelligent sheep. In order for evil to succeed in its endeavours, it must either overpower you or make you compliant with it.

A quote from the CG-animated character Beowulf (from the film: "**Beowulf**") puts what I have just said into other nearly-sufficient words: "The time of heroes is dead… the Christ God has killed it. Leaving humankind with nothing but weeping martyrs, fear, and shame". Of course, it is not "the Christ God" who has killed anything. It is religious Christianity which has left weeping martyrs, fear, and shame in its wake. I will illuminate you on what I have just said soon, and then address it again more deeply later on, but for now, it is important that you know the following:

Even when neglecting the fact that significant portions of the Bible are written in such a manner as to enslave and dumb people down, the Bible for the most part is entirely subject to our interpretation. It is that fact which has given rise to the many thousands of churches in existence today, and it is that fact which has allowed conmen, false prophets, and evil-doers, to thrive with the Bible.

The Bible mostly is a book of stories. It is a historical document as well as a religious one, and this is another reason why there are contradictions in it. Luke Chapter 6, and Verses 27 to 31 is part of a story of Jesus saying specific things, to specific people, at a specific time, and at a specific place.

But people have been misled to believe that each and every word in the Bible can be used as a command from God. People do not understand what the Bible is. They are told "It is the word of God", but from where does that idea come from? Certainly not from the Bible, and I can assure you that it certainly did not come from God.

The Protestant Lie

So let me shock you: The Bible is not the word of God. There is not on any of its pages, scripture that says the Bible is the direct word of God. Not one verse, in any chapter claims so. In fact there are parts of the Bible that refute such a claim. 1 Corinthians, Chapter 7, is one of many examples. Men wrote the Bible, not God. As such, the Bible is a work of imperfection.

One must also consider the fact that we do not possess the original manuscripts of the Bible. We do not have either the Old or New Testament in their original forms, as the original Old and New Testament texts are lost. What we have instead, are copies of the manuscripts. In fact, we have copies of manuscripts which were copied from other manuscripts, which were copied as well from other manuscripts, which were themselves copied from other manuscripts, which were copied from other manuscripts, etc.

You see: Before printers and photocopiers were ever created, copies of texts had to be written by hand. There was no other way. The obvious problem with this is that when texts are copied by hand, things change. Small mistakes are made by scribes, and although the mistakes are small, when those texts are copied by another scribe, mistakes occur again. The mistakes propagate themselves through manuscript copies.

In addition to this problem is the tendency for people to effect changes to text or to correct known errors. Sometimes the correction is not quite correct, as the person making the correction would have to assume what was probably meant by the previous scribe. In doing so, people add information to texts which was not there before, and they can change the meaning of entire verses or chapters by attempting to complete "missing information". Evidence of these man-made changes can be seen in virtually all the New Testament books. Some of the most well-known of these changes are pointed out as such by certain Bible translations.

For example: Mark Chapter 16 of the King James Bible has 12 additional verses which do not belong there. Verses 9 to 20 are not present in the earliest New Testament manuscripts, but King James obviously did not know this, and neither did a few other Bible translators. Some Bibles though, will include verses 9 to 20 of Mark Chapter 16, but place in brackets the fact that those verses do not belong there, and brackets will also be placed around the entirety of verses 9 to 20.

The likely reason for those verses being added, is that it did not make sense to one or more scribes for Mark Chapter 16 to end the way it originally ends. At some point a scribe probably included the extra verses as commentary, but as his work was copied by other scribes, one or more of them decided to include verses 9 to 19 to Mark Chapter 16.

Another instance of Bible texts being added while they do not belong, can be found in the Gospel of John. Verses 1 to 11 of Chapter 8 is a story not present in the earliest manuscripts, but it made its way into the King James' and others' translations. Again, some Bibles will cite in brackets that verses 1 to 11 of John Chapter 8 do not belong in the Bible, and place the texts in brackets.

There are many texts in the Bible which differ from the oldest manuscripts, and there are many instances in history where scribes added information of their own or changed the meaning of certain parts for the sake of their agendas. Ironically, the earliest manuscripts differ from one another far more than the newer manuscripts do from each other, but the true irony is that in the New Testament, there are many discrepancies in different authors' accounts of certain events.

(These are historical facts, of which everybody who knows Bible history is aware. There is nothing new about what I am telling you about the Bible, as scholars and priests [those who are qualified] have known about these things since the18[th] century. However, I am certain that in reading this book, many of you will have heard or read of these things for the first time, because you took for granted what you have been led to believe by religious people who do not investigate anything they themselves are told.)

The account of Jesus' crucifixion is one of many examples where the Bible contradicts itself by virtue of different authors' accounts. Let us look at what the author of Mark says, and let us look at what the author of Luke says. Mark and Luke are similar in their descriptions of what happened to Jesus, but Luke adds things which are not present in Mark's account, and in one key aspect, Luke's account differs from Mark's.

Mark Chapter 15, and Verses 21 to 32 says: "And they compelled a passerby, Simon of Cyrene, who was coming in from the country, the father of Alexander and Rufus, to carry his cross. And they brought him to the place called Golgotha (which means Place of a Skull). And they offered him wine mixed with myrrh, but he did not take it. And they crucified him and divided his garments among them, casting lots for them, to decide what each should take. And it was the third hour when they crucified him. And the inscription of the charge against him read, "The King of the Jews." And with him they crucified two robbers, one on his right and one on his left. And those who passed by derided him, wagging their heads and saying, "Aha! You who would destroy the temple and rebuild it in three days, save yourself, and come down from the cross!" So also the chief priests with the scribes mocked him to one another, saying, "He saved others; he cannot save himself. Let the Christ, the King of Israel, come down now from the cross that we may see and believe." Those who were crucified with him also reviled him".

However, Luke Chapter 23, and Verses 26 to 43 says: "And as they led him away, they seized one Simon of Cyrene, who was coming in from the country, and laid on him the cross, to carry it behind Jesus. And there followed him a great multitude of the people and of women who were mourning and lamenting for him. But turning to them Jesus said, "Daughters of Jerusalem, do not weep for me, but weep for yourselves and for your children. For behold, the days are coming when they will say, Blessed are the barren and the wombs that never bore and the breasts that never nursed!' Then they will begin to say to the mountains, 'Fall on us,' and to the hills, 'Cover us.' For if they do these things when the wood is green, what will happen when it is dry?" Two others, who were criminals, were led away to be put to death with him. And when they came to the place that is called The Skull, there they crucified him, and the criminals, one on his right and one on his left. And Jesus said, "Father, forgive them, for they know not what they do." And they cast lots to divide his garments. And the people stood by, watching, but the rulers scoffed at him, saying, "He saved others; let him save himself, if he is the Christ of God, his Chosen One!" The soldiers also mocked him, coming up and offering him sour wine and saying, "If you are the King of the Jews, save yourself!" There was also an inscription over him, "This is the King of the Jews." One of the criminals who were hanged railed at him, saying, "Are you not the Christ? Save yourself and us!" But the other rebuked him, saying, "Do you not fear God, since you are under the same sentence of condemnation? And we indeed justly, for we are receiving the due reward of our deeds; but this man has done nothing wrong." And he said, "Jesus, remember me when you come into your kingdom." And he said to him, "Truly, I say to you, today you will be with me in Paradise"'".

Ignoring the fact that Luke's explanation contains information which is not present in Mark's explanation, there is one big difference between what Luke says and what Mark says. According to Mark: those who were crucified with Jesus reviled Him. According to Luke though: only one of the men who was crucified with Jesus reviled Him, while the other one defended Jesus. Jesus then had a conversation with the man which led to Jesus assuring him that he would go to heaven with Him.

The story of Jesus' Crucifixion is one example of the kind of minor discrepancies between authors in the Bible, but there are examples of far greater discrepancies and contradictions. The Biblical story of how people found Jesus' tomb empty, is one such example.

Mark Chapter 16 says: "When the Sabbath was past, Mary Magdalene, Mary the mother of James, and Salome bought spices, so that they might go and anoint him. And very early on the first day of the week, when the sun had risen, they went to the tomb. And they were saying to one another, "Who will roll away the stone for us from the entrance of the tomb?" And looking up, they saw that the stone had been rolled back—it was very large. And entering the tomb, they saw a young man sitting on the right side, dressed in a white robe, and they were alarmed. And he said to them, "Do not be alarmed. You seek Jesus of Nazareth, who was crucified. He has risen; he is not here. See the place where they laid him. But go, tell his disciples and Peter that he is going before you to Galilee. There you will see him, just as he told you." And they went out and fled from the tomb, for trembling and astonishment had seized them, and they said nothing to anyone, for they were afraid".

However, Luke Chapter 24, and Verses 1 to 12 says: "But on the first day of the week, at early dawn, they went to the tomb, taking the spices they had prepared. And they found the stone rolled away from the tomb, but when they went in they did not find the body of the Lord Jesus. While they were perplexed about this, behold, two men stood by them in dazzling apparel. And as they were frightened and bowed their faces to the ground, the men said to them, "Why do you seek the living among the dead? He is not here, but has risen. Remember how he told you, while he was still in Galilee, that the Son of Man must be delivered into the hands of sinful men and be crucified and on the third day rise." And they remembered his words, and returning from the tomb they told all these things to the eleven and to all the rest. Now it was Mary Magdalene and Joanna and Mary the mother of James and the other women with them who told these things to the apostles, but these words seemed to them an idle tale, and they did not believe them. But Peter rose and ran to the tomb; stooping and looking in, he saw the linen cloths by themselves; and he went home marvelling at what had happened".

However, Matthew Chapter 28, and Verses 1 to 10 says: "Now after the Sabbath, toward the dawn of the first day of the week, Mary Magdalene and the other Mary went to see the tomb. And behold, there was a great earthquake, for an angel of the Lord descended from heaven and came and rolled back the stone and sat on it. His appearance was like lightning, and his clothing white as snow. And for fear of him the guards trembled and became like dead men. But the angel said to the women, "Do not be afraid, for I know that you seek Jesus who was crucified. He is not here, for he has risen, as he said. Come, see the place where he lay. Then go quickly and tell his disciples that he has risen from the dead, and behold, he is going before you to Galilee; there you will see him. See, I have told you." So they departed quickly from the tomb with fear and great joy, and ran to tell his disciples. And behold, Jesus met them and said, "Greetings!" And they came up and took hold of his feet and worshiped him. Then Jesus said to them, "Do not be afraid; go and tell my brothers to go to Galilee, and there they will see me."".

And John Chapter 20, and Verses 1 to 18 says: "Now on the first day of the week Mary Magdalene came to the tomb early, while it was still dark, and saw that the stone had been taken away from the tomb. So she ran and went to Simon Peter and the other disciple, the one whom Jesus loved, and said to them, "They have taken the Lord out of the tomb, and we do not know where they have laid him." So Peter went out with the other disciple, and they were going toward the tomb. Both of them were running together, but the other disciple outran Peter and reached the tomb first. And stooping to look in, he saw the linen cloths lying there, but he did not go in. Then Simon Peter came, following him, and went into the tomb. He saw the linen cloths lying there, and the face cloth, which had been on Jesus' head, not lying with the linen cloths but folded up in a place by itself. Then the other disciple, who had reached the tomb first, also went in, and he saw and believed; for as yet they did not understand the Scripture, that he must rise from the dead. Then the disciples went back to their homes. Jesus Appears to Mary Magdalene But Mary stood weeping outside the tomb, and as she wept she stooped to look into the tomb. And she saw two angels in white, sitting where the body of Jesus had lain, one at the head and one at the feet. They said to her, "Woman, why are you weeping?" She said to them, "They have taken away my Lord, and I do not know where they have laid him." Having said this, she turned around and saw Jesus standing, but she did not know that it was Jesus. Jesus said to her, "Woman, why are you weeping? Whom are you seeking?" Supposing him to be the gardener, she said to him, "Sir, if you have carried him away, tell me where you have laid him, and I will take him away." Jesus said to her, "Mary." She turned and said to him in Aramaic, "Rabboni!" (which means Teacher). Jesus said to her, "Do not cling to me, for I have not yet ascended to the Father; but go to my brothers and say to them, I am ascending to my Father and your Father, to my God and your God.'" Mary Magdalene went and announced to the disciples, "I have seen the Lord"—and that he had said these things to her".

Even when putting aside the inconsistencies and contradictions in the number and names of the women who went to Jesus' empty tomb, and the time of day, you can see that Mark, Luke, Matthew, and John, differ greatly from one another when discussing Jesus' resurrection. Mark Chapter 16 says that Mary Magdalene, Mary the mother of James, and Salome went to anoint Jesus's body when they saw a man sitting in His tomb with the stone door already rolled over from it. The man then informed them that Jesus had risen and told them to go and tell others, but the women ran out and did not tell anyone anything because they were afraid.

However, Luke Chapter 24, and Verses 1 to 12 contradicts Mark Chapter 16 in that it says the women encountered not one man, but two men in the tomb while the stone door was already rolled over. Neither of the two men were sitting down. The texts then say that the women bowed their faces to the ground before the men, who then told the women to go and tell others that Jesus had risen. The women then went to tell other people, one of whom (Peter) went back to the empty tomb and was amazed.

Now, Matthew Chapter 28, and Verses 1 to 10, tells yet another story which is different. Drastically different, in fact. The texts tell a fantastical tale of how an angel appeared from the skies like lighting to roll the stone door away from Jesus' tomb before Mary Magdalene's and the other Mary's eyes. The texts also claim that there were guards there who became afraid of the angel and became "like dead men". The angel then told the women to go and tell others that Jesus had risen, and as the women ran with excitement to tell other people, they happened upon Jesus Christ Himself in the flesh who told them to inform people to go and meet Jesus somewhere.

However, John Chapter 20, and Verses 1 to 18 tells yet another story which is different, and one which is even more fantastical and drastically different than Matthew's. The verses say that Mary Magdalene by herself went to Jesus empty tomb, but found it empty. She then ran to Peter and another one of Jesus' disciples to inform them of Jesus' body being gone. The two disciples then ran to go and confirm what Mary had told them, but one of them reached the tomb before Peter did. When both Peter and the other disciple had seen for themselves that Jesus' tomb was empty, they went home, but Mary stayed outside the tomb, crying. When she looked into the tomb again, she saw two angels sitting inside the tomb. One where Jesus' head was, and one where his feet were. They then asked her why she was crying, and she told them Jesus' body was missing. As she turned around though, she saw Jesus in the flesh standing behind her. She at first did not know it was Him however, and only knew after He called her name. She then exclaimed "teacher!" in excitement, before Jesus told her he was ascending to heaven and that she should go and tell the other disciples. She then went and told the other disciples that she had seen Jesus.

So… As you can see, it is quite evident that the severe discrepancies and contradictions in the Bible on the issue of Jesus' resurrection alone, point to the fact that the people who wrote those things in the Bible either made things up or just got the wrong information from other people. The entire Bible is filled with texts which are made-up or inaccurate, and yet people are being told that the Bible is the word of God.

Look: God does not contradict Himself. The notion of the Bible being God's word, is man's own fabrication. The word of God is His word, His speech, His voice, and His intonations. When God speaks, you will know it is Him, and you will hear His voice. The Bible was not spoken into existence by God, it was hand-written by men, and compiled by men who in the process of compilation, made decisions about which of the hundreds of stories to include in the Bible, and which stories to neglect. I do not doubt for a moment that when choosing only 73 of the hundreds of books which claim to have been inspired by God, there will be mistakes made.

People who claimed to be inspired by the Holy Spirit, supposedly wrote the books that constitute today's Bible, but even if they are not lying, it is a fact that having the Holy Spirit dwell within you, does not mean you are no longer human. And it certainly does not mean you cannot make mistakes. Human beings make mistakes, and this explains why there are many things in the Bible that should be taken with a grain of salt. 2 Timothy Chapter 3, and Verses 16 to 17 says: "All scripture is given by inspiration of God, and is profitable for doctrine, for reproof, for correction, for instruction in righteousness: That the man of God may be perfect, throughly furnished unto all good works".

Assuming you take the author's word for it, his and others' words may have been inspired by the Holy Spirit, but their words were not God's words. The Bible contains within it, words which were from God, supposedly quoted verbatim. Those you could argue, are God's words, but there are many other words which are not from Him. The Psalms for example, are not words from God. They are a collection of prayers to Him.

Religious Christians are quick to say the Bible is God's word, but they do not even know the Bible's history, and how it was compiled. They do not know why there are so many churches, or why the Catholic Church has 73 books in their Bible, while virtually every other Church in existence typically has 66 books in its Bible. Christians believe for the sake of believing, so they go along with whatever they have been raised to believe, but I have written this book as a drop of potent medicinal truth in the cup of religious lies being fed to them. A very concise history lesson is about to ensue.

Let me begin with a mention of the Roman emperor Constantine. Christianity had been illegal in Rome when he gained power in 306 A.D., but after claiming the throne through war, Constantine soon decreed that Christianity was to become Rome's official religion, and made it legal for people to practice other faiths as well. This was particularly great for the underground Christian movement because it meant they would no longer be persecuted for being Christians, but this decision was not without its problems.

In Constantine's time there was no Bible. Rather, people had a collection of Old Testament books called the Septuagint, as well as hundreds of New Testament books floating around. The Septuagint was an old Greek translation of the Torah, and contained Old Testament books which the Jews had always had. But because there was no definitive "New Testament", things became theologically complicated for Christianity.

You see: It was highly doubtful that any of the New Testament writers had any first-hand experience with Jesus Christ, and Saints like Paul, despite not having any first-hand experience with Him either, would have been a great help in the guidance of Christians. However, Paul died long ago and divisions were surfacing between people about the Deity of Christ and the nature of His association with God the Father. These divisions became more significant over time, threatening the unity of Constantine's Rome.

To put an end to this, Constantine assembled The First Council of Nicaea in 325 A.D., where among other things, a uniform set of beliefs about Jesus Christ was to be agreed upon by church leaders. The purpose of the council was a purely political one, and Constantine organised it for the sake of maintaining order. The decisions which resulted from the council were not based on any God-given prophesies or Holy-Spirit revelations to Church members, but were based instead on establishing consensus among people.

As had been done before with the introduction of Christianity to the pagans of Rome, a compromise had to be made for people who disagreed, to come together in agreement for the sake of the Roman Empire. This tendency to compromise even with pagans, combined with the political agendas of Church leaders, is the reason for the Sabbath being moved to Sunday, and the celebration of things like Christmas.

(Note however, that the practice of praying to Saints did not arise from any sort of compromise with pagans. Like many other things, it came from within the Church itself).

Following the council, disagreements were resolved (somewhat) albeit only temporarily, because Church traditions and beliefs had been decided upon in Nicaea, but the hundreds of New Testament books available were still a problem. The fact that anyone can write a New Testament book and claim to have been inspired by God, led to much debate between people about which books were canon and which books were not. In fact, these debates lasted centuries. Technically they are unresolved even to this day, but not as far as general consensus goes.

The first major synod on the matter of Biblical canons was the Council of Laodicea in 360 A.D., which preceded The Council of Rome in 382 A.D., which preceded The Council of Hippo in 393 A.D., which preceded The Council of Carthage in 397 A.D., which preceded The Council of Trent in 1545. By 400 A.D., the accepted New Testament books had been reduced from hundreds, to just 27. The main criteria for the elimination of all the other books, was whether or not the books conformed to what was being practiced by the Church, what Church elders believed at the time, and whether or not the books served the agendas of the Church elders.

You see: Christianity was being practiced and understood differently by different groups of people, because not everyone shared the same views of Jesus or Judaism. The people who represented a set of beliefs similar to those belonging to what we now call the "Orthodox" Church, constituted a single sect of Christianity amongst several others which existed. It is only because Orthodox Christianity gained political power when Constantine took Rome, that the Church was able to expand its version of Christianity to the extent that the other versions are now somewhat dead. The Church burned many New Testament books because those books' teachings varied from what Orthodox Church elders would have liked for others to believe.

Now, knowing all this information, you would have to be quite naïve, to believe the modern Bible to be complete and without error when compiled by fallible human beings. And you would have to be even more naïve to call it the word of God.

Indeed there were mistakes made in the compilation of the Bible and the selection of its New Testament texts. Of the hundreds of New Testament books available, there were many which fraudulently claimed to be written by Prophets or God-inspired people, and yet had bad doctrine in them. However, there were also many books falsely claiming to be written by Prophets or God-inspired people, and yet did in fact possess good doctrine. This made it especially difficult to determine which of the books were genuine, and meant that the chances of mistakenly including a forged book into the Bible was high.

These accidental additions are clearly evident in a significant number of New Testament books. Take 1 and 2 Peter for example. In the case of Peter's letters, there is the historical issue of the fact that the entire New Testament was written in advanced Greek, even though Peter was a low-class fisherman who spoke Aramaic. There is some debate between historians as to whether or not Peter wrote 1 Peter, but it is more or less unanimously agreed upon that Peter did not write 2 Peter.

However, Peter could not have possibly been the author of 1 nor 2 Peter because the historical evidence indicates he would not have been able to write them. In fact, the Bible itself reveals that Peter was "illiterate" or "unschooled". Acts Chapter 4, and Verse 13: "Now seeing the constancy of Peter and of John, understanding that they were illiterate and ignorant men, they wondered: and they knew them that they had been with Jesus" (The original Greek Bible text referring to Peter and John speaks of them literally as being "illiterate" not just "unschooled" which is used in many English Bible translations). If you cannot read or write, you certainly cannot write a New Testament book.

The earliest Gospels of the New Testament canon are those written by Paul, approximately 20 years after the death and resurrection of Jesus Christ. The other Gospels were all written by anonymous writers many decades after Jesus. The labelling of the Gospels according to John, Peter, Mark, Luke, Jude etc. were later (much later) done by scribes who assumed those people to be the authors of the books now attributed to them. The scribes quite clearly assumed incorrectly, because those books were all written a very long time after Jesus' crucifixion, and in a language which the alleged authors would never have understood.

Now, before we continue, let us discuss what led to the Council of Trent. Let us go to the year 1054. You see, this is when Christianity experienced some turmoil after political differences caused a schism of the Church into the "Roman Catholic Church" and the "Orthodox Church". There had been schisms before, (like those which resulted from the Council of Ephesus in 431 A.D. and the Council of Chalcedon in 451 A.D), but this recent division of the Church caused some people to lose faith in the papacy, as the politicization of Christianity, and its use as a means of government control and manipulation became even more apparent under the power of Roman Catholicism. A few heretics were therefore born from this mistrust, and although the Church had them killed, the spirit of heresy was destined never to die with them.

In 1517, one particular heretic named Martin Luther, took it upon himself to challenge the Church on certain matters, and in a way that eventually led to a new branch of Christianity: Protestantism. A thing by which Luther's rebellion was initiated, was how the Church (a very wealthy entity) was taking money from poor people by telling the people that money given to the Church would grant them remission of their sins.

Luther made his objections quite public, and these objections eventually landed him in formal assemblies where he was to be examined by the Church. During his first examination, a confrontation of outspoken words ensued between Luther and a Church representative, when under questioning, Luther accused the Church of being the antichrist.

Luther was eventually excommunicated by the Church, as he continued to defy it and repeatedly refused to recant his heretical proclamations against the Church. Thus, Luther was forced into hiding for some time when the Church wanted to kill him, but while hidden away, he secretly began translating the New Testament into German. His translation of course was not exact. In addition to making sure his New Testament translation would conform to German vernacular, he translated it in such a fashion that it more resembled his ideals than that of Catholicism (This moulding of Biblical text to suit his doctrine is more apparent in his later translations of the Bible). He also wrote letters to certain people, espousing the doctrines he had manufactured in disagreement with the papacy. False doctrines which he had in fact been teaching for quite some time before the Church excommunicated him.

After Luther's New Testament went public in 1522, it became very popular and facilitated the spread of his doctrine quite rapidly. This was relatively easy to do, considering the fact that the papacy's improper conduct was apparent to anyone to whom it was pointed out. In gaining followers, Luther accused the Church of being the antichrist, having erred in its ways, and mistaking itself for a God-like authority in its own right. Eventually Luther's doctrine spread so well, that he decided to create his own Church, and he did so successfully.

When Luther later translated the entire Bible, he negated 7 books from the Old Testament, and placed them in a section of their own which he dubbed "Apocrypha". These books are: Tobit, Judith, Baruch, Wisdom, Sirach, 1 Maccabees, and 2 Maccabees. He also removed large parts of Esther and Daniel from the Bible because they did not conform to his doctrine.

Although Luther's cause was noble at first, and prompted by the misuse of

Christianity by the Roman Catholic Church, he was quite misguided, arrogant, and proud. None of Martin Luther's beliefs were divinely-inspired. Rather, his doctrine and his rebellion against Roman Catholicism, were inspired by his personal convictions. Luther's doctrine was not from God or the Holy Spirit, although his followers certainly presumed otherwise, and his separation from the Roman Catholic Church was a significant motivator for some of the dogma he preached in opposition to that of the Church's.

Luther, in his presumptuous self-righteousness, manufactured doctrine of his own, modified existing Catholic doctrine, and moulded the Bible in the image of his own agendas. A Bible, which was compiled by the Catholic Church in a manner which served the agendas of Catholicism. As a result, the Protestant Church (the major branch of Christianity which stems from Luther's teachings) only has an incomplete and adulterated version of the Catholic Bible, and in effect, is only practicing an incomplete and adulterated version of Catholicism.

In other words: Every single Church in existence other than the Catholic Church, is practicing an adulterated and diluted form of Catholicism, because the Catholic Church was the first ever Christian Church. And every Bible version which exists other than the Catholic Bible, is an adulterated Bible, because the Catholic Church compiled the first Bible.

The Council of Trent in 1545, was assembled in part, as a response to Luther and his doctrine. It was held not long before his death, and dealt with Catholic doctrine to reaffirm everything the Catholic Church had been practicing (with the exception of the sale of indulgences), to issue a few new decrees, and to condemn the heretical teachings of Martin Luther and his ilk.

Since Luther though, there have been even more divisions within Christianity (countless divisions), and essentially all of them were divisions within Protestantism. The spirit of separation which accompanied Luther stayed with his Church and his set of teachings, and appealed itself to all those who thought to separate themselves from the papacy.

Riding on the back of the aforementioned divisive spirit, is the devil. The devil's work through men like Martin Luther, is the reason for thousands of Churches existing today, the reason that millions of people are enslaved by religious doctrine, and the reason that modern Christianity is bathed in lies and misinformation.

As more Churches began to spring up since the advent of Protestantism, the element of truth they inherited from the first Church of Christ (the Catholic Church) became more and more diluted, whereas the perversion of Christianity by the founders of the new Churches increased in severity. A gradual attenuation and cessation of Church practices, amalgamated with the new doctrines and varied Bible interpretations by the founders of the new Churches, is the principal cause for the ever-increasing phenomenon of ineffective prayers and the lack of Holy Spirit manifestations.

Now let it be clear that being a "Protestant", or a "Catholic", or a "Seventh-Day Adventist", etc. does not mean you are exclusively saved nor cut off from God. God is a God for all of mankind, and Jesus Christ died for all of us. His Holy Spirit will seat itself in the soul of any man or woman who calls for it, and God will respond to all those who recognise Him.

God looks at your heart, not your denomination. Even those who are not Christian, are watched by God and have angels of guidance and protection assigned to them as they are assigned also to the rest of humanity. The notion that "you are doomed to hellfire unless you have the Bible" is a deception originating from Martin Luther and his misguided reformation of Christianity. It is a terrible lie, and it is used to keep people enslaved to religious doctrine. Although Luther's intentions were to free people from the papacy's controlling use of Christianity, he only wound up substituting one system of control for another.

Martin Luther, in his act of stripping down Christian practices (because they were Catholic practices), laid the foundations not only for mindless religious indoctrination of men *"through faith alone"* (as he would say), he also paved the way for the elimination of the rituals and spiritual practices which facilitate peoples' communications with God within Christianity. Man's ability to communicate with God, to think freely, and to live as spiritual beings, has been stifled by religious indoctrination. I will explain later in this book exactly what I am talking about, but for now, understand that in the stead of spiritual development, all that most Christians have is a near-useless blind faith.

Christianity today is about convenience to them. It is convenient to go to Church every Sunday and feel better about yourself, and it is convenient to have certain Bible passages for you to cherry-pick for your friends/associates. Christians will say "It is God's plan" when it makes them feel better to say so, and they will say "I am blessed" when things are going well for them.

When they suffer, they will still say it is "God's plan", or that "God is testing" them, and when opportunities slip through their fingers they will say "God must have not wanted that for me". But after suffering for a long time, their faith will slowly turn to anger and/or hatred. They will start blaming God, and asking why He is allowing them to suffer. Eventually, some people will buckle under the weight of their circumstances and the devil will find room to pervert them against God.

Blind faith is the problem with what mankind has done with the Bible, and it is for that reason the Holy Spirit has lead me to write this book. Matthew Chapter 7, and Verse 7 says: "Ask, and it will be given to you; seek, and you will find; knock, and it will be opened to you. For everyone who asks receives, and the one who seeks finds, and to the one who knocks it will be opened". The irony here, is that despite most people not seeing anything from their prayers, this part of scripture is true. It is not a lie that God will answer those who knock, however there is something missing. The Bible does not mention the things which must be done before doors will open for you, and the little that it does mention, is rather misleading. The Bible does not tell people how to knock on God's door, and how to cause the ground to shake (literally) with His power. Prayer is one way, yes. However it is not the only way, and as a plethora of scorned atheists will attest: nor is it by any means, the most effective.

When people take as the word of God, a book which was written and compiled by fallible human beings, and when they claim it contains all the truth one needs, a variety of bad things will result. The most damaging of which are ignorance and gullibility. It is due to the spirit of ignorance that Catholics will call the recognition of other peoples' ancestors "pagan worship" yet they themselves do the exact same as the "pagans" do when they pray to Saints, and it is due to the spirit of ignorance that Protestants will condemn Catholics for "paganism" yet they themselves place flowers and/or a deceased person's favourite item(s) next to his/her grave with lit candles.

You see: Your typical Christian does not know much, if anything at all about the spirit realm, but will quote from the Bible to talk of things he/she has no clue about. Your typical Christian does not know that by placing objects next to the burial site (or place of death) of a dead person and/or lighting candles there, they are creating a shrine for the deceased. It is a form of what naïve Christians would call "pagan worship". In fact, the practice of establishing memorials for the deceased is descendent from "pagan" rituals. Christians will condemn "pagans" for creating shrines to spirits, but are blissfully unaware of the fact that they (Christians) practice the same rituals. Rituals they practice to a far lesser extent only because their ignorance of the spirit realm will not enable them to do more.

Lighting a candle in tribute to any dead person is an invocation to his/her spirit, and placing any items next to his/her memorial site is an offering to satisfy his/her spirit. If the spirit is so inclined, if it is able, and if it is a good spirit, it might then begin to intervene in your life and protect you, as well as bring you good fortune. Most peoples' deceased loved ones intervene in their relatives' lives anyway, but when the deceased are pleased with particular people, it is only natural that they go to greater lengths to help those people in life.

Erecting statues in honour of spirits (like those of dead people), or performing rituals (like funerals) for them, is not different from the acts of "idolatry" which "pagans" are accused of committing for their spirits/ancestors, but everybody else does these things anyway because they can quite clearly see that there is nothing wrong with what they are doing, and because they do not know how closely their conventions are linked to the "paganism" they claim not to be affiliated with.

This is how the spirit world works, but the Bible does not tell you: The things which Christians condemn as "idolatry" and "pagan worship" are built on the foundations of establishing shrines for spirits and offering things to said spirits. The next step, is the establishment of a two-way communication between the spirit(s) and the human(s) who wish to converse with the spirit(s), but the ignorance of your typical Christian will not permit him/her to ever get to that step.

Going many steps beyond what I have mentioned, can lead to the summoning of forces which can be used for protection, for healing, etc. but I did not write this book to teach anyone of such things, so I will not elaborate. And I dictate that you do not endeavour to find out on your own. These can be dangerous things, and without guidance from the Holy Spirit or from those to whom God has allowed wisdom to be imparted, you will surely run into big trouble.

The last thing you need is to have your life destroyed by evil spirits for whom you have accidentally (or perhaps knowingly) established a doorway.

There are countless stories of peoples' lives being torn asunder by experimentation with things of the occult, because ignorant and naïve people allowed their curiosity of the spirit realm to get the better of them.

Creating a shrine for one's departed family members or friends, as Christians (and many other people) do, is not sinful. It is a means of communicating with, and acknowledging the existence of those who do not exist in physical bodies. It is not worship. Just as Catholics pray directly to Saints and ask for help from them, they are not worshiping the Saints. So Africans who recognise their ancestors, are not "ungodly pagans". I will talk about these things later on to aid your understanding of them, but these things are the means by which men of God become spiritually developed and powerful. These are God's things, and only those whose spirits are strong can wield them properly.

There is no doubt that spiritually-ascended members of the Catholic Church know of the things I speak, and in great detail. The Church definitely knew long before they compiled the Bible, but decided to leave any texts on such things out of the public domain as much as possible, because they can be dangerous to overzealous and ignorant people. The Bible was compiled mostly as a method of control, and only partly as a means by which Christian doctrine is easily accessible. There is no way that the Catholic Church (the few Church members who knew) would place God's secrets into it. Secrets of spiritualism and of God, can do more harm to those who endeavour to discover them, and unless a person is of a pure and dedicated spirit, such things are really not meant for him/her.

Chapter Three: A MATTER OF KNOWING

Just as there is a physical world, so too is there a rather expansive world of what goes mostly unseen. The universe is so massive it exceeds the capacity of the average human being to fathom, and God has brought into existence, an almost innumerable amount of creatures, many of whom are not known to us on Earth to inhabit our planet.

A percentage of these exist in generally perceivable, and physical forms (Cows, humans, fish, apes, etc.), while some exist only in realms that are generally unperceived by most people. I.e. the spirit. The most commonly heard of are the "ghosts", the "angels", and the "demons", but of course having them at the forefront of general knowledge does not mean they are the only things out there.

Ghosts & the Spirit Realm

Before I talk about the spirit realm in slight depth (for now), you should first understand that all living things are comprised of energy such that there is a spiritual dimension to them. As human beings for example, our bodies are shells – vessels through which we navigate the physical world. You might need to get used to the following fact, but your shell (which you probably have grown attached to), is not the actual you. The entity that happens to truly define you is inside of your body: The mind, and its metaphysical extensions, which constitute the spirit.

All living creatures are spirits. Animals as well are spirits encased in a shell, and that is why they are able to think and feel emotions in very much the same ways we can. The degree of intelligence the animal possesses, is what determines the extent to which they are capable of displaying and/or feeling these emotions.

Now, with regards to human beings, the term "ghost" is typically used to refer to people who were once alive in physical-world bodies, and then died now having only their spiritual component(s) to define them. They still live and are fully cognizant, but not in the conventional sense. Unless they have figured out how, they can no longer be felt, heard or known to exist in the physical world by most people.

This is because spirits are energy forms who operate within energy thresholds outside the spectrum of what our bodies can usually pick up on. In the same sense that various forms of electromagnetic radiation can only be picked up by sensitised electronic equipment, ghosts and their activities too, can be picked up via sensitive camera or audio equipment at certain times.

With the exception of some rare cases, ghosts do not have or cannot generate, the energy required to perceptibly phase and manifest themselves into the physical world. As a result of this and other factors, it is the common occurrence that ghosts who remain on Earth are displeased or unhappy most of the time. Everyone feels the need to matter – even when they are dead.

When human beings die in the flesh we become ghosts. We do not simply cease to be in existence when our bodies have given out to the aging process or have been subjected to a fatally traumatic event. Those who would characterise themselves as obstinate unbelievers in the spiritual realm and its components commonly find this out the hard way but the good news is that they have little trouble accepting that they are ghosts, and dealing with what is left of themselves after death. Even though they might initially battle to come to terms with their perhaps untimely passing.

Ghosts are spirits who no longer have physical bodies, so technically we are all ghosts as we are, and before we die, all that happens is that our bodies can no longer facilitate us. Upon death your spirit may or may not be taken/guided to whichever place you are "meant to be", depending on multiple factors. However, for the most part, unless you are evil, and/or to a significant degree, responsible for the suffering of others that you are yet to account for, you should first be willing to go there. Heaven and hell are not the only places people can go when they die, and the Bible certainly does not say that they are. The Hebrew-Aramaic Old Testament does not support the idea of "heaven and hell alone", and the New Testament does not claim heaven and hell to be the only places people can go to. Deceivers and those deceived, have used the declaration of "heaven or hellfire" to scare good people into a life of religious enslavement, but they do not know about the things which they speak and claim to believe.

Speaking of which: There is also the issue of reincarnation, which many people do not understand. Indeed there is such a thing as reincarnation, although it is rarely afforded. People who are allowed to reincarnate include children who died young or who were murdered by the practice of abortion, as well as a very small number of people who are sent to this Earth for a particular purpose.

On the issue of where people go after death: bad people go to bad places, and good people go to good places. It is a bit more complicated than that, but essentially this is the principle. I have personally been to, and seen, some of these places so I know that what most people believe about the spirit realm, is highly inaccurate.

An angel once showed me that there are many different places our spirits may reside after death, and it can depend on many factors. At about age 17, the angel had come to wake me from my body as I slept, and took me to what appeared to be one of many checkpoints leading to various parts of the universe. While there, I saw spirits of different kinds moving through what seemed to be portals, and going to places unknown. Some of these spirits were human, some of them were angels, and some were types of spirits which I had not heard of before. I saw different colours around all the spirits, and it occurred to me that these were their auras. The auras signified their temperaments or highlighted aspects of their attributes as beings.

The angel who had taken me there, had a lot to say. He conversed with me about who he was, why he had come to take me, and that he had some things to discuss with me. I asked a few questions and spoke to him about some of the troubles I was going through at the time, as well as some of the good things in my life. The angel never did laugh or show much emotion of any kind, but he always had a very good word of advice for the various things I had to say.

As we spoke however, a rather unpleasant sensation began to dawn on me: my head began to hurt a lot. It soon occurred to me that the reason my head was hurting was the fact that, that night, before going to bed, I had foolishly sprayed a mosquito repellent onto my bed sheets as well as into the atmosphere of the room, therefore saturating it. I am allergic to the chemicals in most mosquito repellents, so my body reacted adversely to the repellent, and the consequence of that poorly-thought action, was a painful headache.

The reason I became aware of this despite being quite far away from my physical body, is that when we travel in the spirit, we are still connected to our physical bodies in a sense. If ever we lose the connection to our bodies, it is probably because we will never be able to return to them.

When some, or most people have out of body experiences they do not maintain full awareness of their bodies, because they do not know how to. However, I am very different from most people, so I quickly learned to be aware of myself in two places at once. I was aware of both my body that lay sleeping, as well as my spirit that remained in the heavens.

Now, the headache became so bad that a few times, I requested to return to my body and take some painkillers so that I may resume the discussion with the angel at a later date, but the angel insisted that our meeting was of utmost importance. So we kept going. Eventually however, I said "It is really getting bad now, we need to talk another time". The angel then told me that if he left, I would not see him again for a long time. He also proceeded to say that where we were, was a place through which all kinds of spirits were at liberty to travel, and that there were evil spirits who had noticed us and were watching. When I looked around to confirm this, I saw that there were indeed a group of evil spirits in a corner somewhere, and apparently hoping that the angel would leave soon because they could not come close to him. These were black shadow figures, and I realised they were not there by coincidence. They had attempted to prevent the angel and I from meeting, but failed to do that, so all they could do was watch us.

The angel told me that if he left, the protection he was offering me from them by his presence would no longer be maintained, and he asked if I was sure that I was ready for him to leave. I said yes, but enquired about the evil spirits that were nearby. The angel told me that they would try and hurt me once he left, but that they would not be able to overcome me. So I agreed to depart from him, and he left.

When he did leave, suddenly they all came and attempted to envelop me, but as I had fought evil spirits before (long story), I easily overpowered them. These were low-order dark creatures, some of whom were spectral forces, while others took the appearance of spiders. As I repelled them, I transported myself back to my body and awoke with the worst headache I had had in a very long time.

As I said, the Bible does not state that heaven and hell are the only places available to the dead, but people have always felt the need to reference the Bible for what it does not even say, or misuse it for what it does say, as long as it is in agreement with their preconceptions.

Religious Christians need to understand that everything of the physical world has a spiritual connection because God is a spirit, and when He created the universe, and everything in it, He did so from a spiritual perspective. The universe constitutes physical manifestations of processes and entities that were brought into existence spiritually, first.

Given that the universe is so incomprehensively massive, and God Himself is so infinitely diverse, there is a very large number of places where there is life. Human beings are not God's only creations, despite what some very naïve biblical creationists will tell you.

There are many different forms of intelligent life scattered across the universe, but human beings are special and different from God's other creations by virtue of the fact that it is only we, who were created in His image.

Many of the planets we see to be devoid of life or activity, actually harbour spiritual beings of various kinds, as the spirit realm can be seen as being only a soft mirror image of the physical realm. An empty house in the neighbourhood for example, usually is not empty at all. They are usually always haunted, even if the ghosts do not make themselves known. If no one occupies something or claims it to be his/hers, any ghost has the right to claim it.

When people move into such establishments, the ghost(s) occupying the home may object and occasionally cause trouble. The kind of trouble depends on the ghost, but it is unusual for anything serious to happen, except in cases where the ghost is very upset about something. Ghosts are people too, and they still have feelings, so many of them are distraught about having been killed or that no one seems to remember them. Especially distraught, are those who reside in the home they were murdered in.

Some ghosts (because of any number of possible complications) are trapped in a certain space or environment, but otherwise, ghosts can traverse a large portion of the universe. A lot of the time though, the deceased will remain on Earth, as most of them still have family members alive whom they would like to watch over or maintain some form of contact with.

Ghosts are constantly trying to communicate with the living in order to be acknowledged, and are always attempting to establish contact with loved ones in any way they know how to. When they succeed, even people who would consider themselves sceptics, realise there is something trying to talk to them.

Deep down, (sometimes way deep down), every person is aware of the existence of God and/or the spiritual realm. Every single person by virtue of the spiritual attributes that define them, at least knows that there is something there or here that they "cannot quite explain". Something they "feel" often enough to be of significance.

In my experience, I have found that typically, those who vehemently profess their disbelief in "ghosts", "spirits", "God" or what have you, do so from a common and subconscious standpoint of fear. This is of course not always the case, but it seems to be human nature to cast aside what scares you, and run away from it as a means of apparent resolution. To many people, sometimes the easiest way to avoid something is to claim it does not exist, and seemingly denounce its grasp on you.

You might be surprised to find out just how many atheists and admitted sceptics of the spirit realm irrationally fear the dark or the thought of sleeping alone in a dark room. "Irrationally", by their own admission. I can recall how as a child, after watching something scary on television or listening to ghost stories, I would feel so afraid of ghosts that I dreaded the act of sleeping alone in a dark room. Despite having never experienced any activity that would justify my fears, and never witnessing phenomenon that would serve as evidence that these things even existed, that fear was instilled into me.

Ironically, now that I am a little more grown up, live alone in my own apartment, and have dealt with evil spirits of all kinds and for over five years, I am able to rest well at night, and have no interest whatsoever in fearing opportunistic creatures that throw themselves onto people as they sleep.

Strange sounds in the evenings, voices whispering while I lay down to try and sleep, items knocking themselves over from shelves, hearing footsteps in my room, having animalistic and often large creatures, land on my bed and blow wind into my face, being taken in the spirit to unknown lands by beings of darkness, having constant battles with demons, being approached by witches, etc. I have experienced it all, and to an extent that only a few priests would not struggle to deal with.

On many nights I could sense the presence of evil spirits in my room, hovering about and watching me, just waiting for me to go to bed. I used to have to feel both anxious and calm simultaneously on a nightly basis because I knew that the likelihood of an evil spirit paying me an unwelcome visit was high, and that I did not know how dangerous it could be.

However, one does not need to have fought evil spirits to know that they are out and about on this planet, because the evidence is in abundance. It is just that some people choose to ignore it. I personally believe that there are very few people alive who wholeheartedly are convinced by the notion of atheism and its arguments. Most atheists are only doing their very best to convince themselves and others, of the things they wish were true.

Atheism has nothing to do with whether or not one believes in a spirit realm, but the failure to acknowledge the existence of an ever-present God, is usually linked to the declaration that there are no such things as ghosts, and/or that nothing becomes of us after death. I do not currently know anybody who claims to be atheist (because I prove to them that they are misguided), but many of those whom I personally knew to have claimed abandonment of all theism, frequently switched between calling themselves "atheists" and calling themselves "agnostics". It turns out that this is quite the common trend among atheists, and a good is example is a particular "Richard Dawkins". I could see right through his claims to atheism before he ever publically said (on various occasions), that at times he prefers to call himself agnostic. You see, being labelled an atheist tends to have attached to it, connotations of "intelligence" by the ignoramus masses, and atheist propagandists like Richard Dawkins will capitalise on that.

In Richard Dawkin's case especially, being recognised as a key figure of anti-theism, not only brings him a lot of attention, it generates him revenue. Here I am, discussing him in a section of my book because it is likely that you know who he is. And if you do not, it is probable that you will soon find out, as he is somewhat of a mascot, poster child, and spokesperson for the atheist movement. However, that is all he is. He appeals mostly to naïve teenagers, inquisitive lay people, and new-atheists who need somebody to comfort them in their delusions.

At best: Dawkins has not much of a clue about what he talks. At worst: he is a fraud. He avoids any kind of debate with people whom he knows will ridicule his assertions with logic and fact. And when given the platform to address groups of people by himself, he uses the opportunities of his proclamations going unchallenged, to say the most ridiculous of things.

An honest evaluation of Richard Dawkins concludes that he does not know what he is talking about, but because he is a representative of the atheist agenda and a co-operator with the media's bias against theism (whether he knows this or not), he gets significant media coverage and gets to debate a few theists who usually do not seem to know what they are talking about either.

Richard Dawkins, like many atheists, has used the avowal of atheism to attribute to his esteem and to increase his own reputation. However I can see that like many other atheists, he also knows in his own heart that there is a God, in spite of his claims to the contrary. I do not believe one needs to be able to see the things I can see, to identify Richard Dawkins as nothing but an advertisement for atheism. An advertisement for something which he does not truly believe, but which offers him a platform through which he can attack religion. He is a fame-seeker who drives a bandwagon of atheism, while erroneously using arguments against religion to fuel it. Like the vast majority of atheists, he focuses his campaigns on attacking religion because he cannot defend atheism. Atheism is a logically unsound paradigm, and just as much as he seems to lack the ability to determine this, he does not possess the ability to rationalise a logical defence for it. Likewise, he attacks "creationism" because he cannot defend the bogus theory of evolution. As I will later explain: No one can.

You see: what has happened to him, as it has happened to most atheists, is that he has confused religion and its failure to justify itself, with the failure of God or the spirit realm to be evidenced. Of course he does not endeavour to experiment with the manifestation of "supernatural" forces and he instead supposes the God of religious depiction to be the only God. That is the God whose existence he continually attacks. Advocates against religion tend to make the mistake of erroneously associating God with religion and its stupidity, because religion claims to be of God.

In a sense similar in nature to that of the elitist, racially-prejudiced people who link Africans to crime, Atheists link God to religion. It is merely incidental that God happens to be claimed by religion, and it is merely incidental that most Africans in places like the U.S. are so disadvantaged as to be situated in ghettoes and inevitably therefore, linked to crime. Religions have undoubtedly proven themselves to be symbolic of foolishness, but as I have said, they do not represent God or His intentions. What most atheists really mean when they say they do not believe in God, is that they do not believe in religion. Whether or not they believe in God in another matter.

Ask most atheists why they are atheist, and through spite, they will most likely satirically make mention of "a man in the sky casting judgment on mankind", the nonsensical religious notion of being able to make money buy sowing "a money-seed", or the failure of religion to make any sense whatsoever with its many ridiculous claims. Such People's atheism is a product of their ability to discern the irrationality of religion, and their inability to discern its separation from God. They are bitter that religion has lied to, and manipulated them or people they know, and this bitterness makes itself apparent almost intentionally when they speak.

A high percentage of people who formerly belonged to a religion and now identify as "atheist", are people who used to live life very much religiously, until one day their brains started working properly and they realised that the lives they were living were lives that other people had dictated to them. They were lives not based on fact or logic, but rather were based on the arbitrary declarations of people who told them what they should believe.

When people who hold themselves to nonsensical religious standards, finally realise how much of their time religion has wasted, or when people realise how useless religion has been for other people, they angrily abandon their faith, and a lot of the time, they wind up throwing the idea of God out of the window with it as well. They rightfully become angry at religion, but they wrongfully become angry at the notion of God, because it is not really God they are angry at. It is the picture of "God" religion has painted for them which has left them scorned.

The resulting internal conflict from this scorn becomes apparent when God is mentioned before them. Particularly, it can be seen in environments like the web (internet) when someone brings up the idea of God. A statement as simple as "Thank God" by somebody in the comment section of a web page will prompt an impudent atheist to intrude upon the discussion and proclaim "there is no God", or something to that effect.

Such people are deeply troubled, and are never at rest as long as people express a recognition or admiration for God before them. Unbeknownst to them, that thing which prompts them to declare objections to the notion of God, and which constantly worries their soul to say "there is no God", is usually not a natural thing. I will later explain in greater depth what I am about to say, but what I am getting at is that most of such atheists are occupied by evil spirits of deception or pride that often thrive on feeding their host(s) lies about God being "unfair" or "ruthless" in order to try and validate their backs being turned against Him. Pay attention to some of the things these kinds of people say, and you will recognise the talk of demons.

These kinds of people are so troubled that they will mindlessly move from one internet forum to another, making the same declarations against the idea of God. These people, although a minority, can make it seem as though the internet is full of atheists, when in reality all the "there is no God" comments on the internet, are from the very same childish and irrational people who asininely surf the web, saying the same ludicrous things over and over and over again everywhere they go, because they are internally disturbed and spiritually confused. They call themselves atheists, but they are obsessed with God. Their obsession will never cease, and they will continue to endure their torments, almost retributively, until the day they confess in their hearts, the truth of God. Such troubled souls are dreadfully lost, and the more unintelligent they are, the less likely it is that they can be shown any truth.

For it is one thing to discuss the existence of God with someone who claims there is no God, and it is another matter entirely to discuss the existence of God with such a person when he lacks the ability to reason. The aforementioned kinds of atheists will usually absent themselves from the possibility of rational discourse, while not knowing anything whatsoever about the things they choose to believe or that which they choose to ridicule. They are proud, presumptuous children who lack the ability to present sound arguments to support their proclamations, and will normally resort to derision against those who engage, or attempt to engage, them in debate.

These gullible atheists poison their minds with the poorly-founded ideas of Richard Dawkins and his new-atheist brethren, and yet cannot themselves defend their very religious beliefs with anything other than insults and absurdities. "Logic" and "reason" are things far removed from them, but they will claim such things for themselves. They are illiterate on historical matters, naïve on religious matters, and foolish about their own convictions, yet they passionately dive head-first into historical and religious arguments. It is therefore not a surprise that they cannot defend their claims with anything but mockery and ridicule. They are after all, only following in the footsteps of their new-atheist leaders. It would be unreasonable to expect them to behave differently.

Atheists who go through such embarrassing pains to disclaim God do not understand Him beyond the concepts they have blindly endeavoured to prejudicially rationalise, and many of them are so desperately in denial that even the naïve and ignorant religious mind understands God far more than they do.

Considering the fact that religious minds are very much ignorant of Him too, one can see that there is much shame cast upon the heads of vehement atheists, to whom atheism is as much a religion as those they condemn. Even animals know there is God. A man sins against himself when he declares there is no God, and he hurls himself from the cliff of rationality in the process.

You see: Atheists are in a dilemma. Why? Well, what is atheism? It is "disbelief in the existence of a God or gods". In other words: They **believe** there is no God. They certainly do not know there is no God. There is not an atheist on this planet who can claim he/she knows for a fact that there is no God. This means an atheist has no facts from which to draw his/her conclusion that there is no God. All that an atheist can say is "I do not know".

Therein lies the dilemma of atheism. Because an atheist can only say "I do not know" when it comes to the existence of a God, an atheist cannot really be an atheist. An atheist must identify as "agnostic" if he/she wishes to maintain any credibility of at least being a semi-rational person. For an atheist to claim atheism, he/she can only do so religiously. They can only do so by blind faith and irrationality. The same kind of blind faith they accuse religious people of having. There is no logic to atheism, and this is why atheists so desperately and illogically cling to their religion.

Now, because it is rather atypical to encounter an atheist who does not flagrantly pride him or herself on his/her inflexible belief system, and often subconsciously fear-driven "doubts", atheists tend to define themselves by their somewhat radical world view and some go to great lengths in an attempt to advocate movements against religion – and rightfully so.

You see, religion is an infectious tool orchestrated and utilised by evil. God Himself is against religion. Let me explain why: Before and even after, the Bible was ever written, there was religion in various manifestations. Primary of which was the worshiping of useless idols. People expressed adoration for various gods and made sacrifices to beings they believed were of a divine nature.

When the Prophet Elijah challenged the worshipers of a demon god named Baal, he was challenging religious leaders who at the time were believing in a false God. 1 Kings, Chapter 18, and Verse 24 to 29: "And you call upon the name of your god, and I will call upon the name of the Lord, and the God who answers by fire, he is God" And all the people answered, "It is well spoken". Then Elijah said to the prophets of Baal, "Choose for yourselves one bull and prepare it first, for you are many, and call upon the name of your god, but put no fire to it". And they took the bull that was given them, and they prepared it and called upon the name of Baal from morning until noon, saying, "O Baal, answer us!" But there was no voice, and no one answered. And they limped around the altar that they had made. And at noon Elijah mocked them, saying, "Cry aloud, for he is a god. Either he is musing, or he is relieving himself, or he is on a journey, or perhaps he is asleep and must be awakened". And they cried aloud and cut themselves after their custom with swords and lances, until the blood gushed out upon them. And as midday passed, they raved on until the time of the offering of the oblation, but there was no voice. No one answered; no one paid attention".

The worshipers of Baal saw no fruits of their labour. No evidence whatsoever that Baal even existed, but they were held in bondage to silly rituals, and useless practices.

A major aspect of religion's deceit lies in convincing people to rely on blind faith. In doing so, followers stop thinking logically and accept whatever false doctrine you bring them based on this premise. The Bible says nothing (absolutely nothing) of worshiping God with blind faith. Blind faith is a poison tossed into the minds of men by the evil one, and is a platform for severe ignorance disguised by religion and its controlling nature.

It is by blind faith that people worshiped Baal, and it is by blind faith that most Christians, Muslims, Mormons, etc. worship today. Religion operates on the basis of a faith that has not been justified or proven to be of sound reasoning, because if you can make people believe something they have not even seen, they are susceptible to the many subsequent lies you intend to deliver to them.

Look at Islam for example. You see how diligent many of them are. How unbendingly most of them adhere to their religious protocol. They are more dedicated to their God than Christians are to theirs, because Islam is more controlling and forceful. As a result, the culture of close-minded Islam is more widely practiced than the culture of Closed-minded Christianity.

Now please, do not confuse my damning remarks and exposure of religion for what it truly is, with a damnation of Christianity and what it stands for. Christianity, as an acceptance of Jesus Christ's sacrifice, and recognition of God's presence is not a religion. However Christianity as a judgemental system of dictatorships, silly indoctrinations, and false leaders, is.

People do not know what religion is. Anyone who calls him or herself religious, is lost. For religion is a lie, an imposing deception, and a mechanism of grandiose ignorance. Believing in Jesus Christ, having the Holy Spirit dwell within you, and trusting in God, does not make you religious. What would make you religious, is a subscription to the nonsensical ideologies and faulty logic that religion is well known for. Being held captive by the limitations of ridiculous doctrine. That is what religion has always been about.

The devil has been using the Bible and Christianity religiously to mislead people onto a path such that they do not see the true light, for as long as anyone can remember. Religious Christianity impedes the growth of its participants, like any other useless religion does. The self-defined atheist is right, when he/she endeavours to spread awareness of religion and its falsehoods. I agree as vehemently as they do. Famous self-proclaimed atheists like Richard Dawkins and his kind are right in their campaign against religion and the various arguments they often have for the liberation of humanity from its tyranny.

Christians seem to be disturbed by the fact that there are people who claim there is no God, and they tend to seek very strongly to convert such people to Christianity (or back to it, if they once were before). But the rib-tickling irony, is that the Christians themselves are often the primary reason most atheists have abandoned theism in the first place. Anyone with a logical or fact-driven mind-set will see that religion is just another global scam, because the facts are at odds with its claims. "Atheism", is only the inevitable knee-jerk reaction to religion.

Religious Christianity attempts to dumb people down, and often makes preposterous excuses for what does not seem to make sense or what people do not understand. Scientists and men of scientific inquiry have been harassed throughout the ages and accused of witchcraft by religious institutions for attempting to explain things that the church did not agree with, because "The Bible did not speak of them".

For example: The Catholic Church of his time, placed Galileo under house arrest for the remainder of his life, for advocating a heliocentric notion of the Earth and its position in the universe. 'Heliocentrism' is the idea that the Earth is in fact not the centre of the universe (contrary to the church's teachings at the time), and that it orbits the sun.

It is far easier to say "God did it", and remain in ignorance than go and discover the truth for yourself, and Religion would rather keep people ignorant, so as to maintain control over them. Why on Earth would your typical atheist want to revert to an inefficient system of poorly justified doctrine, and slavery to even more poorly justified protocols?

It is only the most honest atheists who realise that there is a God, and stop lying to their own hearts about the fact that He is there. People who do learn to reject the lie of atheism either transition to Christianity, or attempt to explore the existence of God in other ways, because atheism offers no valid explanation.

Everything can be explained, and there is no such thing as 'the supernatural'. Why would I say such a thing? Well you see, the 'supernatural' is defined in the Oxford English Dictionary, as being **"attributed to some force beyond scientific understanding or the laws of nature"**.

So, let us look at the definition of 'natural': 'Natural', is contrasted from the 'supernatural', by the fact that it pertains to everything that is of nature, and not man-made. This means, and only means, that what has been manipulated by man, is not of nature.

Unfortunately, there is a problem here: Mother Nature. You see, 'nature' and 'Mother Nature', are two very different things. Mother Nature, is the universal system that governs everything we see around us, in such a way as to maintain balance or equilibrium between all things. It offers the basis about which all scientific research can be established, and constitutes the fundamentals of all the scientific laws and theories we have derived (and then some) to date.

Commonly, Mother Nature is used by most people as if it were a term to be restricted to the manner in which our planet Earth, and what we see on it, functions. But Mother Nature extends and applies to everything in the universe. In addition, 'Mother Nature' tends to be understood by people as only alluding to the personification of what the dictionary describes primarily as being 'nature', however this is not so. Although the dictionary may refer to 'nature', what it ambiguously defines is 'Mother Nature'.

'Nature', is a term referring to the characteristics of any entity. That is to say, it defines the reason something behaves in the manner that it has been documented to, and/or simply, what it does. This may come across as little more than a discussion of semantics, but there is an underlying and imperative distinction I am making for you.

When something is said to be natural, the meaning is that it remains unaltered from the state it was originally designed to be in, and/or that if it has changed, it has done so by virtue of the mechanisms which caused it to be, in the first place. Bearing in mind the fact that anything and everything that is of Mother Nature is known as being natural, and the fact that God designed nature to behave the way it does, one can easily see how it is impossible for anything to ever be called 'supernatural'. All phenomena adheres to restrictions, such that they can be predicted to a certain extent.

The inception of everything natural and physical that we see around us, is by the means of a spiritual precursor. It is by God's hand, that everything exists the way it does. By His hand, that galaxies induce gravitational pulls on each other. By His hand, that occurrences described by both classical and quantum mechanics, work the way that they do, and it is by his hand, that the Sun rises at a place on Earth at any given time.

It is a scientific fact that inherent to all things natural, are mechanisms of adaptation. Living organisms adapt to their environments, and they change. This does not mean that Charles Darwin's "Theory of Evolution" is correct (and it is not), but it does mean that if it was, evolution would be by God's design, because it is by God's design that creatures can adapt to change the way that they do.

I must point out that the theory of evolution has absolutely nothing at all to do with whether or not God exists. What it throws into argument is whether or not the Bible's account of how God created living organisms is correct. The reason most atheists tend to attribute to evolution in arguments against the idea of "creationism" is that most atheists do not at all know what they are talking about when they discuss things like the Bible, God, or creation. They are only desperate to look for things they can try to use as evidence for their assertion(s).

At its core, evolution can never be used to explain the origin of life. It can also never be used to explain the origin of new animal species. Yes, many atheists and modern-day supporters of Darwinism will tell you otherwise, but as I am about to reveal: many atheists and modern-day supporters of Darwinism are lairs and/or poorly informed. You see: A key aspect of evolutionary biology is the idea of "Natural Selection". Natural selection can account for the survival of animal species as well the demise of animal species. It can also account for slight variations within animal species (micro-evolution), but that is all it can account for. We know it can account for these things because we have observed the evidence. Dog "breeds" are a popular man-made example of such evidence, and the variation in beaks of Darwin's "Galápagos finches" are a popular natural example.

Evolution is a long-known fact of the universe, and nobody who is sensible has denied this. Things are always changing, and there has never been anything controversial about 'adaptation' and 'natural election', because these things are true even commonsensically. However, the evolution of animal species into other animal species, is an unproven hypothesis (to put it very mildly). What Darwinists do, is employ the means of deceptive propaganda and manipulation to advertise "the evolution of species into different species" (a body of nonsensical and made-up ideas) to society, while doing so in the context of "adaptation and natural selection" (common sense and scientifically-proven facts).

When they say "evolution is a fact", what they incorrectly convey, is the false proclamation that 'the evolution of a species into different species is a fact', knowing very well that their statement will be misunderstood by people to that effect. "Evolution is a fact" is a statement which **does not** mean that 'the evolution of a species into different species is a fact'. It means that 'adaptation and natural selection are facts'. Darwinists use this confusion which they have orchestrated, to deliberately sell deceptions and misconceptions to laypeople.

For example: Darwin's finches are used to advertise the development of a new species, when in reality the finches demonstrate no such thing. They demonstrate only adaptation and natural selection. The variation in their beaks is something which fluctuates back and forth throughout the year in fact, and can never (ever) go beyond or below a certain limit. There are limits to variation in all animal species which cannot be exceeded, and in each and every case that such limits are exceeded in an organism, the organism either cannot sustain its life and dies, or becomes incapable of reproducing. Animal breeders are very well aware of this, and have to be very careful about selectively breeding cows to produce more milk or breeding dogs which will have the most physical strength, etc. It is biologically impossible for any species of animal to evolve into another species.

Such realities are never discussed by evolutionists as they propagandise and deceive masses with their fairy-tale. The proclamations by anti-creationists (atheists and evolutionists) that DNA mutations eventually lead to the creation of new species of animals (macro-evolution), and/or that life originated from a "soup" of randomly arranged elements, are nothing but proclamations. There is no evidence for them whatsoever. In fact, all experiments which endeavour to artificially demonstrate the evidence, fail miserably. The justification for the aforementioned unproven assertions by evolutionists is that it takes "millions of years" for an animal species to develop, but that as well is only an empty proclamation. Like evolution's "Tree of Life", it is a postulation for which the evidence intended to support it is highly contradictory, and evolutionary biologists are aware of this, and many other problems.

They use the media to hide such problems from the public domain as they try desperately to find excuses for them, but continually they fail. In the meantime, they lie, they deceive, and they stall for time with the aid of corrupt institutions. For example: You might have heard of a "missing link" (missing transitional form) in the fossil record of human evolution. A link which evolutionists have been desperately trying to find since they first encountered the problem. What you probably have not been told however, is that there are missing links across the entire spectrum of animal fossil records. In fact, there are countless fossils of many animals and plants which date back "hundreds of millions of years", and yet look exactly like the plants and animals which exist today.

You will also often hear deceptively sensationalist talk of crocodiles being "living dinosaurs" in wild-life television programs, as if to imply that the fossil records dating them to "hundreds of millions of years ago" makes them evolutionary exceptions. In reality however, every other living organism that is alive today would qualify as a "living dinosaur", because every other living organism has fossils which date back "hundreds of millions of years". There is nothing exceptional about crocodiles.

This brings me to Darwin's "Tree of Life": A fanciful construct at odds with the scientific evidence. In stark contradiction to what Darwin's Tree of Life portrays, the fossil record does not show the slow emergence of life forms, and the diversification of those life forms into other species. Rather, the fossil record shows a very sudden boom of a multiplicity of complex life forms. A boom inconsistent (in every sense of the word) with Darwinian evolution, for all the life forms which very suddenly emerged back then, have no evolutionary ancestors and remain completely unevolved to this day – more than 'half a billion years' later. The forms in which they appeared then, are the exact same forms in which they exists today. This boom of complex life, called the "Cambrian Explosion" is consistent only with one thing: Creation and its implication.

The false assertion that macro-evolution is due to micro-evolution extrapolated over time, and the deceitful proclamation that DNA mutations give rise to new animal species, are the reasons there are so many missing transitional forms in the fossil record. If indeed animals evolved into other animals, there would be a very large number of fossils of creatures which have slight variations in their physical structures. In fact there would be many millions of them because the evolution of a fish into a land mammal, if due to Darwinian processes, would require many millions of biological adjustments which would have to be present in fossil evidence. The same would be true for the evolution of land animals into other land animals. However this is not the case. All we have in fossil records are different species of animals which evolutionists claim are related to each other. They make these claims with no supporting evidence whatsoever, and rely on mass-media and misinformed children to spread their lies.

The claim that animals evolve over millions of years, into entirely new species of animals is not only unsupported, it is disproven by the evidence. The evidence in support of evolution simply does not exist, and every single diagram of an animal's evolutionary tree is one which has been invented by people. Because it is scientifically impossible to actually prove evolutionary chains of animals or plants, diagrams are drawn by assumption and animal fossils are arranged by supposition.

You see: what evolutionists do, is look at several animal fossils and then assume an evolutionary link between them. They then place the fossils in hierarchies of their supposed evolutionary path. There is no scientific method involved, it is a case of presumption. This is interesting because one might wonder how evolutionary chains would look if certain animals which are currently alive, were extinct.

Let us take dogs for example. There are many different shapes and sizes of dogs. If every dog breed as they exist today, were extinct and fossilized thousands of years ago, and then recently dug up, there is a 100% certainty that they would be classified as different species of animals and assembled in an evolutionary chain. How am I sure? Well, what they would do with the dog fossils is exactly what they are currently doing with other animal fossils. The different shapes and sizes which dogs come in, is exactly the criteria that evolutionary biologists use to construct fictitious macro-evolutionary chains. In reality though, evolutionists do more than just that. They look at animals which are completely different from each other, and then claim that certain body parts are transformations of the other animals' body parts.

This is guesswork, not science. Guesswork with missing links and holes all over the place. If there are "missing links" in evolutionary chains which you have made up yourself, that should be enough indication to you that there is something very wrong with your theory. It is quite evident that the only reason people blindly cling to the theory of evolution's unproven claims, is so they may have an alternative explanation for the existence of living organisms than creationism.

There are also those who are being deliberately deceived by classroom textbooks which present the guesswork of evolutionary theory as fact. The people who read such books take it for granted that these assumptions are factual, without examining the evidence for themselves. Of course this is because most textbooks do not at all mention that the assumptions of evolution are just assumptions, and that they are unproven and unsupported. The many problems which face evolutionary biology are also neglected entirely by most classroom textbooks, so people are accepting the theory of evolution in its entirety as proposed by modern-day evolutionists (fraudsters) without actually analysing it or knowing anything about what the theory of evolution really is.

The theory of the evolution of organisms into other organisms is a very far-fetched body of speculations, with no scientific evidence to support it. Any evolutionary biologist who advertises macro-evolution as a scientifically-proven fact to society, is committing fraud and should be stripped of his/her title as a scientist. Likewise, the creators of each and every single online "news" article or magazine deliberately defrauding its audience with blatant deception in favour of the theory, should be tried in court for misleading the public. It is only because they know they cannot be tried for stating their baseless opinions, that their mendacious propaganda is continued.

Classroom text books have been criminally defrauding tens of millions of students for decades with deceitful images, and staged scenarios, because the fraudsters are confident that the majority of students will not adequately investigate the lies they are being told. Under honest and unbiased scientific examination, it is revealed to be a theory for which there is indeed no scientific support, but its proponents are not honest nor are they unbiased. Their theory does not even abide by the scientific method, but because they are backed by the establishment and its various mainstream media prostitutes, their voice is loudly heard.

There are indeed many problems with evolution across the board, and the problems are such that anti-creationists are constantly having to make new assumptions which eventually prove to be untenable. They are to this day, doing their best to reconcile their baseless assertions with the contradictions which the actual evidence poses for them, and there are concerted efforts by them to do so deceptively.

For example: There are several internet websites and social media groups which are run supposedly by non-scientists, and claim to publish contemporary "science news" for the current generation of young web-surfers. These media groups often sensationalise headlines, and publish the kind of pseudo-science which a science journal would never publish (although, science journals are sometimes guilty of publishing deliberately misleading information). Headlines like "New Supermassive Black Hole Discovered", or "New Research Indicates Presence of Gay (Homosexual) Gene in Humans" are common occurrences with these media outlets.

There is no scientific evidence for black holes, and there is no scientific evidence of a "gay gene", but the audience of the pseudo-scientific media outlets which claim such things are usually credulous lay people who know no better than to believe the nonsense being sold to them. Because these media groups do not claim to be run by actual scientists, and because there is no governing body presiding over the things which such groups publish, proponents of lies can use these avenues to deceive people.

Speaking of black holes – there are a few interesting facts about theoretical physics and the pseudo-science of black holes which I think may interest you:

Black holes are widely claimed to be the results of Albert Einstein's work. But like Darwinian evolution, not only is there no scientific evidence for them, the scientific evidence refutes their existence. You see: black holes are physically and mathematically impossible for a number of reasons. A popular excuse, is that they consume (and apparently destroy) universal information. This violates the laws of thermodynamics, and is a violation known as "The Black Hole Information Paradox". However, this is something "black hole" advocates publically admit only because it is so glaring, and cannot be hidden in the fraudulently complex equations which supposedly describe black holes.

It is due to such paradoxes, that theoretical physicists hypothesise (i.e. make up and construct from thin air) "multiple universes" and "apparent horizons", and manufacture "black hole thermodynamics" in desperate attempts to reconcile the facts with fiction. Something destined never to happen, because the mathematics of black holes is in fact, complete nonsense. Pseudo-mathematical garbage which contradicts itself throughout its presentation, and is filled with arbitrarily defined parameters, made-up circumstances, and grotesque grammatical misappropriation of definitions.

The reason most people (even many scientists) are not aware of the fraudulent nature of modern theoretical physics, is that the faux mathematics of things like "black holes" is so irrational and convoluted by deceptive terminology and blatant fabrications, that many people who are low in self-confidence and esteem, believe themselves simply to lack the intelligence necessary to grasp them. When told of these unscientific things, they accept them without question and place their faith in whoever is advertising these things to them. Others know very well that it is all nonsense, but they lack the courage to confront the propagandists responsible for deluding masses, and even when they possess such courage, they do not get the media exposure required for them to voice their discoveries and concerns.

Do not yourself think that these topics are above your ability to comprehend them. They are very simple and can be easily broken down for anyone who has gone through a basic high school physics and maths course. For your adequate apprehension of the subject matter, which is beyond the scope of this book, I highly recommend you seek the work of a man named Stephen J. Crothers. He very clearly exposes these hoaxes for what they are.

Theoretical Physics has made few significant advancements since the theories of Special and General Relativity, and such relative stagnation is the reason fraudulent theoretical physicists are having to imagine outlandish theories which media outlets sensationalise for unsuspecting laypeople to delude them into false beliefs.

Now the cause of all this boils down to a man named Albert Einstein. I am sure you have heard of him. You are likely aware of the usual things: that he was a "genius", that he "discovered e=mc²", that he "contributed to the development of the atomic bomb", that he "pioneered the theory of relativity". All those things, I am sure have been repeated to you by media outlets for a long time.

What you probably do not know however, is that they are all untrue. You see: Albert Einstein was an individual who's only major contribution to theoretical physics was the worldwide attention he brought to the subject. He certainly was not the first man to work on or study 'relativity', and in fact, he blatantly plagiarised the idea(s) he is most famed for (as exposed by the book "**Albert Einstein: The Incorrigible Plagiarist**"). In the eyes of the general public, he is the man responsible for Special and General Relativity, only because he has acquired tremendous fame through the mainstream media's aggressive advertisements of his name.

Most people have never even heard of James Maxwell, Wilhelm Wien, Max Plank, Ludwig Boltzmann, Henri Poincaré, Hendrik Lorentz, Heinrich Hertz, David Hilbert, or any of the many other people whose ideas and discoveries, Einstein (and the media) claimed to be his own. Einstein's name is synonymous with intelligence, and his face is attributed to IQ (Intelligence Quotient), but Albert Einstein and the pseudo-science of IQ only have one thing in common: They are both not nearly what they seem or are claimed to be by those who naively or deceitfully advertise them.

Albert Einstein was a fraud, so of course, every major idea or hypothesis which stemmed from the fame of his supposed work would be fraudulent as well. Black holes, white holes, worm holes, gravitational waves, etc. are all pseudo-scientific nonsense which the mainstream media advertises because they are incentivised by very wealthy entities to do so. The meaningless nature of these wild theories and ideas is the reason physics has made few advancements since Einstein. To date, not a single useful invention has come out of General Relativity or String theory, because the pseudo-scientific aspects of these things being advertised are not useful. They are based on imagination.

On the bright side: Millions of lives have been drawn closer to the sciences through the Einstein propaganda campaign. But on the other hand: The era of science which Einstein's name helped bring to the fore, is one where wild and nonsensical theories are hypothesised for the purpose of ego and sensationalism, and where the mathematics is intentionally and deceptively bent and construed to fit the ridiculous hypotheses. An era where fantasists run wild after their own tails in the search for enigmas of their own design. An example is String theory, and the imaginary dimensions which had to be dreamed up before the theory could ever be somewhat mathematically tenable.

Such things are not science, they are fantasy. Desperate fairy tales from the pages of an imaginary book. An imaginary book of "The God who never was". It is from this same book that evolutionists have gleaned their pseudo-scientific theory, and they are turning franticly through its pages for something more.

The problems which evolutionary biologists face are too great for them to ignore though, so every now and then they will claim to have discovered a new fossil, and media headlines will make noise that scientists have found the "missing link" in human evolution. Deceitful imaginations of the creature's appearance will then start being circulated, life-size wax constructions and statues of the made-up creatures will make their way to museums, and books will start to mention the "human ancestor" as well. The new discovery will receive much media attention and praise for a while, before quietly slipping away into silence when it is proven once again to be another failed attempt at evidence for evolution.

The scientists at the forefront of the "missing link" media frenzy will have been able to use it to advance their careers by the time attention of their "new discovery" dies down. Their attempts at sensationalising something for the purpose of fame will be successful, while many people will remain deceived due to the lack of media coverage of the fact that the claimed "missing link" was a lie.

(It is due to the deceptive and sensationalist media propaganda campaigns which evolutionists use to market their lies, that to this day there is a surprisingly significant number of misinformed laypeople who actually believe that the fake statues of human and animal "ancestors" displayed in some museums are genuine. Although the fake statues are not representative of palaeontological finds, word-of-mouth misinformation and deliberate misrepresentation by unscrupulous museum officials instils the false notion of the contrary to into the minds of many young and naïve individuals.)

This trend of making things up and then selling fables to society through mainstream media and pseudo-academia, is something evolutionary biologists have been doing for more than a hundred years now. The "human ancestors" which have ever been made famous (e.g.: Neanderthals, Homo erectus, Piltdown Man, Nebraska Man, The Taung Child, Ramapithecus, Lucy, Australopithecus, Ardi, Homo Naledi, etc.) **have all** been pseudo-scientific frauds. I could write an entire book to thoroughly expose the fraud of Darwinian evolution, but here are just a few very brief examples:

Neanderthal Man: The first "Neanderthal" bones were discovered in 1856 and were identified as 100% human. However, the subsequent creation of Charles Darwin's theory of evolution meant that people became desperate to find evidence for the theory. Among other things, evolutionists chose to use the bones of Neanderthals, but in addition to mistakes being made in the identification processes and scientists being deliberately deceitful, artists fabricated fleshed-out images of Neanderthals (the bones of which were proven to simply be that of an arthritic human being) and these fabricated images began circulating. To this day the "Neanderthal Man" hoax is being perpetuated by evolutionists, and completely imaginary depictions of their appearance can be found in school text books and museums, even though their physiology does not differ from humans in any meaningful way whatsoever.

Homo erectus: First dubbed "Java Man", Homo erectus erectus was the result of an ape-like skull fragment, and a few teeth found in 1891, with a human leg bone being found a year later. The bones were discovered by a Dutch physician, who with no justification whatsoever other than his obstinate desire to find the "missing link" (and his only credential being that he was a physician), claimed the remains to be that of a human ancestor. Of course he provided no proof that the leg bone (or even the other fragments) was found within reasonable proximity of the skull fragment, but he wanted people to believe him. They did not. Not until more than 20 years later, when evolutionists realised they could capitalise on the physician's "findings" to sell their religion. Today, the Homo erectus Java Man (and a "Peking Man" friend of his) hoax is still around, with imaginary drawings and sculptures of ape-human hybrids in school books and museums. Wildly imaginary images, from only a few small bones which evolutions assert, belong to a human ancestor.

Piltdown Man: "Piltdown Man" was a discovery of bone fragments in 1912. Fragments, which were advertised as belonging to a human ancestor. This "human ancestor" then had fictional drawings of its appearance disseminated, sculptures placed in museums, lessons taught in classrooms, and hundreds of scientific papers written in its favour over the course of several decades, until being exposed as another "missing link" fraud in 1953. It was discovered that the bone fragments were simply the jaw bone of an orangutan, a human skull, and some chimpanzee teeth.

Nebraska Man: "Nebraska Man" was a 1922 discovery of a tooth, which scientists claimed, belonged to a human ancestor. From this single tooth, evolutionary biologists manufactured and circulated the image of an entire ape-like man (even including his wife and children) and the imaginary ape-like human ancestor began being advertised and positively written about in scientific papers as a missing link. The hoax continued until 1927, when other parts of the skeleton to which the tooth belonged were found. The tooth was discovered to belong to an extinct wild American pig.

Ramapithecus: "Ramapithecus" was the discovery of two jaw bone pieces in the 1930s. With this single jaw bone, evolutionists constructed an ape-like human ancestor and his entire family. This fraud was heralded as a "missing link" until the jaw bone was exposed in the 1970s as belonging to a baboon.

Lucy: "Lucy" was the discovered partial fossil skeleton of a guerrilla-like creature in 1974. As with each and every single "human ancestor" discovery, the skeleton was insufficiently complete and broken so evolutionists speculated wildly about what kind of creature Lucy was. Soon after Lucy's discovery, imaginary sketches and sculptures of fleshed-out Lucys started appearing everywhere with media headlines shouting "Missing Link" as usual. It has since been found that Lucy's bones are identical to modern-day guerrillas, not to humans, and that Lucy cannot possibly be a missing link, but still the Lucy hoax is being prolonged by evolutionists, and the deliberately deceptive human-like skeletal drawings of Lucy (instead of the guerrilla-like skeleton which was actually found) keep being circulated alongside fairy-tale images of Lucy's flesh.

Homo naledi: "Homo naledi" was a 2013 archaeological find of some ape bones in a cave. In 2015, the people who discovered the bones decided to proclaim that the bones found were those of bodies which were buried there by an emotional creature who mourned its dead (like humans). Of course this claim was nothing more than an assumption and a fantastical wish (at best) on the part of the people who claimed to have discovered the bones, but still, they used that to declare a new human ancestor. As has been done with every pseudo-scientific evolutionary fraud in the "missing link" industry, an artist's imagination of the fleshed-out appearance of Homo naledi soon started circulating, and mainstream media went about their "new human ancestor" ritual (while steering clear of the ridiculously gigantic leap-of-faith assumption which the researchers made in order to Justify the "human ancestor" label).

Interesting bit of information about the lead researcher behind the "Homo naledi" hoax: His name is Lee Rogers Berger, and he has a documented history of fraud and corruption in his field. Such as a 2008 'research find' on the small island country of Palau, where he claimed to have found evidence of a dwarfed human ancestor. While in Palau, he exploited some of the country's sacred burial sites for the sake of a (rather embarrassing) National Geographic film he was making to help sell and sensationalise his "new discovery". A discovery in an area of expertise where he was very clearly sorely lacking.

In his documentary named "Mystery Skulls of Palau", the typically fraudulent evolutionists rhetoric was put to work: "It's a discovery that could change what we think we know about the evolution of mankind", "It's simply astonishing", "On a remote island in the pacific lie the remains of a people that are unlike anything discovered before", "Quite shocking", etc.

It turned out however, that "Quite shocking" was the only word applicable to the content of his pseudo-scientific documentary, as the film was riddled with absurd and obvious errors. The likes of which were so appalling, that one of the small number of scientists whose insights and opinions were all largely and underhandedly removed by Berger from the final cut of his documentary (to try and save face) wound up publically disassociating himself from the project.

In addition: Berger carefully timed the release of his ridiculous pseudo-scientific documentary and the publication date of his ridiculous pseudo-scientific thesis, which he wrote to support the poorly-founded claims that his documentary espoused. As he would later manage to do with his "Homo naledi" years later, his intent was to use the hype generated from the documentary and the subsequently sensationalist media coverage, to claim fame with his new hoax. Unfortunately, as I have said, both the documentary and the thesis were highly nonsensical. So nonsensical were they, that fellow evolutionists could not take the chance of supporting his claims. His claims were thoroughly debunked and even labelled "complete nonsense and cannot be accepted as serious science" by fellow scientists.

Berger seemed to learn from this slightly (only slightly), as it is apparent that with Homo naledi, he was far more careful with both the timing of his sensationalist leap-of-faith pseudo-scientific claims, and his utilization of media headlines to quickly advertise, and then keep dead quiet, about his new "discovery" (as is the norm in the business of fraudulent evolutionary biology).

Unfortunately for him: although media headlines have stopped screaming his hoax into peoples' ears, fellow scientists have not ignored it. You see: His habit of allowing his seemingly desperate thirst for fame to overshadow the level of thought being put into his hoaxes continues to betray him. He is accused of rushing his findings, making simple errors in his journal papers, and seeking little more than fame out of his "Homo naledi" work. Nothing he had not already been known for.

Lee Berger also happens to be the same man who was responsible for the 2008 discovery of Australopithecus sediba: Another "human ancestor" fraud, which he claims his nine-year-old son found for him. The perpetration of hoaxes and the passing off as fact, ideas and conclusions which he came to by nothing but guesswork and wild hypothesising, seems to be something Lee Berger has been avidly pursuing for a long time.

In fact: his tradition of trying to sell poorly-supported, factually-inaccurate, pseudo-science to society goes back more than a decade to the publication of his two books: "In the footsteps of Eve" and "The Official Field Guide to the Cradle of Mankind". Two pieces of literature which even his peers view as being a disgrace to science. Riddled with errors of all sorts, and rubbished by scientists from head to toe, these books demonstrate how tragically easy it is to misinform and delude laypeople with pseudo-science.

I need not point out that Berger is almost universally disliked even by evolutionary biologists, as he seems to take his hoaxes to such obviously ludicrous heights, many see him as a liability to the cause of evolutionary "science".

Now, my point with the discussion of Lee Berger is this: If a man with Lee Berger's highly transparent history of fraudulent pseudo-scientific deception and fame-seeking foolishness, can get away so easily with paleoanthropological hoaxes, evolutionary biology is in a terrible state. This is no wanton denigration of Lee Berger. It is a demonstration of how the state of evolutionary biology is such a pitiful one, that virtually any person who intends to delude society with baseless pseudo-science can go far in the field. It is much more of a sham than the things which fantasists are doing with theoretical physics these days, and that is indeed a very low position in which to be for evolutionary biology.

With Homo naledi, Berger and his media circus were careful not to use the term "missing link", because they obviously were very well aware of the kind of immediate problems that would throw into the atmosphere. Instead, they focussed on "human ancestor", most likely so as to minimize instances of people being led to stumble upon all the "missing link" shams throughout history.

You should know: that there is not just one "missing link" in human evolution. There are millions, if not hundreds of millions. Just as there are millions, if not hundreds of millions, of missing links in every other animal's evolutionary tree. Hundreds of millions of missing links for which **there is not a single fossil**. Not a single fossil, and yet somehow the flimsy fairy-tale of evolutionary biology is being sold to society.

The "evolutionary human ancestor" scams boldly highlight how easily pseudo-science can be passed as science, and how easily people can be deceived simply by repeating the same things over and over and over again. The "Piltdown Man" hoax particularly, highlights how easily one can infect universities with rubbish, and how effortlessly one can poison the minds of society with said rubbish.

Establishing and nourishing pseudo-science is a remarkably easy thing to do. You need only have people with an agenda to help drive it, and weak-minded workers who are so eager to blend in with the mainstream, they will accept and advertise your pseudo-science in the hopes that they will be appreciated by yourself and the fraudsters whom they wish to serve, and that they will hopefully be awarded the label "scientist" in media articles selling your bogus theory/idea to the public. You also need money. Lots of it. And it helps if you are good friends with mainstream media houses and universities (but, simply having lots of money is enough to pervert these already corrupt institutions). Once you have those, you need the help of corrupt or weak-minded journalists (of whom there is absolutely no shortage) and one big push from the mainstream media. It is that simple. The highly political environment within which post-graduate academics of most universities must navigate themselves, is one where there is much bootlicking and brownnosing, so people in desperate need to brainwash others into believing "there is no God" are able to easily advertise evolution, while people who desperately want to belong and to be a part of the mainstream, are going along with it.

There is no fossil evidence whatsoever for animal or human transitional forms, Darwinian evolution is nothing but guesswork and conjecture, and each and every single image you have ever seen of an ape-like human ancestor has been a fraud: an imagination of what evolutionary biologists desperately wish was true. But because scientists and teachers are being pressured, bullied, and forced into proclaiming acceptance for the hoax of evolution (with many of them, losing their jobs if they dare to even question the theory), and because journalists are being bribed, bullied, and blackmailed into advertising the theory (with many of them having their careers systematically ruined by the powerful mainstream establishment if they dare report neutrally on the topic [as exposed by the 2008 documentary **"Expelled: No Intelligence Allowed"**]), this joke of a scientific theory lives on.

The next time you see a headline which reads "Missing Link Found" or "New Ape-like Human Ancestor" beside the image of an artist's imagination of the ape-like creature about whom the headline is, you would be wise to be highly sceptical. There is a 100% chance that it would be another desperate lie by desperate evolutionists.

This tremendous sense of desperation is something which has plagued evolutionary biology since Darwin came up with his theory, and this is why evolutionist have not stopped going to great lengths to defraud the public. In the earlier days of evolutionary biology, evolutionists did worse things than simply lying to people. They committed atrocious acts of human rights violations in order to further their agendas.

You see: Evolutionary biology and racism were very closely intertwined. The racial consequences of Darwin's claim that humans evolved from apes were obvious from the start, and evolutionists only started distancing themselves from evolution's implication that "blacks" were less evolved human beings than "whites", when they realised it would cause human rights problems for them. Before human rights ever became an issue, the theory of evolution was used to bolster the stance that whites were superior to blacks.

The most famous of evolutionists' human rights crimes, is the thing which happened to Ota Benga. Ota Benga was a Congolese man who was sold by African slave traders and captured by an evolutionary scientist in 1904, so that he could be placed in a zoo and demonstrated alongside apes as a live ape-like human ancestor in New York. He was caged with monkeys, advertised as a "missing link", and described as a beast. Ota Benga had a terrible life, and so terrible it was that he eventually committed suicide.

It is not at all, a small problem which plagues evolutionary biology. Most people do not hear of the problems associated with the theory of evolution because information of that nature is not broadcast on television, or advertised by newspapers. But people in the scientific community are well aware that there are serious, self-destructive problems, and they have heated discussions about such problems frequently.

If you endeavoured to query individual proponents of evolution within the scientific community, you would find that evolutionists not only disagree with creationists, they disagree with each other. Contrary to what you might have been lead to believe by mainstream media, and public proponents of evolutionary biology, there is much disagreement between evolutionists, and there are many opposing theories held by them. The theory of evolution is a theory of untested and unproven assumptions and declarations, and this is why there are so many problems with it.

Despite the mainstream representation of Darwinism as a unified set of beliefs, evolutionary biologists are constantly arguing about which version of their baseless, made-up, pseudo-science is more likely to be accepted by the ignorant general public. This is due to the made-up nature of the theory of evolution, and the fact that there is no hard evidence to support the theory. People who decide to become evolutionists have to decide what they want to believe by blind faith and/or prejudice alone.

You should know that not much of the things which people are being told about the theory of evolution, is without deceit. Mainstream media, and prominent scientific figures will tell you what they want you to believe, but what they want you to believe, is not necessarily in your best interest.

This book is not dedicated to exposing the lies and hidden agendas behind popular scientists' claims that there is no God, so I will not cover that much of it here, but luckily for you, there is a plethora of scientifically documented evidence damning the ludicrous notion of atheism and anti-spiritualism, by virtue of its adoptees' common claims that there is no spirit realm or that there is no God. All you need to do, is go out there and look for it. To start you off, I highly recommend the following 2006 documentary: "**The Case for a Creator**". I also highly recommend the following 2009 documentary (and its 2011 sequel): "**Evolution: The Grand Experiment Episode 1**".

There is nothing that cannot be explained scientifically. Our inability to interpret and define certain phenomena, merely means we currently lack the information or the skills to be able to do so effectively. There are systematic contingencies about all phenomena, irrespective of the rarity of their occurrences, or the nature of their apparently incomprehensible complexities.

Basically, everything happens such that there is an explanation for it. We may not have reasonable or justified explanations for some things now, but they can still be explained. Even if it means God is the only one who can explain them. And then, even if that means the only one He can explain them to, is Himself.

God is the ultimate scientist, but we are built in his image. It is by virtue of this and our own desire to learn, that we have come so far in crafting models and theories describing various aspects of the world around us, and manipulating them to create other things. I believe we still have a very long way to go before we even begin to reach the limits of our ability to comprehend and solve the many complex problems of our universe.

A few hundred years ago, the idea of electronically transmitted images and sounds would have been denounced as witchcraft. Today, such technologies exist and more advanced ones still are being developed. There is nothing strange about them to us. But when people mention "ghosts" or the spiritual aspects of what define us, there tends to be attached to that, a stigma of insanity or delusion about the person who mentioned them, by the paradigm of prominent mainstream "science".

This is partly due to the conspiracy of mainstream "science" to neglect the works and publications of scientists who have undergone serious study and experiments, which have proven in the very least, that there is something more to the folklore and ancient ghost stories than what a few people in denial want you to believe.

There are very few people on this Earth who genuinely are sceptical of spiritualism, and among them there are very few people who are justified in their scepticism. And I do mean very, very few. So I will use "sceptic" and "pseudo-sceptic" interchangeably from here onward.

In large part, the people who say there is no evidence for God or the spirit realm, are the very same people who without any observed evidence whatsoever, make mention of "black holes", "multiple universes", and "dark matter", because they have heard mainstream pseudo-scientific sources sensationalising them on television, or because they have read about such things in deceptive online news articles.

Ask such people whether they have ever seen dark matter, black holes, or multiple universes, or whether there is even any proof within the scientific community that these things exist, and I guarantee you their answer will have to be "No" if they have any clue at all about what they are saying (and the vast majority of them do not). They will blindly and eagerly accept such "scientific" fairy tales, yet they will claim they have never seen God so He cannot be there. Such a mind is not a rational scientific mind. It is a faith-based closed mind. No less of a faith-based closed mind than that of any religious person's. Both religious people and pseudo-sceptics believe it a virtue to substitute 'intellect' for 'faith'. The only difference is that religious people acknowledge a distinction between the two, while pseudo-sceptics do not.

It is by blind faith that sceptics say "There is no God", but they will claim it is by intellect. Most sceptics will bigotedly assert there is no such thing as God or the spirit realm, and that alone is the basis of all their arguments at their core. When you present any evidence to them, no matter how convincing, they will dismiss it and cite any explanation, even if illogical, in justification of their views, because "there simply is no evidence of God or the spirit realm" is an indisputable declaration to them.

In support of this dogmatism, it is not uncommon for these irrational, pseudo-sceptical, faith-based, naysayers to attribute to "Russell's Teapot" or a "Flying Spaghetti Monster". They claim that not being able to disprove something does not make it true. They will say "If I tell you that I've seen a flying spaghetti monster, your inability to disprove my claim does not make it a fact", and they seem quite oblivious to how unintelligent that statement makes them seem.

It is quite obvious that one's arbitrary claim of something as nonsensical as a flying spaghetti monster does not make his/her claim true! And it certainly does not even make it plausible. Such an argument is irrational. But why? Why does it not make any sense to cite Russell's Teapot as an argument against the existence of spirits or God? The reasons are quite simple, and only a few of them are even worth mentioning here.

Firstly, let me ask you: has a spaghetti monster ever been said to be seen by people in places all over the world? Secondly: Are there any concepts and coinciding descriptions of such an appetising being by people in various backgrounds, ages, and times? Also: where on this Earth will you find somebody who speaks of this creature?

The answer to the first two questions is "No", and the answer to the last one is: "Wherever there is a naïve pseudo-sceptic attributing to it". There are people all over the world who have witnessed undeniably supernatural phenomena and events. The experiences of all these people are indisputably similar to one another, and their individual descriptions of the entities or phenomena they encountered are identical to those experienced by people on other sides of the world.

You see: The ideas of "God", "ghosts", and the "spirit realm", are not like the things imagined in fairy-tale books, or the things made up by unsophisticated pseudo-sceptics. Spiritual things are things for which there is much historical justification and evidence. They were not randomly dreamt up by people.

In as many different cultures as have been found, there are documented descriptions of things pertaining to the spirit realm, and there are innumerable examples of such things which have strong commonalities across the globe. When billions of people are seeing or have seen the same things, or when they are experiencing or have experienced the same things, it is only a die-hard dogmatist and religiously irrational thinker who would dare say "They must all be crazy" or "humans must be genetically predisposed to believing in the supernatural" (something which some pseudo-sceptics have made up to justify their dogmatism). It is logically unsound for sceptics to compare the arbitrarily declared existence of a "spaghetti monster" to the existence of God or spirits, but as I have said: pseudo-sceptics are desperate for anything they can use to defend their mind-set, and they will stoop to illogical depths for that cause.

Sceptics who present unsound arguments in favour of atheism are disingenuous people who often lay claim to "science", but will only do so to misappropriate the term (for which they are undeserving) in defence of their bigotry, because they understand that most people do not really know what science is. In fact a lot of the time, neither do the sceptics themselves. Most people seem to believe that anything a scientist claims to be true, or anything that is written in a Science text book, is of science. However, that is not the case. If a scientist says something which is not true then it is not of science, and if a scientist displays bias for, or against anything, in spite of the evidence, then his/her logic is unscientific.

Science is unbiased and seeks only the truth through observation, analyses, and experimentation. **Prejudice** on the other hand, seeks merely to justify preconceived notions and opinions. Mainstream scientific sources advocate prejudice behind a curtain of proclaimed science, and mainstream scientists ridicule people who have an open mind to the possibility of things in the "supernatural" realm. They call themselves sceptics in the stead of what they really are: prejudiced bigots. They deceitfully hide behind pseudo-science and pseudo-intellectualism, in a poorly concealed attempt to mask both their ignorance, and their real agendas.

In the minds of dishonest, unscientific pseudo-sceptics like these, "There is no evidence of God" or "There is no evidence of a spirit realm" is a fixed banner they hold above their heads, and it leaves absolutely no room for logic or reason. They are comfortable only in the small box of lies and denialism they choose to live. These people are not scientists.

A narrow-minded sceptic will duck and dive sensible arguments and reasonable evidence for things they do not want to acknowledge, by saying things like: "It must be replicable" (never mind the fact that millions of people around the world, and in different backgrounds, are reporting the same things). When it is replicated before them, they say: "It has not been replicated enough times", and when it is replicated many times, they say: "The conditions were not controlled enough". When objectively replicated under controlled conditions, they toss at you, the juvenile declaration that "It is some sort of con-artist magic trick": the hand grenade they keep with them at all times.

But because the aforementioned hand grenade is quite obviously a shamefully last resort, when confronted with evidence suggesting the paranormal, a pseudo-sceptic will typically opt rather to fight the notion of "ghosts", "spirits", "God", or what have you, by asserting that **there must be** a "non-magical", and non-spiritual explanation for whatever it is that is being demonstrated to them or being observed by them, and they will cling to that declaration devotedly. Even if that means playing a game of semantics to describe or attribute to the phenomena in question, to better suit their sensibilities. And even if it means… making things up.

For example: When a self-proclaimed psychic is placed under evaluation and given a set of tasks to complete (Determining the history of randomly selected peoples' lives, for instance), and he/she seems to be passing the test(s), the sceptical people overseeing the experiment will say: "Oh, this so-called psychic merely has the ability to read people's physical reactions and is highly sensitive to their subconscious behaviours. This person has no true psychic ability".

With absolutely no experimentation to justify that assertion and of course no methodology for such experimentation, sceptics will declare that the psychic under evaluation is no psychic at all, but rather is just really good at reading people's subconscious behaviours and calculatingly arriving at the truth about the people they are interacting with. That is quite the dishonourable extreme of blatant prejudice by pseudo-sceptics who call themselves scientists. As I have said, many of these sceptics are simply afraid to admit something, and they know in their own hearts why exactly they harbour their fears. It is fear that leads them to irrational "scepticism", and it is fear that leads them to irrational arguments in its defence.

Recently there has been found, strong mathematical evidence in the field of String theory which indicates the presence of a logical creator (a God) in the universe's design. The evidence indicates that everything in our universe has been programmed.

The discovery was that the information in our universe (which exist as antecedents to other information I presume), corresponds to binary computer code. In fact, not only does the information resemble computer code, it resembles a specific type of computer code. One which has existed in the field of computer science for several decades now.

In addition to this, is the discovery that embedded within the universal computer instructions, are error-correcting codes. In case you do not know why this additional discovery would be particularly important, let me explain.

In engineering and computer science, "Error correction" is a function of signal-rectification (or in the case of my own example below: signal-compensation). You see: In theory, when we input information/instructions to a computing device, the output should correspond to our inputs. In reality though, our input signals usually have to travel a significant distance to their source. Depending on the signal-transfer medium and the type of signal, our inputs can become distorted by the time they reach their processing or output terminals. The output information will therefore correspond to the distorted information and not the original information.

To counteract the signal-distortion, we can add additional information to our input signals (or a slight variation of the original information) in such a fashion that when the signal is distorted, it is distorted to the form we intended it to be in the first place. As with many other things in life, there are many ways to go about error-correction and detection and I have given you a very easily-understandable example of my own. In actuality, and due to the infrastructures most of our electronic systems serve, we run the code/signal through a set of algorithms which serve the function of a comparator, in order to detect and correct errors.

Back on topic: The fact that computer codes with additional error-correcting codes injected into them, have been found in the information that describes our universe, indicates that an intelligent entity (in whichever form) is responsible for the creation of the universe. You see: The source of all intelligent information is intelligence. What do I mean? "What is intelligent information"? It is information with intent. i.e. purpose-driven information.

Whether you are reading simple words on a page or analysing an internal combustion engine's ECU mapping, the source of all intelligent information is intelligence. Random processes are by their definition, incapable of design, so meaningfully consistent, purpose-driven data can never (ever) arise from an environment devoid of intelligence and purpose.

Take DNA for example: The thing without which, biological life cannot be. DNA is a storage system for an inordinate number of very specific instructions which are required to build every protein, and therefore every cell, in a living organism. DNA contains nothing but meaningfully consistent information.

Mindless/random forces are incapable of instruction. There is nothing meaningfully consistent about a random process other than the fact that it is a random process. It cannot produce anything of meaning and intent. It cannot produce instruction. It is therefore impossible for the instructions which DNA contains, to be a result of anything other than an intelligence. Just as it is impossible for the information contained in a computer program to be the result of anything other than an intelligence.

Monumentally, all the evidence is stacked against atheism, and monumentally, all the evidence points strongly to an intelligent Creator. The very foundation of science is the establishment of a coherent world-view and the ascertainment of truth – something by which the world-view abides. When you turn your face from the evidence and refuse to follow it to its logical conclusion, you are not a scientist, and "science" becomes a term to which you are an irrational disgrace.

You become the type of person who advertises to others, that "Humans share 98.8% of DNA with chimps", and yet completely ignore and neglect to mention to them that "Humans also share 95% of DNA with mice", because the former (and highly incorrect) statement serves your ridiculous atheistic agendas, whereas the latter does not. The irrationality of your mind-set and the consequential incoherence of your world-view will lead you to perpetually dodge the truth whenever it unsettles you, and compel you to invent nonsense in its stead. Nonsense leading to dead-end after dead-end. A self-imposed stupidity. This is the current state of mainstream "science". And the nonsense of "gravity waves", "black holes", "gay genes", "multiverse theory" and "macroscopic evolution", are its children.

I listened to a few minutes of a discussion which took place at a conference hosted by Neil deGrasse Tyson pertaining to the discovery of computer codes in our universe. When Dr. Sylvester James Gates (a theoretical physicist who was part of the team that stumbled upon this revelation) said he had found sets of equations describing our universe in terms of binary code, while jokingly alluding to the possibility that all our lives are just a computer simulation, one of the other speakers (who seemed opposed to the obvious God-supporting implications of Dr. Gate's statement) said something in disagreement with Dr. Gates. To paraphrase, he said: 'equations do not have time, as they are abstract. Whereas the real world does.'

Those of you who know a thing or two about mathematics will probably struggle to find anything relevant to the topic of discussion in the above paraphrased text. From somebody who is recognised as a scientist, 'equations do not have time, as they are abstract. Whereas the real world does.' is almost the most ridiculous thing he could have said. You would expect him to understand that mathematics is only a tool. What mathematics does is describe. It describes the world around us, and it often does so with respect to time.

I was mildly surprised when I heard such a reasonably old man in a position as esteemed as his, say something as seemingly irrational as "... a mathematical equation doesn't have a flow of time in it, it just is", as if that somehow had something to do with the implications of the very equations being discussed. I was more than mildly surprised however, when I later found out the man who made the objection was Lee Smolin. A respected theoretical physicist whom I would not have thought of as being likely to give in to the unscientific pseud-sceptic rationale of some of his peers. Perhaps Smolin merely misunderstood Gates, and as a result, said what he said. But in any case, his objection was a textbook demonstration of pseudo-sceptic behaviour.

A pseudo-sceptic in his position would know better than to say what he did, but would say it nonetheless, if it was the nearest stone he/she could find to throw at the window of God's existence. You do not need mathematics to explain or imply the existence of a logical creator, but even in the presence of mathematical evidence, a sceptic (who would jump at the chance to use mathematics to disprove God) will attempt to refute the idea of God or the spiritual realm(s) by any means he/she can devise.

It is ironic that theoretical physicists turn to things like String theory to try and dodge the idea of intelligent design, and yet even there they cannot escape that reality. Like religious people, pseudo-sceptics believe only what they want to believe, and they need no rational reasons to.

Human beings had no idea that there was even such a thing as the atom, before research and analyses of physical matter revealed this. They did not know of electrons, protons, or neutrons, yet these things affected them and the world around them. In this same way, you do not need to know there is a God, or a spirit realm, for it to affect you, and trust me, it affects you and your world every day. It is evident that any scientist who does not believe in a logical creator, has not been a scientist for long enough. Either that, or this "scientist" is intentionally closed-minded to the truths of the matter, because his/her insecurities do not permit the acceptance of truth.

The scientific and historical evidence for the supernatural realm, ghosts, demons, etc. is almost overabundant. There are countless experiments and documented occurrences of such phenomena by both the scientific community and the community of laypeople. Particularly irrefutable however, is the evidence in the medical and law-enforcement industries. There are near-countless experiments and observations of medical practitioners who have confirmed supernatural occurrences from and about people throughout their dying processes and/or after their successful resuscitations. Likewise, there is irrefutable evidence in the official police records of many solved murders through the intervention of psychics.

Endeavour to discover information for yourself, and gain insight into such claims, and you will find the truth by all means. Unless of course, you look only for evidence justifying your preconceptions, like most bigoted sceptics, and religious people all the same. In which case, you will only find and agree with the lie you have chosen to tell yourself. When the sceptic runs out of explanations and rebuttals for evidence of the paranormal, he/she resorts to saying "It is a trick", and when the religious person runs out of explanations for why his/her religious book says what it says, and how such books are true, he/she either beats around the bush about it, runs away from the argument, or blatantly tells you lies.

An ignorant man who claims atheism will say "Because we can explain it scientifically, God did not do it", and an ignorant man who claims theism will say "Because you cannot explain it scientifically, God did it". Proponents of either world view are misguided and misinformed because their bias obscures their vision to the truth that God and Science are inseparable. "Because it is God's word", or "It is a trick" are not acceptable responses or rebuttals for either the religious or the pseudo-sceptical to use.

Angels

Among the spirits who have been in existence since a time before the Earth was created, are angels. Angels are God's workforce, and can be found scattered across the entire universe, doing whatever they were designed to do – most of the time. There are many different kinds of angels, but they all have one purpose intended to them by the creator: to maintain order.

There are angels that govern aspects of Mother Nature, angels that act solely as messengers, angels whose jobs it is to look after and watch over people, and even angels of war. Different types of angels possess varying gradations of intelligence and spiritual power, but they all were created for the will of God.

Contrary to the misrepresentations of angelic beings in the film industry and in fantasy novels (like those written by some con-artist Christians), angels do not look nor behave like the calm, beautiful and graceful creatures they are often advertised to be. They can take on many forms, and they may or may not appear to have wings behind their backs. They can also differ greatly in personalities.

In Luke Chapter 1, and Verses 19 to 20, the angel Gabriel became angry at Zechariah and removed his ability to speak, only because he doubted what Gabriel had brought him: "And the angel answered him, "I stand in the presence of God, and I was sent to speak to you and to bring you this good news. And behold, you will be silent and unable to speak until the day that these things take place, because you did not believe my words, which will be fulfilled in their time."". Another angel might have reacted differently, although not with delight either. Even if Luke's story is not true, it is not unlikely that a high-ranking angel would take issue with being doubted in his God-given message.

Angels are not at all the stereotypically iridescent, and elegantly charming symbols of altruism they are portrayed to be in the invented worlds of film and literature. Angels of war for example, are terribly frightening creatures, dressed in fiery swords and amour, and most of whom are almost cruelly unforgiving, and there are angels so massive, they could eclipse moons. The reality of angels and demons is so far removed from what most people have been led to believe, that I cannot explain even a tenth of it here.

You may encounter an angel with power so terrifying you would confuse it for a demon at first glance, and you could see a demon that would have you believe it to be an angel of God. Demons were angels too, so telling them apart from angels might not always be easy, but one of the main differences between the demons and the angels, is with whom their allegiance lies, and in concordance: their moral principles and how they behave.

I will cover these creatures in slightly more depth in the following chapter, but in short: Demons are filth who have rejected God's will, and by virtue of their loyalty to satan (or to themselves), are no longer in direct service to God. Angels however, are a working aspect of God, in that they take orders directly from Him, and serve as His extensions across the universe.

Generally, angels can take on any appearance, and the most powerful of them can manifest physically to look like animals, or even human beings that go about their day-to-day lives. You sometimes walk past them when you move on busy streets, but would never know, because they act just like everybody else. There are other kinds of spirits who walk among us as well, but that is beyond the scope of this discussion.

Angels are structured hierarchically, and their strength and intelligence increases with their rank. Angels of Mother Nature for example, are some of the most basic forms of angels. Only performing simple tasks, and may or may not be self-aware, whereas high-order angels tasked with responsibilities requiring intelligence, are fully cognizant beings.

Angels that possess intelligence similar to ours, are the ones who move about fighting battles where they are called, travel to and from planets with life on them (like Earth), and/or are assigned to protect certain areas or entities. This is how people have guardian angels assigned to them, and it is these angels who help keep the human beings they guard out of trouble. Were it not for these guides and protectors, the life expectancy of the average human being (males in particular, for obvious reasons) would be far lower than it is.

Have you ever witnessed somebody about to lose his life or about to become severely injured, only to be quite inexplicably "lucky", and escape harm? These are the kinds of cases where it is often their guardian angel who saved them. Guardian angels can come in different forms, with different personalities or attributes, but they all work for the same purpose.

Spirits with enough power and the legal rights (when sanctioned by God), have the ability to change the outcome of events in the physical world, and they do this mainly by discretely making alterations to as few as just one variable in any given environment.

Take the following scenario as an example: A boy leaving his doorstep to cross a street, spots something small sparkle with the corner of his right eye, and very briefly slows his pace of walk to look in that direction, but realizes it was nothing, and keeps walking as fast as he was before. As he crosses the street, a drunk driver quickly speeds past the boy, brushing fierce wind by his face, and almost hitting him. "Oh my God, that was close!" he says. And indeed it was.

Had the boy not slowed down as slightly as he did to momentarily investigate the distraction, his average speed would have been such that by the time the car passed that very spot on the road, the boy would have been right in front of it. And he would have died that instant.

Something as supposedly insignificant as a transient and distant sparkle in one's peripheral vision can save one's life. Apparently negligible changes in our environment can have significant effects, as everything in our world is interconnected. Changing one thing, can result in the change of another, which can result in the change of yet another thing, and such a chain of events can stretch to infinity, with enormous consequences.

Spirits can see into the future because in the spirit realm, the perception of time is drastically different from what it is for us in the physical realm. This allows spirits to see into the future for as far as any given course of events allows them to. This means that today, an angel might not know what will happen in a year's time. But tomorrow it might.

Angels were created by God to serve His purposes, but because they all have free will, and minds of their own, not only are they capable of making mistakes, they are capable also, of doing whatever they want. It is because of this that angels too get punished by God for disobedience, and it is because of this that Lucifer fell prey to pride, and a desire to be like God Himself.

Evil Spirits & Their Nature

Within the spectrum of morality, and at its opposite end, is a characteristic known as evil. We see evil every day in the form of murders, war, and destruction of different kinds. Adolf Hitler, alongside the devil himself are often cited as chief ambassadors of evil made manifest, but why is this? If somebody asked you to explain the definition of evil to them, what would you say?

Evil is not just the act of doing "bad things", or the trait of "being a bad person". Evil as a temperament, is something which is in the greatest opposition to God, and of the highest selfishness. Observe those who do evil, and you will see that the primary component of what drives them, is self-interest and the disregard for others.

It is a fact that all of us have been created according to the perspective, and structured around the basis, of a moral code. It is what defines all sentient life forms above a certain calibre, as this is a fundamental component by which God operates.

Cognizant energy forms (those characterised as living), like human spirits, exist in various orders or hierarchies that represent their ability to make informed decisions, and the degree to which they can be held accountable for their actions.

When people do things in the knowledge that they are wrong, or with the purpose to inflict unjustified harm, they are practicing evil to one of its extents. Unlike very low life forms who cannot be governed by morality, and so cannot be evil, human beings have a lot of responsibility.

A worm for example does not have the capacity to be evil, as it lives only to keep on living, and beyond that, is there to contribute to the dynamism of a multi-dimensional world and its inhabitants for God's purposes. The purposes of Mother Nature.

Now cats and dogs are of a far higher calibre of creature than the worm, and this is why they are capable of expressing emotions like fear, happiness, anger, joy, sorrow, excitement, even jealousy, empathy, and remorse. So they are governed themselves, by morality – however limited it may be about them.

Given that human spirits, are ranked higher than those of cats and dogs, we can feel to a greater degree, and about a wider range of affects. This is by virtue of our intelligence, which is what governs the ability of a sentient being to feel. It is because of this, that we are more responsible for our actions than the animals are for theirs.

It is by God's design and allowance that we all have free will. We have the freedom to do absolutely anything we please, even if it is destructive. The universe operates in such a way that we are rewarded for the good we do, and penalised for the bad. So we have choice, but our choices have consequences.

(For the record: I am not referring to the Hindu laws of "karma". As is the case with most of Hinduism's and Buddhism's teachings, karma is a fictitious concept.)

It is by choice that Lucifer rebelled against God, and by free will that some angels continue to do so even today. The Bible speaks of a war that raged in the heavens in Revelations, Chapter 12, and Verse 8: "Now war arose in heaven, Michael and his angels fighting against the dragon. And the dragon and his angels fought back, but he was defeated, and there was no longer any place for them in heaven. And the great dragon was thrown down, that ancient serpent, who is called the devil and satan, the deceiver of the whole world—he was thrown down to the earth, and his angels were thrown down with him", but what the Bible does not say is when the war broke in the heavens, and when Lucifer was cast out of heaven.

The heavenly war in fact, is an event which occurred long before Adam and Eve. The devil lost his job after being found guilty of wanting to replace God Himself, as he became jealous, and sought to be worshiped by those who came before Adam, not as a god, but as God.

When Lucifer lost his battle, he and the army over which he ruled were severed from the cord of God's blessing and cursed. At the moment he was sacked from the appointed position and its esteem in the heavens, Lucifer lost his name, and became satan "the accuser of our brethren" (his new job description). Not because God needed an accuser, but because that is simply what the devil chose to be doing. Like a bitter child looking to cause trouble wherever he could, and only spitefully so. Deservingly, the devil has been referred to as "the serpent", "the deceiver", "the great dragon", or "the beast". Representative of negativity in its most concentrated form. Where there is negativity, there is a force in general opposition to positivity. The ultimate source of light, and positivity is God. And this is why evil is said to be in darkness: it is far from God.

Fast forward a few thousand years after the devil's defeat, and he is still a problem today. But this serpent does not work alone. Before the 'great dragon's' disgrace, the angels whose responsibility was in the faculty of creation, were in allegiance to God, but were first and foremost at Lucifer's command. Lucifer answered to God, and like a sergeant general, Lucifer sent God's orders down the hierarchy of angels under his control.

Lucifer's authority and position next to God afforded him jurisdiction over many things, and when he found out that God was intending for man, who was made in His image, to be capable of leading and giving orders to angels like him, he rebelled, and sought rather to be the one that mankind would worship and praise. This jealousy is the sole reason for satan and his angels' hatred for mankind.

Also, this is why many angels fell with Lucifer, and how there could have ever been a war in the heavens in the first place. Basically speaking: Lucifer attempted a coup d'état. An attempt to overthrow the known ruler. But when the government in power is an almighty God, your chances of success are as close to zero as you can imagine.

Lucifer was not an angel of war, but he was a leader in a specific department, and ranked over many other angels. The lead angel of war was at the time, and still is, the archangel Michael, and so God commanded him to fight Lucifer. It basically, was Michael and his army, vs. Lucifer and his supporters, so it is only natural then, that the military-minded, and more powerful, Michael was the victor.

Since the relationship Lucifer had with God crumbled, Lucifer has been stripped of not only his crown and title, but of his very definition. He no longer is a light barer, so he can no longer be called an angel of light. His deeds bespeak the degeneration that has become of him, so he is now an angel of darkness.

The angels under his control are known as demons, the devil is their king demon, and they work day and night in the attempt to fulfil the ultimate purpose of spreading chaos and upsetting God's people as much as they can before their time is up.

They are hateful, and bitter towards God for being thrown out of heaven, and they are hateful and bitter towards mankind for being preferred by God over them. This is why their main aim is to destroy and convert to the dark side (and subsequently the lake of fire), as many human beings as possible.

It is a result of this, that not all demons are free to roam the Earth. Thankfully, most of them in fact, are in the underworld and the worst of them, held in bondage by the angels who have defeated and caged them.

Others have been bound and sent back to the underworld by human beings who have exorcized them from people, or banished them from a haunted home, etc. Even amongst the demons themselves there is disobedience, and some in a perhaps ironic sense, are in the underworld as punishment by their own brethren.

If every demon were on Earth, this place would be many times less habitable than the barely sufficient degree it already is. Even so, evil spirits are doing a mighty fine job with what they have at their disposal, and they have a treasure trove of ammunition.

How exactly demons and other evil spirits affect us on Earth and even after we die, could be described in a grand encyclopaedia, as it is extensive and sometimes complicated. But generally, they cannot just go about affecting people, so they rely on various loop holes to establish their presence. This is one of the reasons it is very important that most people be born again, and have the Holy Spirit dwelling within them. The Holy Spirit will probably put you at odds with more people of this world, but it will help keep you on the right path.

The primary avenue through which evil spirits affect human beings, just so happens to be: other human beings. This is because the spirit realm has rules, and one of its rules pertains to individual accountability. Evil spirits work about and within humanity's flaws to take it apart from the inside. This is their greatest tactic, and is multifaceted in its application.

The most commonly known facet is witchcraft: A person's utilization of satanic spirits to serve one's means. You see, many people want power, and the devil will capitalize on this desire by granting it to those who crave it. "Power corrupts" is no cliché. It is a fact. But the desire for power alone, is just as likely to do the same thing. The devil knows this to be very true, so he knows also just how to exploit it.

What demons do, is lend their power to human beings in exchange for their lives, the lives of their family members, and that of his/her entire bloodline. The sacrifices involved can be as relatively simple as having to perform simple rituals, or as extreme and unbelievably evil as having to kidnap and kill new-born babies, whose bodies are sacrificed to the demon(s) and whose blood must be drank. It depends on the type of evil spirit(s), the spirit(s)' desires, etc.

"Where do demons get their power from?"? Well demons are just angels who have turned their backs on God, and as such, they possess many of the same powers that they did before they were denounced by Him. They are of varying levels of strength, evil, and rank, so battles between angels and demons are not always one-sided.

When the archangel Gabriel endeavoured to deliver a message to Daniel, he found himself in a battle with the kings of Persia for 21 days. 21 days, until the archangel Michael came to his aid in Daniel, Chapter 10, and Verse 13: "The prince of the kingdom of Persia withstood me twenty-one days, but Michael, one of the chief princes, came to help me, for I was left there with the kings of Persia".

Power is power, and the wielder of the power can be good, evil, neutral, etc. Power alone is neither good nor evil, but its intent and effects can indicate its origin and whether this origin is evil or good. In 2 Kings, Chapter 2 and Verses 23 to 25, Elisha summoned bears to maul a group of children who were taunting him:

"He went up from there to Bethel, and while he was going up on the way, some small boys came out of the city and jeered at him, saying, "Go up, you baldhead! Go up, you baldhead!" And he turned around, and when he saw them, he cursed them in the name of the Lord. And two she-bears came out of the woods and tore forty-two of the boys. From there he went on to Mount Carmel, and from there he returned to Samaria".

Whose power did Elisha use to do this? He used God's power. It was not by satan's hand that the children met such an unfortunate event. Of course, not long before committing this act against the children, Elisha used God's power to purify the river of a nearby city. Whatever Elisha's motives, if what he did against the children was wrong, he would certainly have to answer to God for it later. God gave him powers, the utilization of which, he was responsible for. If he ever misused them, only he would be to blame.

Power is power, and with respect to witchcraft, the purpose of its power is to destroy things. Especially if these things are upright or decent. When people practice witchcraft, the poison of an evil spirit is allowed to flow through them, to corrode all that is good in this world, and particularly all that belongs to those whom they envy.

You see, demons cannot just go about doing whatever they want to whomever they wish. Well they sometimes do, but the spirit realm has rules, and most demons are painfully aware of this. When evil spirits lend their power to evil people, they do not only receive offerings in exchange for their services. They enter an agreement with the host/slave, such that the host is responsible and to be held accountable by God for everything they do by means of the evil spirits.

Evil spirits cannot heal, or construct. They can only damage and destroy. Witchcraft therefore, can only offer devastation. Nothing else. It can never bring anything good to this world. It devastates the families and bloodlines of those where it is present, and it devastates the lives of many more.

The covenant demons enter with witches is convenient, because when a witch casts a spell on, or commands harm to come to someone by means of the spirit, everything that spirit does is in the name of he/she who sent it. A practitioner of witchcraft also becomes possessed or inhabited by the demons they serve. These demons implant messages, and temptations into the host's mind, and because the host can choose whether to accept or reject these thoughts, he/she is held accountable for acting on them.

For this reason, many witches are afraid of death. Each and every single one of them. They are afraid to face God. They know that whatever awaits them on the other side, is going to be terrible. The devil hates all of mankind, and this includes even those who worship him. Witchcraft uses people to destroy, and turn into ruin everything around them, but it also seeks to destroy the very people through whom it works.

When witches die, all manner of hell awaits them. An eternal suffering the severity of which cannot be explained. The damnation of those who have turned their backs against God and given themselves to filth is proportional to the nature of the filth they have been soiled in, and the extent of it. The worse the person, the more torturous the eternal consequence.

Now please take note, that when I refer to witches I am not writing about those known as the "Wiccans". Wicca, is a neo-pagan practice and philosophy which encompasses a very wide variety of beliefs and rituals. In opposition to what they tend to claim, most Wiccans are in fact not witches at all.

The vast majority of those who practice Wicca or who claim to be Wiccans, in actuality are rather misinformed practitioners of a silly new-age Western spiritual movement which has roots in everything from Hinduism to Aleister Crowley's "Thelema". Its members often call themselves "white witches", in a rather juvenile attempt at euphemising something which is not what it is claimed to be in the first place, but they have little to no idea as to what witchcraft actually is. More often than not, these people are naïve fanatics of mysticism who needed something to do, and happened to have stumbled upon "Wicca" somewhere. They usually do not know what they are doing, and they usually do not even really know what Wicca is.

Wiccans as a whole, operate on various belief systems, as the heritage of their practices is scattered and drawn from several places. However the majority of Wiccans, (by that I mean, those who claim to practice "witchcraft" as defined by its modern and Western interpretations and applications) subscribe to the notion of a spiritual and universal force, that mankind is able to tap into and utilise for various purposes.

Wicca is typically not witchcraft, as it is mostly the misguided attempt to manifest intent and "supernatural powers". However Wicca can also be witchcraft (at least, the naïve children's equivalent), because many different entities are worshiped/acknowledged within the general scope of Wicca, and many of them are without-a-doubt, evil.

The reason for this, is that Wicca is the search for and use of spiritual energy. Its practitioners are mostly highly ignorant of where this energy may come from. Wicca has scattered roots, and although most of these roots lead to somewhat mindless spiritual entities and weak forces, a high number of these roots lead to things of a sinister nature.

Wiccans do not know this because the aforementioned sinister nature of Wicca as a whole, has been obscured from view and increasingly masked over time while being diluted by a variety of beliefs, particularly most recently, by the slow interjection of a new-age movement of "spirituality" of which one example goes by the term "Spirit Science": A messy concoction of deceptive and absurd historical information, crude amalgamations of various mainstream religious ideas and principles, and false promises of "spiritual enlightenment".

This new-age movement is complete nonsense and highly damaging to fragile minds who lack the insight and experience to be able to discern it as the garbage it actually is. As with all of satan's most debilitating work, it preys upon people's emotions, and claims to offer "guidance" and "strength", while simultaneously moulding people's ideologies into something inherently incoherent, fallacious and/or hedonistic.

To any of you who may have been lured into these things, and who are familiar with some prominent new-age spiritualists, I must tell you: Neo-spiritualist cult leaders like "Teal Swan/Scott" (whose real name is Teal Bosworth) are poisons to society whose silver tongues spread messages which ultimately strive to destroy the fabric of your understandings, for the self-deifying objective that you may be rebuilt in the image of their preposterous ideals.

You must stay far away from these kinds of people and their "spirit science" foolishness, for the truth is not with them. They come in all shapes and sizes, and they spout their garbage through all forms of media available to them, but they are easy to spot:

Anybody who loves to throw the terms "vibration" and "frequency" around when describing the spiritual realm, **does not know anything about the spiritual realm**. And anybody who speaks of "oneness" and "alignment" to speak of "spiritual enlightenment", **does not know anything about**

enlightenment. In fact, there is no such thing.

The very mention of "spiritual enlightenment" is a glaring red flag, because it means they have simply picked up useless Buddhist jargon. Buddhists do not know anything about the spiritual realm. "Buddhism" is what results when a self-righteous philosopher manufactures a religion, and the new-age fraud who copies the beautiful-sounding ideas of Buddhism, is about as spiritually knowledgeable as a housefly.

If you took your time to do background checks on many of these fraudsters, you would find that they are very different from their public personas. You would find that they are highly delusive megalomaniacs who prey particularly on the minds of weak, broken people, by selling things of insanity to them. In much the same manner by which daydreamers and imaginative theoretical physicists are spreading pseudo-scientific nonsense to lay people with General Relativity and String theory, new-age leaders are spreading their pseudo-spiritual nonsense to lay people. These neo-pagan charlatans preach irrational and senseless ideas which they mix with some basic psychology, Hinduism, Buddhism, and their own signature blend of convoluted, pseudo-inspirational, psycho-spiritual rubbish (which does not convey any sensible information whatsoever), to confuse and amaze gullible people. Some of these gullible people then start spreading to others, the garbage which they have learned. Not knowing that what they are spreading is garbage.

(To demonstrate how easy it is to spout the kind of beautiful-sounding nonsense which comes from new-age "gurus", some people have created websites which one may visit to automatically generate new-age rhetoric. One such website is "sebpearce.com/bullshit" which hosts some very interesting sentence-generating code: A "New Age Bullshit Generator" as its author calls it.)

Just as those who have been misled by other forms of neo-spiritualism,

Wiccans do not know what they think they know. It is typical Wiccans to want to see themselves as "witches" or "wizards" because they do not really know what those things are. They are proud to call themselves witches, but such a pride is often the only thing they ever have in common with actual witches. I will not go in-depth into the delusions of modern Wicca and the many ignorant and spiritually immature fanatics who subscribe to new-age pseudo-spiritualism, but you should know that these things are not what they claim them to be, and that there is a great deal of confusion within the Wiccan community and neo-spiritualist community at large.

Returning from my digression… Now, Witches (actual witches, not the Wiccans) believe they are powerful because they can do things that they think most people cannot. But their claim to power is all a lie, for there is no power in evil. Only its illusion. It is because of the lie they tell themselves, that witches tend to be very proud people. In fact, I have never encountered a single witch who was not filled with senseless pride and a grandiose delusion of power. I have seen that the more evil the witch the more proud she will be.

They derive immense self-worth from thinking they have control, and lavish their egos with the ability to test both men of God (those who might not yet be developed in their power), and other witches. But they lie to themselves when they think they have any power worth mentioning. Not while All-Mighty-God has some say in the matter.

Note: When I mention "men of God" who witches like to test, I am not referring to the usually poorly fortified priest who lies through his claims of providence. I am instead, writing about people who genuinely are a medium through which God's power manifests.

Typically however, when witches encounter such a man (or woman), they suffer the most humiliating of defeats. Depending on the circumstance, they may even lose their lives, so they tend to be very aware of whom not to mess with. Other witches, whose power casts a shadow over theirs, or men of God, who do not mess around in spiritual combat, are greatly feared by them.

Those few men of God who possess the ability to command thunder and lightning by God's power alone are very rare, and most people will never see such men. They are out there, but typically in small villages, helping people, and preaching the true word of God. Very much unlike most priests today who appear on television to sell themselves and their word, true men and women of God take no interest in the absurdity of mass-media and sensationalist spiritualism.

For even if they did, their sermons would only have a few attendees, as most people fear the truth as if it were death to them. The few places in this world where true wisdom resides, are frequented by few. And fewer still, actually appreciate them, for the truth tends not to cater to the kind of selfishness and superficial talks about "sowing a seed of money", that charismatic churches are so eager to discuss.

Moving on: Witches themselves are almost always very evil people, because they are characteristically, and unbelievably selfish. If ever they help someone else, there is an ulterior motive. In addition, witches challenge each other spiritually all the time, and usually belong to groups, through which they act to fulfil their evil spirits' commands. Should a member of the group ever indicate a desire to leave, she will be threatened and likely killed.

This is why it can be very difficult for people to leave witchcraft. Witches who operate in groups often are given assignments by group leaders to bewitch or destroy things, and whether or not the witch tasked with the job(s) really would want to do such things, she must – or face the wrath of her superiors and other group members.

This may all seem extraordinary to most people, as not many people knowingly encounter witches, but there is irony here, because each and every one of you knows a witch, and/or regularly encounters one. The thing is, they tend to be very good at hiding themselves in plain view. Even the elect among us sometimes struggle to discern the true nature of some of the people we come across.

You do not see them for who they truly are, but these people are in our schools, places of work, on the street, in the government, in our churches (especially in our churches) and of course, even in our own homes. There are millions of people on this planet who live unaware, that their mothers and/or sisters are witches. Usually that is because spells have been cast on them to prevent them from finding out.

However, sometimes family members find out. If not because the behaviour of a witch becomes apparent, then rather because the witch will attempt to recruit other family members (usually their children), and normally their recruitment is successful. You see, when a witch's child is young, he/she will attempt to implant a seed of evil in the child that will pave the way for the passing down of the satanic practice of witchcraft in the family, and unless the child's spirit rejects it, the child will wind up on the devil's side of the fence quickly in life. The rejection of the spirit tends to lead to the child's death, or monumental failure at life, as the demons will attack the child incessantly.

For most people, the only way to combat the witchcraft of a family member or anyone else, is through God and His angels. Sadly, going to church and reading one's Bible is rarely enough. To fight evil, one must strengthen him or herself, and employ the powers of the Almighty Jehovah. Powers which require much dedication, wisdom, and fervour. Unfortunately the secrets of such things have largely been destroyed by religious indoctrination. There is a great lack of these things amongst people because religion has deceived people into being timid sheep who cannot defend themselves, but I will discuss that later.

Now, it is very common for demons to demand human sacrifices from witches, and family members are the first ones picked. The demons do not disclose the following (for obvious reasons), but people in the family who the demons can see as highly likely to become successful and admirably accomplished human beings, or those who are destined to do God's work, are the one's chosen to be sacrificed to the demons. The otherwise useless ones in the family and those who are wicked themselves are left alone and will probably be introduced to witchcraft by the witch(s) in his/her family.

There are witches everywhere, but still a shocking number of people live life ignorant of the reality in their own households. In addition, the demons that work through witches maintain connections to one another, and this is such that certain people whose futures are extraordinarily bright, or who are doing the work of God to a highly dangerous effect on evil spirits as a whole, are persistently targeted by them.

Most people are not doing anything of enough significance for evil spirits to focus their attention on finding ways to attack them, so the things I am about to say will not be all that relevant to most people, but there are a few (very few), to whom what I am about to say applies, and they know who they are. Many of them are in sorrowful situations because they see the world for what it truly is, and are being attacked for it, yet they are not strong enough to fend off the evils which fight them. The knowledge which would empower them to fight has been all but eradicated by religious movements and globally-concerted efforts to silence such people.

Most people are really quite dull in the sense that they do not shine bright. People who shine attract attention, and the attention they attract tends not to be in their favour. The brighter they shine, the greater the attention on them will be. As a person through whom the Holy Spirit shines bright with truth and potential, a witch near you may be targeting and plotting against you by a command or influence from demons in your vicinity, or by another witch thousands of miles away.

Remember that the sole purpose of the satanic spirit is to destroy you as a human being, but not before using you to destroy as many other people as it can. That is the purpose witches serve for the devil. They exist to destroy and to be destroyed. The devil is a friend to no man, and practitioners of witchcraft are his pawns in line to be stripped bare and discarded as soon as they have served his purpose.

In the spirit, witches are connected in the sense that evil spirits who exist for the same purpose are free to move between them, and therefore, if you are targeted as one of God's people, you cannot really run away from a witch. Nor should you need to. Leaving town does not usually mean leaving the witch there, as it is likely that in your new location, there are several witches too, who the first witch may use to target you still. I will explain in deeper detail how these things are so, soon.

Evil spirits typically work through the people they possesses by inducing jealousy within them about their neighbours. When witches see that you are prospering, or that you have the potential/capacity to excel in life, they will work relentlessly to ruin you.

Human beings are prone to jealousy, whether they have access to voodoo or not. The only difference between a jealous man, and a jealous man influenced by witchcraft, is the means with which he tries to impede the progress of those he envies.

So as a word of caution: be informed that people only ever become jealous of others that they know. The reason your neighbour covets your new car or hates to see that you have found something great, is that he/she has come to know you, and therefore associates himself or herself with you in a sense. When people prone to envy are unsuccessful in certain areas of life, and they see their friends becoming successful, they think to themselves: "How come they get to have this, and I do not? I clearly do not deserve these things, so why should they?"

People do not envy celebrities or other people they do not know, because the very fact they do not know certain people implies to them that they do not deserve to. Thus, they do not deserve any of the nice things that those people have. Once a person prone to envy gets to know someone, he/she begins to feel they deserve what the other individual has, merely through association.

Witches are certainly not immune to such stupidity, so they are known to prevent many people from being successful by targeting their health, or influencing what many would call their "luck". What a witch will independently do to attempt to lay waste to someone, and what she will target, depends on what it is about the person of whom she is jealous that causes the envy. If you are a highly intelligent student or 'stand out from the crowd' for example, evil will seek to ruin your academic life and stagnate the development of your opportunities.

Evil spirits tend to combine various forms of attack in order to achieve a goal. This is why witches typically cast spells and curses of ailment and despair, so as to deteriorate their targets' defences as rapidly as is possible. This weakening makes the target susceptible to other forms of attack, and depression is a common avenue that makes someone more likely to indulge in addictive or destructive behaviours that pave the way for more problems in the target individual.

Jealousy is the number one cause of people bewitching others, so if you are the mother or father of a highly intelligent child for example, the evil spirit will seek to ruin your child's chances of positively contributing to the world by various means. One common route of destruction, is through drugs and alcohol, but inflicting disease upon him/her can be more effective. Have you ever wondered why so many highly gifted young children (mostly males), wind up on hard drugs and fail to make something useful of themselves? Or why many of them are sufferers of some sort of illness? These are not just universal accidents, there is a purpose-driven cause behind most of them.

Now look: It is not always the devil's work that a gifted child feels heavily depressed, decides to abuse alcohol, or smoke marijuana in excess. And it is not always the devil's work that a gifted child winds up diagnosed with a mental illness, so you certainly should not start seeing demons where there is none. You cannot start pointing fingers at spectres as soon as things start going wrong, but at a certain point getting suspicious might not be a bad idea.

It is within everyone's control to decide what they want to do, and what they do not. If you do not want to do drugs, then do not do them. An evil spirit can plant whatever temptations it wants, but you are still in control of your own life. You choose what to do with it and you are in charge of what steps you take to counteract difficulties in life, regardless of their nature. This is why a surprisingly effective defence against witchcraft in some cases can be that of simply not to believing that it has any power.

To any extent possible, evil spirits work with other people's beliefs. If you believe that walking under a ladder will give you bad luck, then that is the avenue an evil spirit will explore in order to indeed give you that bad luck.

If you believe that no one, and absolutely no one, has any power over you spiritually, especially when you know that God the Almighty supports you, then indeed no one can overpower you. Belief is almost everything, and this is why every successful motivational speaker to walk this Earth speaks of it so much. Believing in superstitious curses of bad luck or the idea that ghosts are coming to get you at night, only strengthens an evil spirit's resolve and gives it leverage by virtue of your belief system, to affect you.

Nevertheless, take heed not to be ignorant of the truth when it stands out in the open. Where there is smoke, there is probably a fire, and the fire will not go away simply because you do not believe it exists. You can only find the fire by investigating the origin of the smoke, and you can only extinguish the flames by cutting its oxygen supply. Pray for guidance and that facts may be revealed to you, so that when there is a problem, you can learn how to fix it. Whether the cause is spiritual or not. This way, if a demon does indeed come to get you at night, you can at least find solace in the fact that you did not call for it. A firm belief in yourself and your power source, coupled with some proactivity, will equip you with the tools to destroy the footholds of all those who curse and fight against you unjustly. Demons do not fear scripture, they fear people who can mess them up.

The devil has no power over he/she through whom God's power is channelled, and evil cannot overpower he/she who has the blood of Jesus with them. As long as you remember and firmly believe that, no evil can overcome you. Evil certainly will try to touch you though, and it will probably try to touch you a lot. Just make sure you punch in return.

Now, what I just covered was some of the bad news, and there is more bad news to follow, but some of the good news is that one does not always need the gift of spiritual discernment to see a witch where there is one. Evil will almost always manifest itself in a person's outward character every now and then. If not blatantly, it will be revealed to you subtly, when you pay enough attention to the details that present themselves to you either in person, or through dreams and other revelations.

People who do not possess sufficient intelligence, or who have an unashamed pride in their witchcraft (what they call their "power") are the easiest to spot out, as the evidence will jump out at you on multiple occasions. You will know when someone desires to cripple you.

If you are a witch yourself, then you too will use your power against them. Fighting fire with fire, until one concedes defeat – or dies. If not, you will fight them with a power greater than they could ever hope to possess. You will turn to the Lord your God and deliver to Him your enemies. You will get the angels to wage war with them, and you will ask God to descend His fury upon them, so He may consume them with His fire if they do not repent of their evil.

This is contrary to the modern teachings of religious Christianity which through the devil's deception, have been numbing God's people to the devil's threat for some time now.

I have mentioned early in this book, how Christianity has gone through a white-washing and watering down of God's principles and teachings, and I will mention it again because it cannot be stressed enough. People are being taught that they are to send hugs and kisses to their enemies who send demons and curses their way. People are being taught that it is OK to be defenceless, and bear the burden of their enemies' attacks because Jesus Christ has once said to "turn the other cheek".

There is nothing wrong with defending yourself. The problem lies with vengeance and hatred. For among other things, these are the things which afflict your enemies, and you do not want to wind up just like them. You must never keep hatred in your heart for such people, as hatred only corrupts the person through whom it is generated. People who hate have no peace. They are ever-presently at war within themselves but believe rather that it is the person being hated they are at war with. When you hate, you corrupt yourself.

But do not take the foolish religious advice of sitting by and bearing the brunt of your enemies' attacks while you pray for their salvation. Everybody has a Bible, including themselves who go to church every Sunday to blend in. You are not going to repent on their behalf. Wish evil upon no one, but set the snakes of your enemies against them. Unless they repent of their ways their own snakes must continue to bite them. You must never allow any tool of the devil to think it can affect you. Be red-hot, so that the oppressive hands of your enemies will burn.

The devil himself is beneath your feet. Pray for reflective protection, and every curse they send your way will go back to them with greater force than they intended it to be for you. Allow your words to be fire, and the Holy Spirit to manifest your intent through your prayers.

A strong will and a hardened faith (not a blind one) is something creatures of the night cannot break, and such a strong belief is cultivated mainly through spiritual practice. There are many ways to develop yourself spiritually, and there are many ways to fight the devil. I will not dedicate much time to teaching you such things here, but I will at least show you a thing or two. The following is a very simple procedure, but it can be powerful:

Take a cup, and fill it half-way with water. Then pour some salt onto the palm of your right hand (only a little bit). Place the salt into the cup of water and pray over it. Whatever your prayer is concerned with, pray over the glass of water in Jesus' name and thereafter drink all the water.

This above ritual can be effective in many areas and is particularly useful against spiritual sicknesses, but if you are having continuous and/or severe spiritual problems, and you are certain that the problems are spiritual, there is something else you can do, and which is more involved.

This is one of the areas in life where the Bible becomes very handy, for there is scripture in the Bible which can be used as an effective weapon against the devil and his cohorts. The Bible may not be the word of God, but it is useful. It is a collection of texts which it would be a mistake to disregard, despite the fact that it is certainly not what it has been advertised for centuries to be. Concerning many things in life, most people swing in one direction or another to a fault, and develop biases which prevent them from seeing the larger picture. I did not write this book to turn anyone into such a person, I wrote it to empower humanity and to solidify the will of man in searching more intelligently for the things which God has made. For a more holistic treatment than the one above, do the following:

Buy 7 white candles, get a bucket, and find one of the earliest Bible translations you can find (or one which has not altered the Bible's texts for the sake of contemporary English). Newer translations of the Bible alter the meaning of some of the passages and this can negate the effectiveness of some of their texts. You will also need access to 7 flowers readily available. The flowers must have a pleasant aroma to you. This is important. It does not matter which type of flower they are, as long as you like them. If you can, you must also acquire 7 bottles of floral water.

The following is a cleansing ritual you must perform for seven consecutive days, and during which period, you must not engage in sexual relations. On day one: Fill a bucket with water. Then take 1 flower and add it to the water. If you have a bottle of floral water, pour all of it into the water as well. Then take one of the 7 candles and break it into 7 pieces, and place the candle pieces into the bucket of water. The pieces need not be equal. Next: open your Bible to Psalms 51, and read it to the Lord from your heart with the bucket of water next to you.

You must then bathe yourself with the water in the bucket. As you are about to bathe, say: "In the name of the Father, the Son, and The Holy Spirit, wash away my sins, and break the chains of every evil cast against me". As you bathe, proceed to condemn every evil which afflicts you and every ailment which you suffer. Wash them away from your head to your toes repeatedly (bathing the water in that order). Do not use soap or a sponge. Use the water alone. Once you have bathed to your satisfaction, lift the bucket and gently pour all the remaining water onto your head. The used flower and candle pieces must then be discarded after you have gotten dressed.

Perform the ritual like that for six days. On the seventh day, the procedure will be the same, except that you will read Psalms 121 on the seventh day, not Psalms 51.

You must bathe as you normally do (e.g. in the shower) to be clean before you perform the cleansing ritual each day, because the water itself is the cleanser and must be scooped up with your hands as you wash yourself from head to toe. And if you bathe more than once a day, you must ensure that the ritual bath is your last bath for each day.

It is that simple. A very big problem with religious Christianity, particularly the charismatic church movement, is the sensationalism of God and the spirit realm, as well as the profound detachment from God and the spirit realm. Most people are very much disconnected from their spirit, in the sense that they have become materialistic. By that I mean: they are mostly unaware of their own spirits (themselves). Beyond the feelings of emotional energy and the odd occurrences of unexplained intuitive abilities, they lack knowledge of the true things in this world, and they do not know how to fight spiritual battles when circumstances call for such action.

No one is born evil, for even Lucifer was not created that way. People who are evil have allowed themselves to become evil over time. You see, as people move through life, things happen to them. Some things change them for the better, and others, a little for the worst. Most people go through major personality-altering events by the time they are 30 years old, and people who are not strong at times of misfortune, tend to develop as a result, various spiritual weaknesses or personality faults that are to their detriment. These faults are the kind of loopholes evil spirits exploit in people.

A large portion of the negative changes that people go through, is often done by themselves. This is because other people's actions have consequences which they bare, but your response to worldly stimulations is yours too to bare, as they may determine your future actions. For example: when you are made angry, you have chosen to be angry. You cannot be blamed for what you may feel under certain circumstances, but you must understand that the power to dictate to yourself what you will and will not respond to, means you are held accountable for your decisions and their effects to varying extents. Emotions cannot be used to validate every one of your actions, although in some cases one can be universally excused for some things.

Emotions are characteristic of our sentience, and from a "real world" standpoint, emotions serve many necessary functions. They are influenced by our biology, but because our ability to feel emotionally is predicated upon our design as spirits, there is a spiritual component to every single one of the things which we feel.

Emotions themselves are not only a reaction to our perceptions, they are representations of energy. From a simplistic perspective, emotions like happiness and joy are generally in correspondence with good. While emotions like jealousy and anger, are of the bad side.

Emotions are energy forms and can be generated from us to an effect. This means they can attract certain kinds of spirits as well as repel others, because such energy signatures are identifiable in the spirit realm. The fact that emotions are forms of energy, means they can have many kinds of effects. If for example, someone made you angry, and while angry, you wished and thought about that person paying for what they did, your intent to harm them as retribution would be transmitted as a thought form.

This can then actually have a negative effect on the target, if they are susceptible to your curse. Among other things, what determines whether or not your wish will have an effect, is the amount of energy you put into that wish, and the level of protection the target has against the curse.

The same is true for positive emotions, in that they can have positive effects. If for example, someone performs an act of kindness which is appreciated by you, your appreciation, when directed at the person, becomes a blessing in the person's life, and that is one of the ways people can be rewarded for doing good things. There are other ways too, but I will leave that for a later part of this book.

This section is devoted to describing evil spirits and their nature, so of course I am now going to reveal how demons manipulate people's emotions to carry out their motives. You see: when you channel negative energy through yourself consistently or frequently, you expose yourself to manipulation by anything that can induce or capitalise on this energy. Negativity not only can be the cause of evil, it can attract it.

Because emotions are energy forms representative of what is generated by the spirit from whom they came, spirits who have the same energy signature about them are like-minded and compatible with one another. This is why certain people get along so well, and why certain types of people are seen in groups. They are similar, and share common interests. This is true at the psychological level for people, usually because it is also true at the spiritual level.

Spirits who have hate and anger in them such that it is in prevalent, tend to be evil. Such spirits can feed on these emotions, so when a person generates these emotions frequently, they attract unwanted (sometimes wanted) companions of that nature. When a human being and a certain spirit are alike, communication that is in agreement between the two of them is established with more ease than would otherwise be the case.

As human beings, we communicate with one another audibly, but what is communication? Communication is the establishment of meaning between two or more entities. Spirits communicate via intent and thought forms. When we speak any audible language, what we are doing is translating our intent into an audible format to be received and retranslated by the recipient into a form that establishes meaning to him/her.

The words of artificial languages like English, are only encapsulations of the meanings widely known to be attributed to them. Spirits do not need to speak audibly with one another, as they transfer information through the intent and meaning generated between them. This means that when a spirit communicates with a person, he/she can acquire information without needing to have heard it audibly.

This is preferred and is more efficient because communication by spiritual means, transfers information in its raw format. It is understood accordingly by the recipient, and so misinterpretations and mistranslations cannot occur. This is evident in many animals, who seem to transfer ideas and messages to one another without making any noises or specific movements.

Now, what happens when people are in a negative emotional state for whatever cause, is that they are less likely to think rationally about the decisions they make in attempting to deal with their feelings. If this emotional state is persistent (lasting for a few days, for example), as stated, they will attract certain energy forms. This leaves them open to manipulation via certain thought forms and temptations.

Human beings have shown to be perfectly capable of allowing anger to make drastic decisions for them, and an evil spirit is not usually present when someone becomes annoyed and does something he/she may regret, but in cases where there is a long-term anger problem, there is almost certainly an evil spirit to be found feeding off of the energy being generated, and perpetuating outbursts of anger from the individual(s) it manipulates.

You see: Emotions are things which arise from within you. Things you are responsible for generating. If you do not have control over your emotions, it might be because something else does. Many people are suffering serious spiritual problems that they mistake for being "normal" afflictions. They struggle to control their emotions, and often find that they persistently ruminate about things which have offended them in the past, or about people who may have angered them. They do not understand why it is that they continue to fixate on things which hurt them, or why they are frequently reminded of something which made them angry or sad, or why it is that they are tormented by a severe and ever-present depression.

Evil spirits expose or attribute to flaws of many kinds (such as the craving of power, the pain of jealousy, or the vengefulness of anger) in order to establish themselves in people's lives, and once they are established in someone's life, they try to make it difficult for the person to get rid of them.

They do this either by making the person feel that there is nothing wrong with him/her when everyone else can see that there is, or by making the person feel that the act of changing and letting go of what he/she clings onto (whatever delusion facilitates their problem), will cause them to "lose something". Indeed they will lose something, and that something is the evil spirit.

Pride, for example, is something which hinders many men and women from being free of certain things. The unwillingness to let go of one's pride can contribute greatly to his/her downfall, and if there is a spirit of pride inhabiting a person, the spirit will remain when the person clings onto the pride. This does not mean all proud people have such a spirit with them, but it certainly means there is a considerable number of them who do. A spirit can only be harboured by a like-minded host, or one who has facilitated its stay by other means.

A like-minded person will accept a like-minded spirit because although most people are not consciously aware of their spiritual selves, their spiritual selves are still there. It is your spirit that defines the true you, and most people only behave in accordance with socially-dictated norms.

It is because people are conditioned by society to operate on a high level of consciousness, that they lose the ability to knowingly keep track of their true spiritual selves at the lower level. Because our spirits are our true nature, even if you openly declare not to like something, such a declaration will not matter if your spirit does in fact like that certain something.

It is not quite as simple as I am about to explain, but if there is anything (like a bad habit) you want to cut out or get rid of, yet are unable to, it becomes a weakness, and so can be used against you as such. This is another common route evil likes to work through. Everything from the prominently bad habits like drugs, and alcohol abuse, to the rather unexpected ones like an addiction to television, can be exploited by an evil spirit to maintain a presence in someone's life. This is because the focus is not necessarily on the activity that the person engages in. There is nothing wrong with watching television.

The area of exploitation is the connecting link between the activity and the person who participates in it. You see, when people do things (any things) such that those things are detrimental to their wellbeing, and yet they cannot let go or quit, that addiction is what an evil spirit exploits.

What I mean by this, is that when something begins to have a control over you, and you cannot find the determination or courage to stop, there is a doorway of opportunity for a sprit to associate itself with the activity, and hence, with you.

Of course one can have a healthy addiction. If you were healthily addicted to learning and building things, for example, or advancing society through science, nothing bad would come of it. The problem arises when your habits or addictions are of a filthy and/or destructive nature. That negativity will attract more negativity.

When anything becomes addictive and destructive in your life, it constitutes a source of manipulation and control. That negativity makes for a habitable environment for a negative energy form or spirit. As long as you continue to cling to the activity, you cling also, to whatever evil spirit may have become involved with it.

This is why simply stating that you will quit something is not enough, and you find yourself soon running back to it because a part of you has still clung onto it. I am not saying there is an evil spirit involved in all cases of destructive addictions, but it may surprise you to find that there is one or more involved in a very large number of them.

Should there be an energy form or spirit attached to your alcohol addiction for example, it will only leave when in your heart, you make the firm and honest decision to quit, and leave the drinking. I am sure there are many of you who have struggled with some sort of addition, and after making the firm decision to stop, have found that something left their chest area, or that they suddenly felt lighter, happier, and more spiritually unburdened.

The good news about all this stuff of evil spirits and addictions, is that all psychological problems can be solved by natural means. Therapy, and counselling are almost always effective ways of getting people to change their perspectives and behaviours.

This is because no spirit can control you. The only power they have over your actions is what you allow by what you choose to listen to. The scenario of a spirit egging you on to do something is no different from that of another person telling you to do something, because it is your choice to either comply or disagree with other people's suggestions.

In the same way you can ignore what any person says, so too can you reject whatever a spirit says to you, even at the subconscious level. If you do not want something around, simply refuse to accept it. Tell it to get away from you, and it must leave, as you do not sanction its presence. You have that right with regard to other people, just as you do with regard to other spirits, because you too are a spirit and were made by the same God that allowed them to exist.

Remember though, that evil spirits also use pain to manipulate people in a number of ways. We have all personally seen this. The most obvious evidence of this can be found in the ghettos and slums of any country. The impoverished are not only financially destitute, they tend to lack both the intellectual and spiritual development that the devil would find a formidable force.

In the ghettos of developed or developing nations, there is an abundance of crime, hatred, and senseless slaughter. I am sure you have noticed as well (if you are familiar with ghettoes and the people that live in them) that there also seems to be discrimination of anyone who displays that he/she has a functioning brain, and is capable of intelligent thought that distinguishes itself from that of the average person. Why is this? Why is intelligence frowned upon in such places?

You see: the men and women of the ghettos, as a result of their circumstance, are regularly subjected to torment of various kinds by the people around them. As children grow up, they are influenced by their environment. They desire to fit in, and their insecurities lead them to emulate their peers and the figures around them who have the most influence.

This is where the problem begins. When a child's environment is polluted with the decay of morality, and the advocation of lawlessness, gangs, and ignorance, it is only a few who do not succumb to the tendency to be one with the madness. This is made worse in certain places (like the U.S.) where the music industry deliberately pumps out garbage which it cunningly brands "music", and which glorifies gangsterism, lawlessness and stupidity to children of the ghettoes. Ironically, the musicians advocating such evils do not engage in those activities which they glorify to foolish children. Rather they live in big comfortable mansions, and surround themselves with luxury, as the feeble-minded children who look up to them and their music, kill each other in gang wars and constitute societal menaces. In desiring to be like the fools they look up to or are surrounded with, children (or anyone who wants to fit in with fools) wind up not only accepting the behaviours of their foolish brethren, they also accept the spirits that are of them. The people of the ghettos who do the terrible things they do, are not merely trying to get money, or survive, they are doing those things because it is evil which drives them.

But you cannot blame the devil for everything. If he is somewhere to be found near a person, generally that person has given him a reason to be there in the first place. Gang wars, and gunpoint robberies may be influenced by evil spirits, but evil spirits are never in 100% control.

Any way you look at it though, ghetto, uneducated, people are some of the worst individuals anyone can come across. The evil spirit moves through the ghettos like an infectious worm. Permeating every layer of these people's hearts and turning them into mindless fools. Making them hate, making them destroy, and making them target what is good in this world.

A manner in which evil spirits gain access to individuals is through the people's acceptance of certain ideas, or their succumbing to specific temptations. What I mean, is that if for example a thought, or idea that is morally wrong (i.e. one that is of an evil spirit, or that is cannot be in agreement with the Holy Spirit) is accepted by you as desired or true, you grant permission for a spirit who believes in the same thing, or who operates according to the same principles of this thought/idea, access to you.

What this means, is that committing a crime such as murder, for example, if not done so under the influence of an evil spirit already, will establish an entrance through which an evil spirit who is inclined to do the same thing(s), may enter. This opens you to demonic possession of many kinds.

In 2007, two 19-year-old Ukrainian teenagers gained widespread internet notoriety when it was found that they gruesomely and arbitrarily murdered at least 21 innocent men, women, and children, over the course of one month in Dnepropetrovsk, Ukraine. For this they are labelled the "Dnepropetrovsk Maniacs". What made this particular string of murders so horrifying, is not just the perpetrators' ages, but the fact that the boys filmed themselves mutilating their victims, and did so in a fashion that very few human beings could tolerate being told about.

The typical human mind cannot comprehend that anyone would do something like that. It does not make sense for a person to be so evil and twisted. Perpetrators of such crimes are called "monsters", "beasts", and any other names which attribute to the undeniably inhumane characteristics of their actions. Such killers are not born. They are made.

Just as evil spirits can take advantage of your addictions, they can also induce them. When you are on the same wavelength as any given evil spirit, you are more likely to take advice from it via subtle spiritual communications. If the spirit that stays with you craves something, it can affect you into craving the same thing.

It is no mere coincidence that a significant number of serial killers are discovered to have begun their habit by killing and/or decapitating innocent animals (like cats). Evil spirits take advantage of people's insecurities, and this includes their fears as well as their desires. If you look into the story, you will see that in the case of the Dnepropetrovsk Maniacs for example, the children had low self-esteem and were often afflicted by feelings of powerlessness. So they started torturing animals in their spare time to compensate for their mental illnesses.

When they began killing animals as an expression of power, their corrupt souls became open to demonic forces whose nature it was to take the lives of the innocent. The feeling of being powerless, is generally accompanied by the desire for power, and this is where demons see the window of opportunity to use that fear to overpower their targets, to capitalise on their targets' desire for power by granting them the illusion of it, or to become a part of the people to internally instigate and justify certain behaviours.

The Dnepropetrovsk Maniacs went from killing animals, to committing robberies and killing human beings, relatively quickly, but now that these boys are in prison, and their lives are ruined, the demons that worked through them get to laugh about how not only they have managed to get the boys to kill 21 or more people, but via their influence, the boys themselves will rot in prison, likely be molested by inmates, and never be free even after the day they die.

Despite obviously being demon-possessed, the boys are accountable 100% for what they did, because they were in 100% control of their actions, and perfectly sane. It is not insanity that does something this, it is perversion. This is why, even after death there will be no peace for them. People who do bad things, whether under demonic influence or not, will be convicted both in court and in spirit, as "guilty". The devil cannot make you do anything. He can only advise or tempt you to, and you are at liberty to deny or accept such temptations.

On the topic of demonic possession: there are varying degrees of it. There exists the subtle form of demon-possession as well as the more cinematic extreme, where the possessed person's body twitches, speaks in tongues, or demonstrates unusual strength (as you have probably seen in a number of horror films). Something like that is very rare, but it does happen.

Now, "What do demons look like?" you might wonder. Like angels, they can take on any appearance they desire, and the most powerful of them can manifest into physical forms to appear human, and walk the streets beside us. People expect demons to appear scary, and horrid, but most of them merely choose to be so. Some of them can in fact look like whatever they want. They can appear as angels of light, and this is one way in which they deceive some people. Beauty is only skin deep, and because demons tend to be spoken of as foul, unattractive beasts, people are able to be misled by angels of darkness who do not fit the description of evil at first glance.

Luckily, demons may change their appearance, and even their words, but their nature stays the same. The difference between a heavenly angel and a demonic one, is the way they behave. Evil bespeaks corruption and selfishness, and no matter how subtle, you can wise up to its lies if you are not willing to be a part of them.

This is why even though false prophets and new-age liars present themselves as "men/women of God" and "enlightened beings" respectively, they (particularly, the new-age clowns) preach and teach complete nonsense to deceive unsuspecting people who are genuinely looking for answers and guidance.

If you are one of the people who has been fooled by the likes of Benny

Hinn (a fraud who tells people he is a man of God) or Aum Shinrikyo (a Japanese man who tells people he can levitate), do not be ashamed. There is no shame in having been deceived as long as you now realise the truth. The devil comes in many forms, but if you can discern lies from truth, it matters not in which form he comes.

Now, when appearing before most people (in a dream or perhaps physically) demons generally choose to take on the appearance of reptilian humanoids, snakes, ghouls, or cloaked spectres, because they know those are what frighten the general public. The form each demon decides to take as well as the way each demon behaves, are what differentiate one demon from another, and why there are demons with the names: Rape, Murder, Mutilation, Melancholy, etc. The names they take after are symbolic of their nature.

Most demons are weak, but some can be powerful, and it requires a certain level of spiritual development to be able to deal with some of them. Some of these creatures are masters of intimidation, and will frighten people who do not know where they stand with God and/or their own spiritual strength.

There are demons who can break walls and set buildings on fire, or who can bend palm trees, but here is the catch: The rocks and the trees vulnerable to abuse, were not made in God's image. They have no authority over the devil. However you are made in God's image, and by the authority God has given you over the likes of demons, you can command them. It is because of this rule: the fact that you are above them, and that God prefers you over them, that the devil hates people so much. The devil and his legions are envious of humanity, so they strive to taint and destroy it.

But it is spiritual power that allows one to have the kind of confidence and belief that demons fear. If you are spiritually underdeveloped, and therefore shaken in your ability to conquer evil, your chances of success with some of these creatures is probably not that high.

To people who encounter demonic activity (for whatever reason), let me say: Demons know all the neat little tricks that make people's hair stand on end. They are quite capable when it comes to making ridiculous noises, and creating filthy illusions that make people fear, and make the demons seem more powerful, because it is crucial to your enemies that you perceive them in a certain way. They want you to believe, that you cannot fight them, that they are more powerful than you, and that you do not stand a chance. They may knock things off from shelves, walk around the room to generate the sounds of footsteps, or whisper sounds when you are alone in a room, but these are only attempts to scare you. Typically they will try to prevent you from sleeping, because if they can deprive you of rest, you will be weaker, and it will be less difficult for them to overcome you.

But remember that fear is irrational. In the same way some people are unreasonably afraid of rats, most people are afraid of ghosts. I would not blame you for fearing the idea being attacked by demons, because they can be quite provocative, but a bee can be quiet nasty too. That does not mean you should fear it. A bee can be swatted, and a devil can be rebuked.

Once they realise you are not afraid of them, they will back off, because surely if you are not afraid, that means you have good reason not to be. Remember, the power of God is greater than the power of any demon's. Through fervent spiritual practice, you will be able conquer any evil that challenges you.

Demons have learned what they know throughout the ages by studying people, seeing what scares them, how these things scare them, and by analysing the films and media they are influenced by. These creatures are not perfect, and they are very blatant copycats, which is why when something is of an evil spirit, it tends to wreak with the stench of unoriginality and an almost 'cheesy' sense about it.

It is typical of demonic entities to say things like: "Give up, you're outmatched", in an attempt to intimidate, "Yada, yada, yada" when they do not want to listen, or "You're pathetic", "You're worthless", "Victory is mine", etc. when their intent is to inflict self-esteem woes upon the person they are communicating with. These are things they have picked up from studying people's communications and how people react to what is shown on most television sets.

Demons rarely speak to people, but when they do, it is either a lie, an attempt at coercion (always wanting to strike "deals" that they will never stay true to), or an attempt to intimidate. They also frequently make attempts to enter people's minds or possess them, and investigators and residents of haunted homes plagued by demonic forces, will confirm these facts.

When a person is said to be demonically possessed, this usually does not mean the evil spirit takes over completely and begins to do as it pleases (as seen in the film: "**The Exorcism of Emily Rose**", for example). What it means is that a demon has been allowed access into the mind and at times the body, of the person afflicted. That is all it means.

People in charismatic churches who claim demonic possession, and the pastors (like Bob Larsen and T.B. Joshua) who purport the ability to exorcize them, are scandalous deceivers. The church people making silly noises and adopting animalistic mannerisms, are fanatical and perhaps hopelessly delusional actors, while the pastors who perform the public exorcisms on them, are conmen who deceive the willing and the gullible.

In the case of real demonic possession where the access granted by a demon is such that the demon directly manipulates and influences the host into doing what the demon wishes, the person may begin to exhibit drastically strange and/or inhuman characteristics. They may try and hurt themselves and people around them senselessly or perform various acts of sacrilege, usually in blatant hatred and opposition to Jesus Christ.

Real demonic possession is no joke, and the exorcism of the person demon-possessed is not something one can do in the presence of just anyone. When evil spirits are made to leave their hosts, they immediately begin looking for somebody else to enter. Not all people are guarded from certain types of spirits so at times a demon may be exorcized out of somebody only for it to enter somebody else who is nearby.

Although "Full-blown" demon-possession is very rare, some religious people jump to conclusions about such things needlessly. There is such a thing as a mental illness which did not inflict itself upon a person 'supernaturally'. Some people are just crazy, and the psychiatric ward is where they need to be.

Regrettably, this does not mean that most of the mentally ill, are naturally, or biologically so. You see, demonic possession and/or oppression is not always as drastic as Hollywood films make them out to be. Oftentimes demonic possession can mean the host being possessed while not knowing it, or being possessed while seemingly showing only signs of hallucinations commonly associated with ailments like schizophrenia.

Demons do not like to be known to exist. They do their best to evade detection, and will work tirelessly to convince everybody else that the sufferer of demonic oppression or possession is "just crazy". This is a highly effective tool of psychological warfare against the people evil spirits oppress. As a result, there are many incidents of people who suffer demonic oppression, being misdiagnosed and mistreated by psychiatrists in the Western world. Often patients are fed wave after wave of anaesthetizing drugs by medical 'professionals' who neglect the very real possibility of something 'supernatural', and they can make the problem worse for the afflicted party.

On the flip side, there are also many people who suffer from mental illness that is not of an evil spirit, and yet are tortured, and harassed by religious or superstitious people who do not have the medical or spiritual background to be able to justify their allegations. A balanced and educated perspective is imperative about all misunderstood phenomena.

Now let me point out that there is quite the difference between demonic possession and demonic oppression. In the case of demonic oppression: a demon, or evil spirit who is sent by a demon, attempts to hinder an individual's progress in life by arranging events of misfortune for them or by inflicting emotional disturbances, like a plague of depression.

Evil spirits' preferred method of attack is depression, because by nurturing negativity inside their victims, and making them feel inexplicably unhappy, they are more likely to seek comfort in activities which are notorious for their symbiotic nature. Drugs and alcohol abuse are typical choices.

These destructive habits then allow the evil spirit greater control and access to the individual, as they have made their bodies habitable by filthy spirits who thrive in environments of corrosive addiction and the disorganization that comes with it.

This is one manner in which witchcraft is used to affect people, but demons do not like to get their hands dirty at too great a risk of their own. Each time an evil spirit runs an errand for a witch or another demon, the spirit risks being cast back into the abyss of the underworld and bound there, or even being destroyed, should the intended victim be powerful. Being destroyed is a fate feared by all of them, and hell is not the kind of place most evil spirits are happy to call home.

On the topic of evil spirits and the places they call home: All spirits are energy forms, and as such they are often forced to draw from finite sources of energy to maintain their strength. All living creatures must absorb and/or generate energy by some means in order to have any effect in the world.

Spirits too can become tired, and require places of refuge like we and animals do. This is where inanimate objects come in, and where I show you how they can be of use to spirits. Spirits can absorb energy from multiple sources, and they can do so in unexpected ways. Any object which contains or receives energy can house and sustain a spirit looking to settle itself around the object. If the spirit can declare the object to be its property, then it will be the case that the spirit owns it.

This means everything from a rock to a puddle of water can be occupied by a spirit for whatever reason it is able to. Things which human beings may take a liking to as well can be occupied. As I am sure you have anticipated, the implications of this can be highly unpleasant. You see: when an object is adored by a human being, that human being tends to send energy to the object.

If a spirit is able to associate itself with the object, it will begin sapping the energy thrown in its direction. When a person has an attachment to something they possess, a spirit can become a part of the possession, and if this spirit is evil, it may bring you misfortune. This is why people sometimes encounter spiritual problems with old antique furniture or statues which they bought. Spirits love statues because they represent living entities, and second-hand goods can come from anywhere.

However, I hope you can recall that we too are spirits. We can claim things too and if we know how to do so effectively, a spirit cannot be granted access to what is ours. This does not mean it is alright to be worshiping objects (like a fancy ring which you picked up from a flea market), as you do that at your own peril, but it does mean you can have greater control of the things you own and the things you love.

An aspect of the spiritual rules pertaining to what we own, allows us to fight for something that always was, or has become, ours. The antique (and probably highly overpriced) statuette you bought, might be possessed by a spirit (not an unlikely event), but once paid for, and declared yours by the previous owner, you have every right to evict whatever entity might remain attached to it. Stubborn spirits may try and put up a fight about things which they want for themselves, but ultimately they must go the things do not belong to them.

This applies to homes as well. In homes where there is spiritual activity similar in nature to hauntings, the spirits that reside in them believe that they have the right to. When spirits, evil or not, inhabit a home, it is either because they have been called/invited there at one point, or because the home was not belonging to anyone else specifically before they came.

The difference between a haunting which is ghostly and a haunting which is demonic, is the nature of the haunting. Most ghosts prefer to be undisturbed, and in accordance with that, they prefer not to disturb. There are many people who live in large homes inhabited by a few ghosts, and they never know.

The larger the home, the greater the chance of there being a ghost or two living in that house with you. Generally, the rules that apply to us all as spirits, state that your home is yours, but if a ghost can occupy a space in the home as well, without becoming a problem and without alerting you, it will try.

Demonic hauntings on the other hand differ from most ghostly ones, in that they are characterised by blatant attempts of the evil spirits' to make their presence known, to bother the occupants (especially the children in the home) and sometimes to drive people out of the house. The only ghosts who behave in a somewhat similar fashion to demons are the ones known as "poltergeists". Poltergeists are human spirits who have acquired the power and knowledge that allows them to manifest themselves physically, and are inclined to use this power and knowledge to derive pleasure from scaring people (by moving objects or making noises).

Most of them do the things that they do, to force occupants out of what they believe to be their home, but some disturb human beings for the fun of it. As other troublesome or evil spirits do, they may try to harass and attack people as they sleep, or pop themselves into one's line of sight every now and then to make the person who sees them scream or panic.

Some assaults on people include what is known as "The Old Hag syndrome". This is when an evil spirit attacks and disturbs a sleeping person while paralyzing his/her body, thereby preventing the person from being able to move or speak. While rendered immobile, the victims of such attacks are subjected to trauma that can include sexual molestation and other forms of mental and physical abuse.

The reasons for this type of attack vary, but anything from witchcraft to an angry spirit claiming to own the place of residence where the attack took place, can be the cause. This has fraudulently been denounced as nothing more than a "hormonal problem" by bigoted deceptive conspirators in the "scientific" community and biased individuals with agendas against any evidence suggesting the paranormal, but it is far from a hormonal problem.

On one hand though, people who say sleep paralysis is natural are partly right, but only partly. You see, there can be natural explanations for why you may feel conscious on your bed, yet unable to move your body. When we sleep, our bodies automatically are rendered immobile so as to prevent us from acting out our dreams or 'sleep-walking', and when it is time for us to wake up, our brains re-enable movement.

Sometimes, this mechanism can malfunction and our bodies fail to wake up, despite the fact that we have consciously done so. This is natural and can happen to some people from time to time. It is a form of sleep paralysis with no spiritual causes. However, when this happens to you as described above, and instead of merely being paralyzed, you experience things like strange smells and/or the appearance of ghostly spectres whose very apparent intention is to torment you, then you are not suffering from natural sleep paralysis, but are in fact coming under attack by a wicked spirit. If this currently happens to you, the truth is: you are not dreaming. However I understand that you probably desire to be told otherwise.

Sometimes the spirit stares at its victim for prolonged periods of time so as to accumulate fear and frustration. Other times, the spirit moves the victim's body across the bed, or grabs a hold of his/her arm. There are also spirits who are known to sit on top of their victims' chests in order to make breathing difficult. The foul smells are indicative of a demon, but demons are not the only beings who do these kinds of things.

If you have encountered all these things, then you know that these creatures are cowards. They can only attack as you sleep because they are powerless against you otherwise. They are aware that most people do not know how to fight spiritually anyway, so most of them attack when their intended victims are slumbering and are even less capable of defending themselves. If a hostile spirit is able, it will go beyond limiting itself to your bedtime and attack you at any time of day, but such spirits are cowards as well. Fight such things, and they will leave as soon as they realise you can defend yourself.

Any evil spirit can do this to you if it is able, and the fact that a majority of people on this Earth are not naturally guarded against them, means it happens to most people during their lifetime. Millions of people have reported experiencing the same things: An inability to move, retained eyesight, the movement of shadowy figures around them or the appearance of a demonic or frightful creature on top of them. Millions of people also report a coincidental cessation of these kinds of attacks as soon as they happen to move away from their house, and into a new one.

When so many people (regardless of their geographic location, background, or upbringing), voice the same experiences, you can be very sure that any sleep expert worth their salt will confirm the existence of something that mainstream science and media will not openly declare, by virtue of their hidden agendas.

Demons work through a surplus of loopholes that I have not even covered the half of, but if I aim to ramble on about these things to completion, this book may never come to an end. So let us move onto the next topic of discussion: Religion, and how the devil works through disinformation to spread it.

Jesus Christ spent a considerable amount of time teaching the people around Him of the gospel, curing the sick, healing the wounded, freeing the demonically oppressed, and even raising people from the dead. He came to reveal the truth to people, but this unfortunately got Him killed by religious leaders.

This is because: To a mind ensnared by religious bigotry, nothing except their doctrine is correct, and anyone who exposes flaws or lies in their doctrine, is an enemy. It is for this reason that the Jewish Pharisees harboured an undying hatred for Jesus Christ, and it is for this reason they conspired with Roman leaders to kill him.

They called him a heretic, a blasphemer, and a deceiver for claiming to be the Son of God, in spite of the wonderful things He did, and the wisdom He spoke. The evil spirits whose whispers manifested themselves through these people's cries of heresy and blasphemy, had Jesus Christ crucified because the peoples' religious mind-sets could not tolerate Him. They could not tolerate **the truth**.

It is unfortunate that although Jesus came to inform people, and even died doing so, religious manipulation remained after Him. It is also unfortunate that it has rapidly expanded itself since. You see, the evil people who called for and succeeded in the crucifixion of Jesus Christ may have long since died, but the evil spirits which were embraced by them have not. Those devils have just moved on, and found other bodies to inhabit.

It is the devil who worked through Judas when he betrayed Jesus, and it is the devil who worked through the religious men who rebuked and killed Him. The serpent works through so many men, not because satan is some omnipresent entity with the great power, but because there are so many people corruptible enough to be used.

Note that when I mention the devil and his accountability for the perversions of this world, I am citing the actions of any evil spirit under his control or who works towards an end similar to his. The devil as an entity is represented by not only satan, but by all those who support his cause. Both indirectly and directly.

Influencing people around a target individual is a common avenue of the serpent. Evil attacks people through other people by exploiting internal vulnerabilities in them. For example: evil spirits make use of people's insecurities to manipulate them into doing certain things. Access to a person is gained primarily in one (or both) of two ways: The planting of a seed that can be sustained by the host environment, or the conscious acceptance of evil by the host. This allows evil spirits to move freely between individuals who allow them access both subconsciously and consciously.

A large number of people are at risk of the exposure to, and influence of, internal spiritual sabotage by things they cannot see because a large number of people are mentally unfortified (or unintelligent) and spiritually unaware. There are other factors, but such pertain to ancestry, universal debts, unknown spirit world communications, etc. and that is currently beyond the scope of what I am here to tell you about. What I can tell you that the ability is within all of us to protect our minds and our souls from demonic influences.

There are probably some of you who have noticed that you are receiving apparently unsubstantiated amounts of hatred from select individuals, and there are some of you who have noticed that you suffer from feelings of jealousy and hatred that can direct themselves to different people. The latter of the aforementioned are most likely unsuspecting tools of demonic oppression, and the former of the aforementioned are most likely people gifted by God to some extent or who have potentially bright futures ahead of them. The more connected to God an individual is, the more problems he/she will face from evil spirits. People perceived as threats by the devil will be fought at every major juncture in their lives.

Regrettably, many gifted people find their paths derailed by the efforts of evil against them, and wind up in all kinds of messes that they do not know how to dig themselves out of. If you know yourself to be one of them, and are experiencing opposition from people that you have identified as 'unnatural', know that you are not alone. I for example, throughout the course of time spent dealing with spirits, have noticed evil moving between people around me and those I would encounter, in a persistent effort to annoy me (to negligible effect).

You see, part and parcel of being human and having to associate oneself with other humans, is having people be jealous of you when you are accomplished at something. If you are destined for any kind of greatness, you will have to deal with people who envy you. In fact, years before you even begin to actualise your goal, let alone achieve it, you will have to deal with people who show jealously towards you, and you will have to deal with people who attempt to spoil you through spiritual as well as non-spiritual means.

People will envy your attributes, they will envy your intelligence, and they will envy your blessings. Those who do not endeavour on their own to attack you or ruin your name before others are almost always usurped by an evil spirit who capitalises on their jealousy to dictate to them the way they are to treat you. Such have been my experiences, and augmented these experiences have been, by the fact that I am spiritually aware.

It is such a shame about people who endeavour to soil the lives of others, because where these people often wind up reflects the fruits of the seed they have sown and allowed to grow deep inside them. Eventually they stagger and fall into the filth they have allowed to fester in their lives.

Having wasted energy and resources being jealous of somebody else, and attempting to sabotage him/her, instead of aspiring to accomplish things of their own. Such people know they will never be able to achieve what you can achieve, so they will hate you for it.

As I have said many times before, an evil spirit cannot make you do what you do not want to do. When people envy you, it often is their desire to witness and contribute to your downfall that allows an evil spirit who wants the same thing, to attach to, and use them for such a cause.

If you know how to detect such things, you can sometimes tell that a particular evil spirit is working through someone, when that person tends to say the exact same offensive thing(s), word for word, as people you have experienced before them, or when they act in very similar ways. You see, an evil spirit's character does not change, and it does not get tired of what it wants to do. It is only the higher-order evil spirits who formulate new plans, and become more effective at executing them over time. Even they have characteristics particular to them that encompass their individuality, so they can be picked apart from one another, but they do adapt and evolve their strategies.

Now, when an evil spirit living inside someone recognises somebody else as having the Holy Spirit, it reacts with hatred. It then communicates this hatred to its host, and he/she responds accordingly.

If ever an evil spirit manages to get the target individual to rationalise and justify reciprocal anger, contempt, or hatred towards the offending person, this spirit will then have established a hole through which to enter and attempt to destroy the target from within him or herself.

Do not to pay any mind to fools who try and incite anger inside you by indicating distaste or by insulting you. You do not want to wind up just like them. They are suffering from spiritually driven emotions that torture them every time you succeed at something, and they will continue to suffer until they manage to rid themselves of the weeds which suck them dry.

This brings us back to the discussion of how the devil uses religion as a tool. Remember that religion is not the belief in God, or Jesus Christ. Those things are not what religion is about, although it hides behind them. Religion is the acceptance of a blind unsupported faith, and the restriction of one's freedom such that it makes its participants feeble-minded, and ignorant of the truth.

Religious people did not know much of the truth when Jesus came to set things straight, and they do not know it now. People are raised in different households, and by no fault of their own, in different religious backgrounds. The Hindus and the Muslims are only Hindus and Muslims, because their parents were. Not because they have any valid reasons to be. Likewise, most Christians are only Christians because their parents raised them that way.

Most Christians are therefore, only lucky to have been born in a family where the God of the Bible is accepted, and the false God of Islam for example, is rejected (although I am sure that Muslims feel that it is the other way around). People often make the mistake of thinking the God of Islam to be the God of the Bible, but Jehovah, Creator of the universe, whose Son died for humanity's sins, and 'Allah', are not one and the same.

Since their fall, demons have had an impact on the people of Earth in many ways. The devil sought worship from man before Adam and Eve, and still he seeks worship from man after them. In addition to achieving this via witchcraft and satanism (where the focus is more on 'evil' and 'destruction', than 'worship'), they do so via religion, where they masquerade as divine entities.

Hinduism is one good example of this. There is an almost innumerable amount of spirits in existence, so it should come as no surprise to you that the Hindus have an almost innumerable amount of Gods/gods. Hindus will claim that they only serve one God, but this is not so. Hinduism acknowledges many millions of gods, and declares that all these gods lead to one God, the creator. If you have your wits about you and/or have been involved with Hinduism long enough to experience evidence to the contrary, you will realise what kind of deception that is.

Hindus worship a very high number of spirits, and almost none of them are related to God in any sense other than the fact that He (or His creation(s)) made them. Most of these spirits are demonic entities. Examples of demon-worship which one can find in Hinduism are the practices and beliefs of the "Aghori sadhus". The Aghori are a group of misled occultists who worship a demon 'God' called Shiva, and enter themselves into all manner of abominable rituals and lifestyles for the sake of their false and useless 'God'.

Although the majority of Hindu practitioners condemn the Aghori, the majority of Hindu practitioners do not know anything about the origins of their beliefs. They oppose the beliefs and practices of the Aghori only because those beliefs and practices are deplorable at face-value. 'Regular' Hindus themselves worship cows and even consume the urine and faeces of cows. Their beliefs are not any more defendable than those of the Aghori's. Like "Wicca", Hinduism has many scattered roots and is drenched in false and nonsensical beliefs. Something which is common to all religions, but in variation.

Islam for example, is different from Hinduism in the fact that a single demon deceived and possessed a man named Muhammad and claimed to be the angel of one God. Religious Christianity is different from Hinduism in the sense that people who really knew not what they were talking about, wrote several books which were then in conjunction with other books, compiled into a single document for colonialists and conmen to use for the dissemination of lies and foolishness. Mormonism is different from Hinduism in the sense that a sexually perverted and demonically-influenced habitual liar called Joseph Smith, founded a highly ridiculous religion for the sake of self-deification. These religions are different from Hinduism, but the devil has a hand in all of them. Hindus, Muslims, religious Christians, and Mormons are not intrinsically bad people. But Hinduism, Islam, religious Christianity, and Mormonism, are very bad. They are not equally bad, because Islam for example, is a far greater evil than Mormonism, but both Islam and Mormonism are evils unto this world.

They trick people who do not care much about investigating the truth for themselves.

Those who accept religious lies are people who have not done, or show no interest in doing, research to validate or invalidate religious beliefs. Sometimes it is fear that restricts them. The fear of discovering that what they have chosen to believe all their lives holds no water. Other times, it is because those who they have been indoctrinated by, have brainwashed them into thinking that the religious way of thinking is the only good way to think.

This is good news for the devil, because when people are so brainwashed by religious misconceptions that they will believe anything, you can use them as multi-dimensional ploys for your grander schemes. Religious people will stay in darkness, knowing little of significance, and as they go out to evangelise, they are spreading their misconceptions to a larger audience. Some of whom, will join them.

In addition, when religious people say or do the often silly and apparently unintelligent things that they are well known for, those who think rationally about what they witness religious people doing, as well as observe the futile efforts of their practices, will think twice about why they should be Muslim or Christian, when only foolishness is to be gained from it.

It is the devil who used Muhammad to create Islam, and it is the devil who turned Christianity into a religion as well. The conmen and televangelists we see on TBN (Trinity Broadcasting Network) for example, are the exact kind of religious evil which serves satan's agenda. Whether or not these conmen know it, they are pushing people away from God.

The sole purpose of religion is to either capture and enslave people into senseless indoctrination, or to push them away from it, and in effect, away from God, by making them think religion and God go together, when the reality of the matter is that God hates religion as much as sensible atheists do.

Many people are leaving religious Christianity, and often adopting atheism, because religious Christianity claims to be the only Christianity. Practical people rationalise that if that is the case, then Christianity must be a lie. Do you see how well the enemy has worked to permeate even the theology of the truth? Jesus Christ, The Holy Spirit, and God, are the source of truth, but satan has managed to use the message of Christ against mankind. This should not be a surprise to anybody, because satan has been around for a very long time. There is hardly anything you can tell him that he does not already know.

People say "the truth will set you free", but freedom can be scary for the fearful and the naïve, who would much rather stay comfortable and warm in a house of delusion, than open the door for the breeze of truth to sweep awakening past them. They slam the door to reality, and lock themselves in a warm room of ignorant, like-minded people because they would much rather not see the world for what it is. A breath of fresh air would do religious people some good, but they do not seem willing to come to terms with the fact that fresh air is usually cold at first.

It is the evil of mankind and the manipulation of religion that successfully invaded and indoctrinated the African continent. Men of the West enslaved African people, raped African people, murdered African people, and treated African people like currency. All this was done by callousness and greed personified. Ironically, by people who carried Bibles with them. In addition to their human rights violations, they programmed their slaves with their versions of Christian doctrine, making them feeble-minded and foolish. They infectiously, spread religious Christianity to the slaves and to their slaves' families.

If you are an African, who believes in the gospel of Christ today, it is probably only because it has been forced onto your ancestors, who by no intention of God's, spread it down their generations, until it reached you, and those whom you know to share the same belief(s).

It is on religious grounds, that the slavers justified the slavery and abuse of other human beings. They used the Bible and a few passages that referenced slavery to justify their evils, claiming that it was acceptable. And because the Bible was identified as "the word of God", it was seen as blasphemy to oppose the slavers.

It is by means of religion that slavers justified slavery, and it is by means of religion that people still are slaves today. The spirit of religion, is a spirit of deception, and it works in those who allow it to. When a false preacher or false prophet speaks lies, and you agree to accept them, you allow the spirit of religious deception access to you. This is what has happened to the millions of Benny Hinn supporters who fail to see the blatant sacrilege of such evil shepherds.

If you have ever argued to exhaustion with a religious man or woman, you may be of the opinion that religious people seem "stupid", or "lack sense". This is because religion breeds ignorance and an undying servitude to false prophets and a false God. The devil is notorious for distorting and moulding what God has made into something that it was not intended to be, and religion is one of these moulded things.

People entangled in the web of religious doctrine have been lured in by a most insidious arachnid masquerading as a bringer of salvation, but has only trickery to deliver to them. Religion offers no Holy Spirit of God, but a religious spirit of the enemy. Such a vile spirit this is, that even people who have the Holy Spirit living inside of them can have it bound and restricted in its affects by the acceptance of the kind of lies the spirit of religion brings. We can only be thankful that the devil is not perfect, and that the imperfect nature of his devices makes itself apparent when you scrutinise them.

If one were to have the adequate tools to deeply scrutinise the things of the natural world, one would find that underlying the interactions and states of physical entities and spaces, are spiritual aspects that go unnoticed by most people as such. One would find that human beings in particular are teeming with spiritual activity.

I have covered spiritual activity in humans before, and as with many other things in this book, I will cover it in greater depth later. You should recall the association I made clear between spirit beings and the human beings who often host them without being aware of it.

The influence of a spirit on a human being can change the way a person thinks, it can change the way he/she acts, and it can even change the kind of things he/she is interested in. A minor example would be the craving for a specific type of food, and a major example would be the alteration of a person's sexual preferences.

The possible effects are many. A person may develop a specific sex fetish, he/she may suddenly become physically attracted to certain types of people, or he/she could experience an increase or reduction in sexual cravings. The consequences of one's association with a specific type of spirit will be in line with the nature of the entity.

Relatively benign things could come about from a relatively benign spirit (although bad things can occur also), but the very worst of things can come about from the very worst of spirits. If a person's sexuality were to be influenced by a highly perverse demon for example, he/she could turn into the kind of revolting abomination who rapes people habitually.

The most common alteration to a person's sexuality by a spirit inclined to do so, is the development of a fetish. A slightly less-common, but still prevalent spiritual alteration of a person's sexuality is one where an individual's sexual orientation is entirely perverted.

Yes, the fact that there is a connection between spirits and their hosts can also explain why there is such a thing as homosexuality. Homosexuality in many cases, is a corruption of the mind or soul. A corruption of what was once natural, to make it unnatural.

There is not always some sort of spirit involved, but from what I have personally seen, instances of non-spiritual causes of homosexual attraction in people are highly outweighed by instances where a spiritual problem underlies said attraction. I will briefly discuss both the "natural" and "unnatural" causes here, beginning with the latter. In circumstances where one's homosexuality is rooted in spiritual afflictions, being gay in and of itself is not the biggest problem. The problem is the reason behind his/her homosexuality.

You see, when a spirit who is perverse in nature, inhabits or imposes itself upon a person, that person will tend to develop the same filthy desires and cravings as the spirit whom he/she is influenced by. The devil will tell you otherwise, but homosexuality in human beings is unnatural, and not at all by God's design. I have personally seen the foul spirits that move through the gay and lesbian community, so I know exactly what I am talking about.

At times it is a spirit which must inflict itself on a person to effect a change in his/her sexual orientation, but a common cause as well for homosexuality in people after a certain age, is a psychological instability such that it affects the calibration of their minds. Incidentally, where such an instability exists, there is opportunity to be infiltrated, and when evil spirits see a hole anywhere, they will attempt to enter it. The aforementioned psychological loophole can be a combination of any number of things.

A change in someone's sexual orientation may be the result of something as extreme as sexual molestation, or some other similarly traumatic event, but some people even turn gay after a bad or damaging breakup from a girlfriend/boyfriend. Sexual molestation tends to be the cause, and this is indicated by the very high number of homosexuals who were molested as children, but you would be surprised at some of the other possible causes.

As stated, the instantiation of homosexuality within and about someone can begin by virtue of a psychological instability or disruption. When this happens, unclean spirits who can capitalise on whatever gateway internal mechanisms are occurring in the human being, will afford themselves the right to dwell within the man or woman when the man or woman subconsciously accepts the spirits (and whatever else that spirit brings), or is spiritually open to them.

It works the other way around as well, as spirits can tempt a person to indulge in certain activities, or plant seeds in a person that can be nurtured to a particular effect. If the person is susceptible to the temptation, or if their environment facilitates the growth of a certain seed, they will grant the relevant spirit access to them.

You must understand that because evil spirits are beings who have been corrupted, it is their nature to act in accordance with corruption. Things which are contrary to God's designs or things which can destroy and are unpleasant, are the very things that evil spirits partake in, and the fact that there are different kinds of corruptions, means there are different kinds of evil spirits who thrive on different kinds of things. Some spirits like to molest children, while others desire rather to commit murder. Some spirits are kleptomaniacs, and others are torturers. Evil spirits differ.

When God destroyed the infamous Sodom and Gomorrah, it was not just because homosexuality was rampant. Homosexuality was merely a symptom of what the real problem was. You see, the people of Sodom and Gomorrah were morally depraved, and highly sinful. A plethora of abhorrent acts were being committed by them, and the place was a hotbed of foul spirits. Where there is corruption or discord, you will see its fruits, and the nature of evil is to bear foul fruits. This is one reason why among other things, people of the gay and lesbian community are generally known to be very proud and very promiscuous.

You also need to understand that a person's sexuality (like a number of other things) is directly related to his/her systematic integrity. Both biologically and spiritually. For example: People who are attracted to small children, are either spiritually and therefore psychologically out of balance, or are biologically and therefore psychologically and spiritually, out of balance. When there is something wrong within or about a person, it will typically manifest itself as a dysfunction.

Such is the case with homosexuals. A very small percentage of homosexuals are people who suffered developmental problems in their infancy (not at birth), and therefore chose to identify themselves with the opposite sex even when they were toddlers. Of this percentage, a high percentage of the children eventually normalize and live life in accordance with their biological design. A very small percentage of them do not normalize due to environmental factors, but studies have shown that they too can be successfully treated.

The vast majority of homosexuals on the other hand, are people who have been perverted or psychologically damaged later in life, and chose to engage in homosexual behaviour as a result. These people know that something is not right with them, and any and all attempts to pretend otherwise are only in spite of such an awareness. They as well can be treated, but of course it very much depends on them.

Gay men who go to great lengths to strain their faces and pout their lips in the desperate desire to appear feminine (often with one hand raised in the air), and gay women who sag their pants, and inflate a perception of masculine bravado about them, are people who are showing blatant symptoms of a systemic imbalance.

Any man who believes he is a woman is a sick man, and any woman who believes she is a man is a sick woman. The same is true for people who think they are cats, dogs, bears, horses, garden tools, or any other things which any sane and rational human being can see they are not. Something is terribly out of balance within such people. Equilibrium, is a state sought by every working system in the universe. There must be balance, and where there is no balance, especially in human beings, there will be conflict or a recognised disturbance. Given that most human beings lack balance in one form of another due to the nature of our lives, human beings in general are plagued by a number of problems. Same-sex attraction is one extreme.

Most homosexuals are in very serious need of help. Unable to reconcile their desires and choices with their knowledge of homosexuality's unnaturalness, gay people tend to struggle initially with homosexuality, and many claim that they would never choose to be gay. However, this is contrary to what is really happening within them.

The only reason some gay people lament about the fact that they are gay, is that society will not accept it. Their inability to change their desires, is primarily due to the fact that they do not want to. They like being "gay". Remember: homosexuality is a symptom of dysfunction. In many homosexuals, this dysfunction is due to spiritual depravity. This is why many gay people are rudely extravagant in said dysfunction, and/or seem to possess an overt sense of pride which can be seen as being particular to homosexuals. Such people (mostly men) are demonstrative of the unfortunate corruption that has befallen them, and many of them are very much aware of their corruption. They are guilty of sexual perversion, and they know it.

You see, it is not God who damns mankind, it is mankind who damns himself. It is by virtue of your own actions that you will receive punishment or reward. When you cross a busy road without looking, and a speeding truck crushes you, you have no one to blame but yourself. After all, you have probably been told before, that carelessly crossing a busy road can get you killed.

In that same sense, when someone happens to warn you of something, and you refuse to accept it, you cannot blame anyone but yourself when the truth is painfully discovered by you.

There are however, some gay people who are too confused to know that they can do something about their sexual dysfunctions (especially now that pro-gay activists are affirming these dysfunctions through the media). God understands them and will take their circumstances into account, for it is their circumstances which have inflicted their dysfunctions upon them. Many of such people, upon reading this book, will see where they have erred and will either change, or seek help from someone who can help them change. Those who are gay by virtue of their associations with unclean spirits or filthy activities and desires however, are unlikely to ever change. They already know they are perverse, and their perversions will ultimately be their undoing.

Those who want help will seek it, but those who are immoral and corrupt will not bother to. Religious people at times attempt to cure homosexuals from their mental illness, but often fail in their endeavour because religious people generally lack the means to address the problem from the psycho-spiritual dimension that facilitates its cause. There are some mental health professionals who do in fact know how to cure homosexuals, and although they are being oppressed by the mainstream media (and the satanists who have infiltrated it in support of the 'gay movement'), these health professionals have not lost their expertise.

There is often only a deep psychological problem behind a person's reason for being gay, and if that reason can be found, his/her sexual disorientation will end. Typically, it is resultant from an issue with a same-sex role model, a father/mother figure, or a need for affection of some kind that has not been met. There is a very high number of ex-homosexuals who will attest to this. Your typical gay man or woman moves promiscuously from lover to lover never quite finding fulfilment, because the root cause of his/her problem(s), and his/her homosexuality, is still there.

Worse, are the tales of people who underwent sex-change surgery, only to find that the surgical procedure worsened their psychological problems, in addition to the mutilation of their genitalia. There is a reason suicide rates are so high for the transgendered, and it has nothing to do with not being accepted by other people, but everything to do with still being unable to accept themselves. They are afflicted by a mental illness for which "sex-change" surgery is no cure.

So now you know the truth about what is really going on with individuals and their sexualities. What mainstream media sources and gay activists propagate on the other hand, is something very far from the truth. You see, even when neglecting the spiritual aspects of our sexuality and the things which occur within us as human beings… even when pretending these things 'do not exist', the facts of the matter quite objectively and regularly ascertainably, differ greatly from what the mainstream media and the so-called 'gay activists' are telling people.

Popular Western media sources and the "liberals" who have been duped into agreeing with them, are pushing a gay agenda on people under the pretence of "gay rights", and are ploughing soil for a seed of tremendous ignorance and foolishness for the masses so that the dysfunction of homosexuality can be accepted by them. This is especially true in the United States of America (a place from which this gay agenda has stemmed). Great lengths have been gone to in attempts to mass-brainwash people, and these lengths include the falsifying of scientific data, the manipulation of media sources, and the bullying of people who oppose the gay agenda being encouraged in Western society.

Mainstream Western media sources advocate the acceptance of homosexuality as something "natural", as if they do not know the truth, but you can be sure that the people who control these media sources do, and they have alternative motives for supporting the 'gay movement'. The anchor-men/women of the deceptive mainstream media news stations are just servants of higher authorities dictating to them what they should read to you on teleprompters. These men and women do not have anything to do with the decisions made about the kind of information to be broadcast.

This does not mean they are blameless however, because in order to be a long-term and 'accomplished' mainstream media journalist, you need to be a certain kind of person. You need to be weak, corruptible, and preferably unintelligent. In the very least, you need to be a short-sighted individual who cares not for things in the relatively distant future, and whose strings can be pulled by whoever decides your employment status.

People who are not any of the aforementioned, cannot survive in corrupt establishments which promote terrible lies to millions of people. Media puppets are working towards the destruction of the world as we know it and the destruction of their descendants' lives, but they are too mindless to comprehend the enormity of their complicity with evil.

As the renowned Yuri Bezmenov (a KGB defector) said: These people are "useful idiots" who will be "lined up against the wall and shot" by their rulers once they have served their purposes for "the Big Brother government". Liberals, Leninists, Marxists, "social justice warriors", "progressives", etc… once they realise their perverted libertarian plan for their country, and finally see the true face of the creature they seek to set free, they will never again see a day which does not bring them anguish. "Equality", "tolerance", "acceptance", and "social justice" are meaningless words written on the mask of their impending tormentor, and they themselves are not in search of those things, but are rather in the pursuit of selfish and carnal evils. Evils which they will pay dearly for.

Their self-serving, short-sighted minds of corruption and evil will never allow them to see what they are heading towards, but those among the mainstream media news networks with whom the spirit of truth abides (as few as they are) have been breaking away from the corruption which surrounds them, and driven by integrity, have been turning into whistle-blowers to the detriment of their jobs, their freedom, and even their lives, because: strong, incorruptible, and intelligent people cannot survive in establishments as corrupt and evil as those which drive the U.S., and Britain. Men and women of intelligence and integrity either quit, or are soon fired by such establishments.

The mainstream news media does not broadcast these whistle-blowers or the things they reveal, but indeed their revelations are out in the open, and anyone who searches for them will find them. There are many of these truth speakers, but here are the names of just four of them, if you desire to get started: 'Annie Machons', 'Udo Ulfkotte', 'Aaron Russo', and 'Charlotte Iserbyt'. Beware of deceptive government-planted fakes like 'Edward Snowden' and 'Julian Assange'. Those people get mainstream media attention for a reason.

The likes of Machons (an ex British Intelligence agent) and Ulfkotte (a German journalist and former editor of a large mainstream newspaper company) have exposed that Princess Diana was murdered by British Intelligence agents for political reasons, that Britain and the United States are arming and funding terrorist organizations to overthrow Middle-Eastern governments, that the American CIA (Central Intelligence Agency) have infiltrated media houses to manipulate society, and much more. But Machons and Ulfkotte get no media attention whatsoever.

Russo (a famous Hollywood film producer), has revealed that the

Rockefeller family (and their friends) control the government, much of the media, and are among the beneficiaries of the U.S. Federal Reserve. He has also revealed that in addition to the creation of phony wars like the "war on terror", they create destructive movements (like the 'gay' and 'feminism' movements which have been rotting society since their inception) to break the unity of society's family structures and to normalize perversions and mental illnesses. Something to which the increasing divorce rate in the Western world is owed.

Russo claimed, that since he was a prominent film producer with much influence, Nick Rockefeller approached him in the hopes that he would become a part of their plot to control society through film and television. But being that he was no greedy fool, Russo declined and opted rather to expose the whole thing, because such are things of which everybody ought to be made aware. Despite these revelations though, for which there is much evidence in his favour, Russo gets no media attention.

Iserbyt (a former Senior Policy Advisor in the Office of Educational Research and Improvement for the U.S. Department of Education) has revealed that there is a deliberate dumbing down of society via school systems worldwide (through the Carnegie and Rockefeller foundations) for the purpose of eliminating individuality and severely dimming the intelligence of society.

She has revealed that destructive school curriculums like the "Outcome-Based Education" system which was introduced to America and spread to other countries around the world, was designed intentionally to produce a less intelligent workforce of people for the benefit of psychotic individuals who want to rule the world through the formation of a world government and a New World Order. But Iserbyt also gets no media attention.

Snowden on the other hand, has not revealed **any** valuable information whatsoever which people did not already know, and Assange is a fraud who was used to plant disinformation into the minds of the general public with his "Wikileaks" for the purpose of America's agendas. Both Snowden and Assange are advertised rather cinematically, as heroes by the media. In fact, Assange has his very own Hollywood movie.

Many prominent media sources are influenced strongly by people whose objective it is to deceive society, because the entities who run such media houses are persuaded by greed and stupidity to comply with the agendas of evil. The U.S. and British mainstream media houses are fraudulent entities whose magnitude of deception stands unrivalled. You cannot trust that these people really are about homosexuals when they put forward the semantically incorrect notion that being gay "is normal". There is nothing normal about being gay, and only a dishonest or brainwashed human being will tell you otherwise.

People are being bullied into accepting lies, and "human rights" is the spiked shield with which they try and ram through any opinions against things like homosexual marriage. People whose opinions are not in favour of homosexuals' blatant and overbearing campaigns are condemned and labelled "ignorant", "intolerant", or "homophobic" in order to try and marginalise them.

Slowly, "gay rights activism" is driving away common sense, and replacing it with a mind-set of pseudo-liberalism which cannot be distinguished from idiocy. Case in point: Gay rights activists and apologists are stating that homosexuality is "normal" because animals have been seen engaging in homosexual acts.

These are people whose brains do not serve them well. Their sentiments probably do not deserve to be addressed, but I can tell you this: If I was gay, I would feel quite insulted that someone had to liken me to a wild animal: A creature that lacks all manner of sophistication and whose brain commands it to defecate on the floor whenever it can. Creatures, many of whom are so vile as to consume their own faeces and devour their own offspring not long after their babies are born.

For them to scrape the bottom of the barrel this hard for evidence, pro-gay activists must be in a very desperate situation. If someone is so unwise as to try and justify abnormal human behaviour by citing the activity of senseless wild beasts, then it is doubtful that such a person is qualified to be casting judgement on any human matters at all.

Such foolishness brings itself to light as such even more glaringly, when you consider the fact that there is no such thing as a gay animal. Not anywhere in the Earth's oceans or on its lands will you find an animal that outright refuses to have sexual intercourse with a fellow animal of the opposite sex. A male dog can be seen experimenting with other male dogs when there are no females around, and perhaps even when there are some. However, a male dog will never refuse to procreate with female dogs when there are female dogs around. Gay men on the other hand, claim that they simply do not feel any sexual attraction to females, and lesbian women claim to feel the same about males. This, despite the fact that a high percentage of gay men also sleep with women, and that a high percentage of lesbian women, also sleep with men. The erroneous notion of a fixed homosexual identity is unobserved even in the kingdom of senseless wild animals.

There are many holes in the theories and conclusions of pro-gay activists. Nevertheless, they are selling closed-minded, and deceptive information to people while claiming it to be of an open mind. You cannot tell people that 'children of gay relationships fair as well as, or better than, children of heterosexual relationships' when the facts are, that children of gay couples are deprived of an important diversity only present with parents of opposite sexes to one another. Scientifically, and in accordance with common sense, a child needs both a male and a female parent in order to grow most efficiently. In fact, the research shows that having gay parents is often detrimental to the child.

Gay marriage activists like to say: "Well, there are many children being raised by single parents and many of them turned out fine", but those are scenarios of dysfunction. A child who is raised by a single parent is a child being raised in a dysfunctional environment. The function of both the mother and father cohesively parenting the child is absent in such cases and therefore the child is at a much higher risk of having psychological problems, abusing drugs, etc. as verified by multiple scientific studies (which by the way, no one needs to perform in order to determine that being raised by a single parent is not an ideal situation).

The children "who turn out fine" do so in spite of the fact that they were raised without a father/mother, and certainly not because of it. Most children suffer the consequences of an absent mother/father to a degree that impedes their positive growth. Of course gay marriage activists must ignore that and many of the other facts which refute their cause, as they continue to scavenge for any shred of evidence in their favour. They will say: "But married heterosexual people get divorced", "Some heterosexual people abuse their children", "some children are raised without a father/mother" etc., so according to them, gay people should also be allowed to get married and raise children. They will regularly cite situations of dysfunction or abnormality, and say: 'See? There are bad things happening elsewhere, so we too must be allowed privileges which you might deem abhorrent or detrimental'.

Divorce is a bad thing, infidelity is a bad thing, and single-parenthood is a bad thing. These are things which nobody wants. The fact that they happen does not make them right, and it certainly does not give homosexuals any logical reason whatsoever to attribute to those things in favour of the dysfunction that is 'homosexual marriage'.

'Homosexual marriage' is in fact an oxymoron. It literally makes no sense, but gay rights activists are not about to let 'things not making sense' stop them from ensuring that men can marry men, and women can marry women, as if men were marrying women, and women were marrying men.

Homosexuals do not need gay marriage, they want it. Gay people say they want "equal rights", but what they are actually asking for are 'special rights'. They want special treatment, because in fact without gay marriage making special provisions for homosexuals to purposefully deny a child the right to a mother or father, (so that the child can instead be raised by two fathers or two mothers), gay people's rights would be just like everyone else's.

As time has passed, more people, having been raised by homosexual parents, are speaking out about how damaging having gay parents was to them, or how it occurred to them that homosexuals raising children, was not a good idea. Not only because they were deprived of the mother-father dynamic (and that many children became gay as a result of gay-parenting), but because it dawned on them brightly, the fact that as children of gay parents they were being used as political tools to further an agenda of some sort. They were like ornaments that gay people could parade in the public domain while saying: "See? We have children, and they will turn out fine" (even though many children do not).

There are many people, being products of gay parenting themselves, who are afraid to speak the truth, for fear of being called "bigots", "ignorant", "intolerant", "self-haters", etc. by 'gay rights activists' and the mainstream news media. Disingenuous 'gay rights activists' in high places are constantly trying to merge a gay agenda into as many facets of our lives as possible, and they see no shame even in distorting and mischaracterising scientific data and making pseudo-scientific claims of statistical analyses in their favour in an effort to do this.

There have been claims that 'homosexuality is genetic', that 'gay people were born that way', that 'homosexuality and sodomy are healthy', that 'gay parents are better parents', etc. and all these nonsensical and disproven claims were made in fake research papers by fraudulent researchers, many of whom were homosexuals themselves, and whose papers have been exposed as deceitful. The data which the deceitful researchers would claim to strengthen an argument in favour of homosexuality, not only contradicted what was being observed by other researchers, their data also turned out to be significantly fabricated. To date, there is absolutely **ZERO** scientific evidence that homosexuality is "healthy", "natural", "normal", or "genetic", but homosexuals who are in desperate need of justification have been compelled by their chronic denial to say otherwise to themselves.

To rub salt in the wound, despite pro-gay pseudo-scientific data being fraudulent, often the data will contradict the headline atop the news article advertising the "research". I saw one where they claimed homosexuality was genetic, and yet the results published were that 52% of identical twin brothers, and 22% of fraternal twin brothers, were concordant for homosexuality. That figure of 52% (although a highly inflated one due to the fraudulent research methodologies of the pro-gay researchers), is quite far from the '100%' figure which would have to be the result before any argument for homosexuality could be made on a genetic basis.

Similar to what fraudulent evolutionary biologists have been doing for decades in order to push their nonsensical 'theory of evolution', every now and then a deceitful "new discovery" will pop up in the field of fraudulent gay research which claims to prove that homosexuality is genetic. The "new discovery" will circulate the very fringes of science journals and deceptive online media groups before dying shortly after being imagined.

Science is the worst place to go when trying to argue in favour of homosexuality, because science tells the truth. Science reveals:

- A very strong correlation between homosexuality and paedophilia.

- That most homosexuals are suffering severely from the denial of reality.

- That homosexuality is a mental illness.

- That a significant percentage of homosexual people experienced sexual molestation of some sort before becoming gay.

- Sexual promiscuity is a more prevalent problem among homosexuals than heterosexuals.

- A high percentage of homosexuals suffer from depression and associated mental disorders, while societal unacceptance of homosexuality (i.e. bullying) accounts for a negligible fraction of the reason(s) for said mental illnesses.

- That therapy is effective at curing same-sex attractions in homosexuals.

- That homosexuality is a choice.

Examples:

"The Proportions of Heterosexual and Homosexual Paedophiles among Sex Offenders against Children": A 1992 study, found that although less than 2% of the population were homosexual, homosexuals were responsible for the majority of child rapes. Roughly one third of all child molestation was by homosexuals.

In 1979, a comprehensive survey of homosexuals called "The Gay Report", revealed that 73% of homosexuals surveyed, had experienced sex with boys, teenaged or younger. The Gay Report also revealed: that 35% of those surveyed claimed to have had 100 or more sexual partners, 77% had taken part in 'threesome' sex, 59% had taken part in sex orgies, 38% had engaged in sadomasochistic practices, etc.

(Ironically, The Gay Report's surveys were done by homosexual activists whose own research wound up condemning their lifestyle.)

A 2001 Dutch survey: "Same-sex sexual Behaviour and Psychiatric Disorders", found that physical and mental health problems were systematically higher among homosexuals and bisexuals, despite the Netherlands being highly accepting of LGBT (Lesbians, Gays, Bisexual and Transgender) persons.

(Conclusively, homosexuality and the homosexual lifestyle are both causative and consequential factors of psychological and physical illnesses, irrespective of how homosexuals are treated by others, because homosexuality itself is a mental illness.)

A 2001 study: "Comparative Data of Childhood Molestation in Heterosexual and Homosexual Persons", found that homosexual men and women reported a far higher rate of childhood sexual molestation than heterosexual men and women. 46% of gay men, and 22% of lesbian women claimed to have been homosexually molested as children, whereas 7% of heterosexual men, and 1% of heterosexual women reported homosexual molestation.

(Mind you, the study does not account for the large number of lesbian women who were molested by men, and who, through their acquired fear/disdain for the opposite sex, became active lesbians.)

"The dubious assessment of gay, lesbian, and heterosexual adolescents of add health": A 2014 study, found that over 70% of adolescents who identified as homosexual or bisexual, later identified as exclusively heterosexual as young adults.

These are the things which science reveals. Pseudo-science on the other hand, claims the opposite of what science will reveal, so pseudo-science is the only place pro-gay propagandists can go to defend their cause. The internet is littered with debunked pseudo-science and deviously deceptive articles and "research" results written by homosexuals for the purpose of mass trickery, and with the co-operation of a certain popular online search engine, such pseudo-science and deceit is readily available for pro-gay deceivers and those deceived, to cite in favour homosexuality, and to further the gay agenda.

To this day ridiculous disinformation is being spread by unscrupulous pro-gay propagandists, so that preposterous things can be proposed by the gay movement. For example: There have been several incidences of gay rights activists going as far as to push for the incorporation of blatant homosexual identities into children's television programs, and proposing that sexual education be reformed to include the discussion and presentation of homosexual acts in school classrooms while claiming them to be normal.

The worst part is that they are succeeding. The pro-gay movement have managed to establish new school curriculums which advertise gender-confusion, homosexuality and sexual perversion to small children, and they have successfully managed to place books which demonstrate and celebrate homosexual oral and anal sex to children, in schools across North America. An example is a pro-gay book called "**Little Black Book: V 2.0 Queer in the 21st Century**". In this book, they even advertise illegal narcotics to children and inform them on which kinds of bars to visit for anonymous homosexual sex.

No, I am not joking about any of this. It is as immensely revolting as it is unbelievable, but indeed they are managing to pull it off, and mostly because mainstream media turns a blind eye to these things, working alongside homosexual activists to bully and condemn anyone who opposes their evil. Do not let them get away with what they are doing. You must not allow these devils to rob society of the things which allow it to function properly. Band together, and oppose them unbendingly. If you do not, you will dreadfully regret ignoring your chance. It is because the establishment has conspired so aggressively against the people, that the homosexual agenda is making such strides. As long as content-producers and media personalities cowardly and fearfully continue to add "… not that there's anything wrong with being gay" whenever the words 'gay' and 'homosexual' are mentioned, the evils associated with the gay agenda will continue to push forward successfully.

The goal of pro-gay activism has, and will always be, to destroy "the family" and to target children. Their first objective was to normalize the sexual perversion of homosexuality. After they have accomplished that, they will try and lower the age of consent at which a person is allowed to have sex with an adult. After doing that, they will attempt to normalize paedophilia. Eventually, they will look to normalise bestiality. The ultimate goal of the people responsible for the gay movement is the perversion of society's morals, the destruction of family units, and the establishment of perversion and sin as a norm.

All this, while campaigning such evil behind the "tolerance" and "acceptance" veil. Anyone in his/her right mind would find it quite fishy that pro-gay activists would go so far beyond simply getting the world to "cease its hostility towards homosexuals". When people openly declare themselves to be gay, the mainstream approach is to celebrate and cheer for them. However, should a supposedly formally gay person declare that they are no longer gay, and that they are now sexually attracted to the opposite sex, they are criticised by mainstream bigots and frowned upon. Ask yourself: "Why would individuals who genuinely care about gay people do such things?" The answer is simple (as it always is): It is because the driving force behind the pro-gay movement, is a very sinister one.

You see, the pro-gay movement is an elaborate plot to disintegrate the societal perception of sexuality in order to make way for the acceptance of perversions. The history of sodomy, homosexuality, and the gay movement is a very long one, and another book would need to be written to address it fully, but I will tell you some of the most important information you need to know about what has been happening regarding these things:

The modern homosexual movement essentially began when a homosexual paedophile named Henry 'Harry' Hay (who was himself, sexually molested by a man when he was a child) founded an organization called "The Mattachine Society" to promote the act of sodomy in America, and to deteriorate society's Judeo-Christian values in the late 1940s. Henry Hay was a member of a satanic cult called the O.T.O (founded by Aleister Crowley) that glorified child molestation, so he publically endorsed sexual activity between men and boys, and also openly supported the paedophilic group: NAMBLA (North American Man/Boy Love Association).

The creation of The Mattachine Society ignited a flame of pro-sodomy activism that spread quickly and operated in several underground groups. As the rapidly expanding pro-sodomy groups were in their infancy, one of the activists of such groups, named Alfred Charles Kinsey (who was also a member of the satanic cult Hay belonged to), founded what is now known as "The Kinsey Institute for Research in Sex, Gender, and Reproduction" after receiving funding from the Rockefeller Foundation to do so.

Like Hay, Kinsey despised Christianity and its rejection of sexually deviant acts like sodomy and pederasty, so he founded the institute to advocate these sexual deviancies through "research" dedicated to the endeavour of weakening public resistance to these acts.

Through his new institute, Kinsey published 'research' (garbage) in the form of two books known as the 'Kinsey Reports'. The 'research' approved of sodomy, paedophilia, homosexuality, promiscuity, and sexual deviancy in general. He acquired a significant portion of his 'data' from pederasts who recorded information of themselves molesting almost 320 boys (some of whom were only a few months old), and published the results of the molestation in his reports. He claimed that sexual molestation was healthy for children, and that children were sexually viable from birth.

This 'research' of Kinsey's was launched into fame by media attention and advertised to millions of people as "revolutionary" "science", but media headlines never mentioned the child molestation. Rather, the mass-media focussed on Kinsey's claims that sexuality was fluid, and that men and women were more naturally promiscuous and sexually deviant than society believed.

Although his faux research was later exposed as nonsense by legitimate scientists and anyone who actually read his bogus reports, it went publically unchallenged for some time, and mainstream media kept well hidden, the nonsensical nature of the so-called "research". This, as well as the fact that a man named Hugh Heffner later capitalised on the hype around Kinsey's reports to launch a pornographic magazine called Playboy, thereafter contributed to a rapid degradation of the American society's moral standards.

Because of this "sexual revolution" which Kinsey started and Heffner pamphleteered, certain types of bars and nightclubs began to spring up in some areas, and in addition to a rise in heterosexual licentiousness, acts of sodomy started frequently occurring at nightclubs, bushes, public bathrooms, etc. Public acts of sodomy eventually became so much of a recurrent problem that authorities had to shut down public toilets, and cut down the trees and bushes of one of New York's parks, in order to prevent homosexuals from performing their activities behind them.

Because authorities began to intervene, sodomites started protesting and demanding the right to perform their public sex acts. Eventually these protestors became violent, and on the 28th of June 1969, they attacked officers who were performing a raid on a bar which sold liquor illegally and was frequented by sexual deviants (homosexuals, cross-dressers, etc.). The protesters caused much damage to public property, and ultimately, they set fire to the building being raided. Their riot lasted the entirety of the day.

The events which took place that day are remembered as "The Stonewall Riots", and the yearly anniversary of these violent attacks are celebrated by pro-gay activists today in the form of "Gay Pride Parades": Festivities of sexual deviancy where homosexuals, transsexuals, and crossdressers, prance about naked or in strange costumes, while exposing their private parts and often performing lewd acts in public view of children and anyone else watching. Sometimes the participants will even recruit children to partake in the activities as well.

Because of the strong link between homosexuality and paedophilia, the first gay parades included the paedophilic NAMBLA organization, but for the sake of the pro-sodomy activists' large-scale political endeavours, NAMBLA was later prevented from continuing to march in the parades. Inevitably though, pro-gay activists' constant recruitment and manipulation of children does defeat the purpose of their tactical decision to ban NAMBLA from the gay parades.

Back to the discussion: Shortly after their "Stonewall Riots", pro-sodomy organizations sought to continue the use of aggressive tactics for their cause. A pro-sodomy group called The GLF (Gay Liberation Front) therefore was formed, and one of their first targets was the medical community. The medical industry (Psychology and Psychiatry in particular) was the most damaging to the reputation of homosexuals, as they identified homosexuals as being disordered and were also becoming increasingly successful at treating same-sex attraction. The GLF would harass and intimidate the medical community at any conventions or conferences held by them, and they would disrupt entirely, whatever meetings were being had.

The GLF quickly collapsed due to internal disagreements, however The Mattachine Society and other pro-sodomy groups realised how effective the GLF's methods of harassment and intimidation were, so they picked up from where the GLF left off, and continued to target resistance to sodomy and homosexuality through harassment and political intimidation.

They eventually pushed, shoved, shouted, and manipulated their way into a position where they had direct access to the APA (American Psychiatric Association): a governing body for mental health treatments and research. You see, the APA had homosexuality listed as a mental disorder, and such a listing had to be removed if pro-sodomy activists were to ever achieve their goal of normalizing sexual deviancy before the general public.

After successfully infiltrating the APA through militant political activism and abusing its members in order to garner support within the association itself, pro-sodomy supporters within the APA (although a minority) eventually managed to pass a vote to effectively remove homosexuality from the list of mental illnesses by changing the definition of what a "mental disorder" is, and downgrading homosexuality from an "illness" to that of a "Sexual Orientation Disturbance", in 1973. This motion was passed with absolutely no research to justify it, and marked itself as one of many significant moves to follow, by the political pro-sodomy movement.

Recently, the former president of the APA, Dr. Nicholas Andrew Cummings (the man who declassified homosexuality as a mental illness), admitted in an interview with Canadian journalist Michel Lizotte, that the APA is now sponsoring fake, pro-gay pseudo-science, and that any legitimate research into homosexuality is being deliberately ignored and not being funded by the APA. He admitted that the APA is now run by corrupt, "ultra-liberal" homosexual activists who hijacked the APA in order lie to the public through the sponsorship of fake research.

After perverting the APA, the next significant move for pro-sodomy activists came in the mid-1980s, in the form of a magazine article called "The Gay Agenda", written by Marshall Kirk and Hunter Madsen (both homosexual paedophiles). In it, they stated that in order to win the war against those opposed to sodomy, pro-sodomy activists would need to shift the emphasis of the fight from the act of sodomy, to a faux identity called "gay", which would therefore force people to look at the issue in a manner which made peoples' very identities the focus, instead of the morally repugnant behaviour of sodomy.

About two years later, Kirk and Madsen wrote another article titled: "The Overhauling of Straight America". In this article they elaborated upon "The Gay Agenda", and presented a strategy to deliberately deceive society into believing that people who engaged in same-sex intercourse were born "gay", and about two years after that article, in 1989, Kirk and Madsen expanded "The Overhauling of Straight America" into a book called "**After the Ball**".

In this book, Kirk and Madsen, without shame, admit that homosexuality is a choice, but that those who engage in such acts must claim otherwise, in order to fool people. They write that all sexual morality should be abolished, and that society must be manipulated through the media to accept sodomy and other such perversions as "normal".

According to the agenda they laid out, society must be brainwashed in three stages: First people must be "desensitised" to sodomy. Then perceptions about homosexuality must be "jammed". Heterosexuals must then be "converted", such that eventually some heterosexual people will begin to consider that perhaps they could have been born gay too. They write that homosexuals must be portrayed as victims, should be made to look good by the media as superior pillars of society, and should be endorsed and advertised by celebrities to further brainwash society.

Most of the book is filled with instructions about how men can attract and seduce young boys, but the rest of it is dedicated to the manipulation of society and the establishment of sexual perversions as a norm through the media.

Within the United States of America, the nonsensical idea that homosexuals were "born that way", is something which came from the devious minds of these two homosexual paedophiles: Marshall Kirk, and Hunter Madsen. Their idea is an outright lie, and they themselves admit that. The following, are some excerpts (just some) of the plans outlined in their book: "After the Ball". Plans which are being executed by the 'gay movement' as I type this.

(Please note the meanings of the following words, and letters used:

Straights: heterosexuals

H: homosexual/homosexuality

Bigot: heterosexual)

> "To desensitize straights, H inundate them with conscious flood of H related advertising, presented in the least offensive fashion. If straights can't shut the shower off, they may at least eventually get used to being wet. (Page 149)"

> "Propagandistic advertising can depict homophobic and homohating bigots as crude loudmouths and assholes – people who say not only "faggot" but "nigger," "kike," and other shameful epithets – who are "not Christian." It can show them being criticized, hated, shunned. It can depict H experiencing horrific suffering as the direct result of homohatred – suffering of which even most bigots would be ashamed to be the cause. It can, in short, link homohating bigotry with all sorts of attributes the bigot would be ashamed to possess, and with social consequences he would find unpleasant and scary. (Page 151)"

➢ *"Conversion of the average American's emotions, mind, and will, through a planned psychological attack, in the form of propaganda fed to the nation via the media. We mean 'subverting' the mechanism of prejudice to our own ends – using the very process that made America hate us to turn their hatred into warm regard – whether they like it or not.* (Pages 153-154)"

➢ *"Success depends on flooding the media, and that, in turn means MONEY, MAN HOURS, and UNIFYING THE H COMMUNITY FOR A CONCERTED EFFORT.* (Page 157)"

➢ *"Three characteristics distinguish propaganda from other modes of communication and contribute to its sinister reputation: 1) Relies on emotional manipulation – through desensitization, jamming and conversion; 2) Use lies, and 3) Subjective and one-sided. Tell our side of the story as movingly as possible. In the battle for hearts and minds, effective propaganda knows enough to put its best foot forward. This is what our own media campaign must do.* (Pages 162-163)"

➢ *"Three points of effective propaganda: 1) Employ images that desensitize, jam and/or convert bigots on an emotional level. This is, by far, the most important task; 2) Challenge homohating beliefs and actions on a (not too) intellectual level. Remember, the rational message serves to camouflage our underlying emotional appeal, even as it pares away the surrounding latticework of beliefs that rationalize bigotry; and 3) Gain access to the kinds of public media that would automatically confer legitimacy upon these messages and, therefore, upon their gay sponsors. To be accepted by the most prestigious media, such as network TV, or messages themselves will have to be – at least initially – both subtle in purpose and crafty in construction.* (Page 173)"

➤ *"Help straights view homosexuality with neutrality rather than keen hostility. In the beginning, seek desensitization and nothing more. You can forget about trying right up front to persuade folks that homosexuality is a good thing. But if you can get them to think it is just another thing – meriting no more than a shrug of the shoulders – then your battle for legal and social rights is virtually won.* (Page 177)"

➤ *"The fastest way to convince straights that homosexuality is commonplace is to get a lot of people talking about the subject in a neutral or supportive way. Talk about gayness until the issue becomes thoroughly tiresome. In the early stages of the campaign, the public should not be shocked and repelled by premature exposure to homosexual behavior itself. Instead, the imagery of sex per se should be downplayed, and the issue of gay rights reduced, as far as possible, to an abstract social question. As it happens, the AIDS epidemic – ever a course and boon for the gay movement – provides ample opportunity to emphasize the civil rights/discrimination side of things, but unfortunately it*

also permits our enemies to draw attention to gay sex
habits that provoke revulsion. (Page 178)"

(I should note that the very first cases of HIV and AIDS were in the United States of America in the late 1970s, and that the HIV virus was first detected among white homosexual males. In the 1980s, if you had HIV, it was assumed that you were a gay man, or that you were a woman who slept with a gay man. Or perhaps you were a man who slept with a woman that had sex with a gay man.

HIV started as an American 'gay disease', but as part of a cover-up, deceitful stories about HIV originating in Africa have been spread by mass-media. This, despite the fact that the HIV virus only became an African problem after the World Health Organization embarked on a "smallpox vaccination programme" in West and Central Africa, as revealed by a 1987 article from The London Times headlined: "Smallpox vaccine 'triggered Aids virus'". Needless to say, that article did not get much media attention. Today, Africa is known as the land of HIV/AIDS, but the virus did not originate there.)

> *"Accuse religious people: Gays can use talk to muddy the moral waters, that is, to undercut the rationalizations that 'justify' religious bigotry and to jam some of its psychic rewards. Portray such institutions as antiquated backwaters, badly out of step with the times and with the latest findings of psychology. Where we talk is critical. TV, films, magazines – most powerful image makers in the Western civilization.* (Page 179)"

> *"Gays must be portrayed as victims in need of protection so that straights will be inclined by reflex to adopt the role*

of protector. If gays present themselves instead, as a strong and arrogant tribe promoting a defiantly nonconformist lifestyle, they are most likely to be seen as a public menace that warrants resistance and oppression. (Page 183)"

➤ "*We argue that for all practical purposes, gays should be considered to have been born gay, even though sexual orientation, for most humans, seems to be the product of a complex interaction between innate predispositions and environmental factors during childhood and early adolescence* (Page 184)"

➤ "*Use anti-discrimination as the campaign, not homosexual behavior. Our campaign should not demand explicit support for homosexual practices, but should instead take antidiscrimination as its theme. Fundamental freedoms, constitutional rights, due process and equal protection of laws, basic fairness and decency toward all of humanity – these should be the concerns brought to mind by our campaign.* (Page 187)"

➤ "*The objective is to make homohating beliefs and actions look so nasty that average Americans will want to dissociate themselves from them. The best way to make homohatred look bad is to vilify those, who victimize gays. The public should be shown images of ranting homohaters whose associated traits and attitudes appall and anger Middle America. In TV and print, images of victimizers can be combined with those of their gay victims by a method propagandists call the 'bracket technique', e.g. Rev. Fred*

Phelps picketing at Matthew Shepards funeral saying "God hates gays." Then people are disgusted by him, so they dissociate from him and his hateful attitude. Every time a viewer runs through this comparative self-appraisal, he reinforces a self-definition that consciously rejects homohatred and validates sympathy for gay victims. Exactly what we want. (Pages 189-190)"

➢ *"TV is OK, but advertising campaign is necessary to be successful, in order to desensitize, jam and convert people.* (Page 199)"

In 1988 (a year before writing the book), Kirk and Madsen took part in a "war conference" in Virginia U.S.A., where more than 170 of the most prominent pro-gay activists gathered to discuss an official agenda that gay-activism would adopt. The result of that conference is the agenda revealed in "After the Ball", and virtually every satanic plan of attack against sanity, rationality, morality, and Christendom, expressed in their book has since been executed by them.

(If you would like to know much more about the history of sodomy, homosexuality, and the gay agenda, I recommend you look up the work of a man named Ryan Sorba. I have summarised parts of his highly informative speech: "**The Born Gay Hoax**".)

Having read the excerpts above, and seeing what is happening in America today, you can see that the gay agenda is going exactly as planned, and beyond that, the agenda is spreading across America's borders. It has already spread quite far and will continue until people like myself do what we are doing, and help expose the truth. The gay rights movement is from the devil, and as with most of the devil's work, the evil and deceit of the homosexual movement is exposed by the homosexual activists themselves. The mainstream media and pseudo-science are their battering rams, but all you need is the shield of truth to stop them knocking you down.

I must inform those of you in the United States that the beast fuelling all the lies of the media, is the very same beast working towards the destruction of Christendom and the subversion of humanity. By paying any attention at all to what is really happening in the world you will see that this is no "conspiracy theory", for the evidence of mainstream media and U.S. government manipulation is abundant and clear. The evidence is there if you look for it, and you do not have to look very hard. Just look in the right places, and do not waste your time with things of the "Illuminati" and the "Freemasons". These groups do exist, but for the most part are not much more than labels of nameless amorphous entities for naïve conspiracy theorists to play with, and for ridiculous stories to be spread by junior investigators, highly naïve "truth speakers", and sensationalist liars.

If you want evidence for the penetration of evil people into the U.S. government, the planning and executions of large-scale hoaxes and "false flag attacks" by them (and the British monarchy) to justify wars, the infiltration of nations to overthrow governments/dictatorships, the social engineering of the world's youth through the film and music industry, and the fabrication of pseudo-scientific money-making schemes for world-unification like that which surrounds the "Man-Made Climate Change" hoax, you need to find names. You need to find video evidence of people admitting to these things, you need to find written evidence, and you need to trace such evidence to organizations and people. There are names, there is video evidence, and there is documentation in many other forms which points to certain organizations, and to certain people.

For example: In his book (Memoirs), David Rockefeller boasts of his involvement in the plan to establish a New World Order: *"For more than a century ideological extremists at either end of the political spectrum have seized upon well-publicized incidents such as my encounter with Castro to attack the Rockefeller family for the inordinate influence they claim we have over the American political economic institutions. Some even believe we are part of a secret cabal working against the best interests of the United States, characterising my family and me as "internationalists" and of conspiring with others around the world to build a more integrated global economic structure—one world, if you will. If that's the charge, I stand guilty, and I am proud of it.* (Page 405)"

You will hear quite often, talk of the Rockefellers and the Rothschilds, but although their part in the world's problems is not a small one (the Rockefellers' especially), they constitute a few large pieces of a rather sizeable puzzle. There is a large number of societies and families of conspirators who work alongside one another, but they all have their own interests. It is because they have found ways to compromise with one another when their paths were bound to cross, that they are united by the same evil for the pursuit of global domination. However, despite making huge strides they are far from ruling world. They still have much brainwashing of humanity to do, and they can only make large steps as long as enough people are asleep.

Ultimately, the ruler of those who conspire against humanity is the devil. satan is not sitting under some burnt tree in the infernal abodes, twiddling his thumbs as the world turns. he is instead actively working at the highest levels of power and plotting fervently against humanity. The devil and his people must be stopped. They are cowards, and what they fear more than a knowledgeable population, is a population which stands up against them. They are ravenous vermin whose infestation must be removed from this world. Spread the word of what is going on in the world so that you may play an active role in stagnating and preventing their activities. Once you learn of their deeds and their intentions, you will have all the motivation you need to revolt against them. If you would like to begin investigating these things, I recommend the following book by the renowned historian, Dr. John Coleman: "**Conspirators' Hierarchy: The Story of the Committee of 300**". He made a speech regarding this as well. It should be available online. Also recommended, is the 2010 documentary: "**Invisible Empire: A New World Order Defined**"

The picture is much bigger than "the Illuminati". Fixating on the "Illuminati", the "Freemasons", and the "Zionists", will only lead you to the places where very silly things are being said with those buzzwords by people who let their imaginations run wild with them. Look for the evidence. Do not allow yourself to turn into an ignorant fool, but you must also not allow thieves to steal sense and rationality from you. Look for the evidence.

Whether you believe there is such a thing as "the devil" or "evil spirits" is irrelevant to the fact that there are lunatics (many of whom identify themselves as "satanists") who have infiltrated established and powerful institutions like government so they can lie to society through the aid of mass media. A few of these sick individuals had the gall to write a book (After the Ball) explicitly detailing some of the intentions of these kinds of people.

They are depraved devils, and the nature of their depravity is the reason they are so proud. They are mentally-ill, spiritually-bankrupt, libertarians who care not for a distinction between freedom and sin. They know the difference, but accept their disease with pleasure because something sinister drives them. Their perversions will be their ruin, and their intent is for their fate to be everyone else's, but with the power of truth and the Holy Spirit, we will fight them.

Chapter Four: SINS OF MAN & THE MODERN-DAY CHURCH

Holy Ghost Fire

The Holy Spirit has received much acclaim for the salvation of mankind. Unfortunately though, it has also been given undue credit for some of the most ridiculous things I have ever encountered and documented. The concept of the "Holy Ghost fire", (its West-African demonstration in particular), is right up there with the worst of them.

The "Holy Ghost fire", is a nonsensical, noise-polluting ritual that entails the chanting of the word "fire", and an almost unbelievable amount of shouting and roaring. The first time I ever encountered this evil (yes, it is an evil, and I will tell you why), I was on holiday visiting a West-African friend in her beautiful country of Ghana.

It was about 9:00am, in a seemingly quiet neighbourhood. I had woken up a few minutes earlier, and was conversing with one of the maids. The local church had begun a morning service at around 8:00am that Tuesday, and since their building was not sound proofed at all, we could hear everything they said via their microphones and surprisingly loud speaker systems.

The church's pastor and his blatantly disingenuous associate had with them, much enthusiasm when they spoke of "prosperity" and "success", and when they spoke about how sowing a financial seed in the church would bring wealth upon those who did, because "God rewards those who give". They then began speaking their native tongue.

I was in the process of frowning my face at the possibility that an audience member might take those deceptive words seriously, when abruptly, and very unexpectedly, the pastor began shouting "fire!", and making what I thought to be extremely distasteful animal noises.

I literally, could not believe it. "What was this man doing?" I wondered. He would scream, and he would howl, in a manner I have never heard any living creature do. It was worse than what one would hear from a crying child in a state of tantrum, or a group of cats preparing for war with one another. It really was undeniably cataclysmal.

I wanted very much to laugh, for I had never before witnessed such insanity from any church. However the repulsive nature of what that man was doing strongly compelled me against doing so. I was confused by it, and so ambivalently, that I found myself standing in one place, pondering the unbelievable lunacy.

What is worse, is the fact that this noise-making went on from that time of the morning until about 3:00pm in the afternoon, with almost no breaks in between. This man would shout "fire!" and chant things which sounded exactly like you would imagine the following to sound: "Hoooorrrrhhh! Haaaarrrrrhhh!! Aaarrrgh! Eeeeeaaaaarrrgh! Hoaooaorrrrrgh!" Over and over again, for hours.

On occasion, he would take a break of one minute or two, to shout 'in tongues' and then without warning, and for no apparent reason other than to create a disturbance, he would continue his animalistic behaviour. Very much to the frustration of those of us outside this church who just wanted some peace and quiet on a Tuesday morning.

That was the first time I had ever encountered something like that, and the maid found my reaction hilarious. She agreed that the "Holy Ghost fire" was beyond ridiculous, but told me that it occurs so frequently and in so many places in Ghana, that it is quite normal. She said (and I quote): "This is not even the worst of it. The church by my place is far worse". This "Holy Ghost fire" is indeed a serious problem.

The problem with the Holy Ghost fire and the notion of its purpose lies not only in the absolute uselessness of the act, but also in the potential ramifications of it. You see: When you create such disturbance, and in the manner that pastor was doing, you run a strong risk of drawing various kinds of activity to you as the centre of the disturbance.

In my confrontations with evil spirits I have found that evil will capitalise on anything and everything that it can, in order to disseminate a disorder and establish dysfunction. The noise which pastors the one discussed make, contains a lot of energy. Energy which will attract a lot of attention. Often the kind that no one really wants. No one who is good, anyway.

As that fool shouted and roared, I detected an energy signature of only rambunctious disorder. It was his intent to make noise, and only noise, under the insincere premise of a "Holy Ghost fire" burning evil from his vicinity. Doing or saying certain things is not necessarily what attracts evil. What attracts evil is the intent with which they are done or said. The intent of such shouting was not only opposite to a just cause, it was in agreement with causing chaos, and where there is chaos, evil spirits will soon be found. If they are not already there for being the cause of it. Many of those who are within the proximity of the "Holy Ghost fire's" audible sphere of influence, do not react well to it either. The "Holy Ghost Fire" is a disturbance in which there is no value.

When one of my friends (a very quiet, apparently shy, and highly respectful boy), came to visit me later that day, I told him about what the local church was doing and how ridiculous it was. He agreed. But when I said to him that these people were fools, he very calmly expressed shock (as if he would expect me of all people not to say such things), while saying: "Don't say that. The Bible says you should not call anybody a fool". In immediate disobedience to his response, I quickly said: "But they are fools". Again in shock he said: "I said: don't, say, that. Don't you read your Bible?" I smiled in disappointment as I was reminded that the squeals and grunts of the pastor nearby, only scratched the surface of ridiculous religious doctrine and behaviour.

Let me take a moment to clarify the difference between religious doctrine, and the sound doctrine of the Holy Spirit: Religious doctrine makes way for arbitrarily defined barriers and constraints that limit people's scope of thought, while making room for unqualified authority figures to tell you what you should think or what you should do. Sound doctrine of the Holy Spirit however, does not focus on nonsensical trivialities that have no reasonable baring on whether you are a good person or not.

Religious establishments are forever guilty of imposing nonsensical rules onto people, and they think these rules can be justified with the Bible. For example, there are churches that believe it is wrong for there to be musical instruments in churches because "it is not biblical", or that it is wrong for women to wear pants because Deuteronomy Chapter 22, and Verse 5 says: "A woman shall not wear a man's garment, nor shall a man put on a woman's cloak, for whoever does these things is an abomination to the Lord your God".

Know this: God does not care whether there is a drum set in your church hall, or whether your sister dons denim jeans. He cares about whether or not you are a good person, or whether or not, you are on the right path. Does not being allowed to call someone a "fool" specifically, mean that you are allowed to call him/her every other dirty word in the dictionary? Of course not.

For the record, the word "fool" is mentioned more than 180 times in the Bible, and in virtually every single one of those instances, the word is used insultingly. After I had explained all this to my friend, he finally admitted to the senseless of attempting to restrict people's use of the English language because of misused Bible quotes and interpretations.

Recently, I had decided to tune into another television channel depicting a sermon by Pastor Benny Hinn, merely to entertain myself with the silliness I was surely about to witness, and in doing so, I was surprised to find that this

"Holy Ghost fire" is happening in charismatic churches on television too. I saw Benny Hinn speaking gibberish that he claimed to be "tongues", and shouting "fire" at a susceptible audience who were eager to knock themselves down in response. It then made sense to me where all this nonsense began.

You see: when liars like Pastor Benny Hinn, are seen doing something which succeeds in tricking their followers, the conmen who look up to the likes of him, take notes. After all, if it works, it does not matter that it makes them all look foolish, because it brings them popularity and money.

Speaking in Tongues

Let me get straight to the point: Absolutely anyone can chant incomprehensible babble, and claim to be speaking in tongues. Religious Christianity has been a joke for a while, but as of late, what Modern Christianity has degraded itself into, sickens me to my core. Religious people do not know what it means to speak in tongues, nor do they even know what these "tongues" are about.

If you are familiar with the foreign 'tongues' some religious folk are keen to chant, then it is likely you have also noticed, how all these 'tongue' speakers sound identical to one another. Supposedly they are a hub of personal messages from or to God, but how can they be speaking in tongues, and relaying their own message to whomever the intended recipient is, when they are saying the exact same things they have heard their neighbours blabbing?

You see, most of these new-age religious people who claim to speak in 'tongues', are not in fact, speaking any tongue of the Holy Spirit. What they do when they utter the gibberish typical of the charismatic church movement, is recite what they have heard on many occasions from other deluded church goers.

You need to understand that the tongue of the Holy Spirit is an ancient language, and as it is a form of communication, each and every utterance, and every intonation, has a meaning behind it. The spiritual 'tongue' is made up of grammatical structures, just like any other audible language is.

The genuine ability to speak in spiritual tongues, is only by virtue of a spirit who dwells within. Human beings cannot by themselves speak in tongues they do not understand. The original stories of people speaking in tongues after receiving the Holy Spirit are true, but the reason they spoke in tongues is that the Holy Spirit possessed them completely, and began to speak through them. A person speaks in tongues when the Holy Spirit aggressively or powerfully channels its intent through the individual.

Take note that demons can speak the very same 'tongue' that the Holy Spirit does. The only real difference, is in what the evil spirit will be saying. This is why people known to be demonically possessed, have been known to speak in strange languages and gesticulate odd patterns with their hands.

Church people who claim to speak in tongues do not even know what they are saying. They just, at whim, start making silly sounds with their mouths, and sadly, this is not how it works. However they have so greatly been fooled, both by others and themselves, that they think what they are doing makes some sense.

Religious people believe that when they speak in supposed tongues they are speaking to God, when the reality of the matter is that God does not care, at all, about the language in which anyone communicates with Him. As I have pointed out in the 'Evil Spirits' section, our words are only an audible representation of our intentions and meanings. Behind every word is meaning, and when your words have no meaning, even and especially, to you, you are not communicating anything sensible. Not to anyone. Your gibberish is only gibberish.

Some time ago I turned on the radio to hear a group of about five West-African Christian pastors who were featured in a segment of a certain radio program, holding a small sermon. Shortly after their speeches, they began to pray… in tongues.

As you can imagine, their prayers began calmly, and were somewhat coherent at first. But after less than a minute, it quickly devolved into a locomotion of madness, and arbitrary chanting. They were all shouting over one another, but I decided to focus my ears on one of them in particular.

The man I had my attention on, amidst all the shouting, was literally making the following sounds with his mouth: "Lolalalala, lalalalala, lalalala, lelelelelele, blebleble, blebleble, lelelelelelelele, bloblobloblobloblo, aaaaaagggagagagagagagchachachachacha". He waved his tongue from side to side as one would do when playing with a small child. The fool carried on like this for minutes alongside his charlatan friends.

This man obviously thought his blasphemous noises could not be picked out from the others, as indeed they were all shouting 'tongues' at their audience in a chaotic fashion. You see, that is the kind purposeful mockery going on in charismatic churches every day, and only the religiously indoctrinated… those swindled by the spirit of deception, accept such insanity.

It is why you must be very careful of evangelists who prowl the streets, spreading deception. Knowingly or unknowingly, evangelism is pushing people away from God, because evangelists generally do not know what on Earth they are talking about.

Evangelism

I am sure most of you have had somebody knock on your door, or stop you on the street, only for you to find out that it is another annoying religious evangelist who has endeavoured to bother you with their doctrines. I too have encountered these folk, and I can tell you that these people are wasting their time more than they are wasting yours. They slave away on streets and doorsteps for the benefit of the devil.

You see, evangelism is a movement of religious indoctrination by religiously indoctrinated people, who have been led by men to believe that God wants them systematically interrupting the days of random people in order to spread their interpretation of the gospel.

Perhaps you know that the 'Jehovah's Witness' is the most notoriously annoying form of this nuisance, as they seem to be multiplying like rabbits. It would appear that these people are being manufactured rapidly, and especially in the United States of America, as a few of my associates in the U.S. regularly express their grievances about such people.

Evangelist Christians are a nuisance to both God and man. Their door-to-door propagandas were never sanctioned by God, but they take it upon themselves to spread a gospel of deception on His behalf. Their motivations, being the lies they have been told by those who were evangelists before them.

A few weeks ago, I was approached by two people on the street who offered to preach to me, "the gospel". I am generally not interested at all in entertaining such people, as there is no helping them. Jesus Christ Himself could descend from the skies right now, in all His glory, and I guarantee you that there would still be religious people claiming it is not time yet, or "not as the Bible says", so it cannot be Him. Jesus tried to convince the religious people of His time that their beliefs were poorly founded and false, yet they killed Him anyway. If religious people would not listen to Jesus, they surely would not listen to me or anyone else who brought them the truth. Matthew Chapter 15, and Verse 14: "Let them alone; they are blind guides. And if the blind lead the blind, both will fall into a pit". It is not recommended to pay any attention to religious people who are fervent in their attempts to convert you, for such people cannot see beyond the scope of their indoctrination. They cannot see reason.

But when the evangelists approached me on the street, I noticed something a bit more ridiculous about them than what I was used to seeing in evangelising Christians. I agreed for them to entertain me so that I could at least see what they were all about. I was expecting them to tell me something unreasonable, and was mildly surprised when they more than satisfied my expectations.

These people told me that the God we all know is false. That there is not only one God, but two. A female, and a male. A God the Father, and a "God the Mother", as they put it. I laughed, and asked them to prove it to me. They tried to, by using the Bible of course, and said that when God made Adam in His image, He made a female Eve as well. And that the fact that Jesus is known as the Son of God, means God has a wife.

I laughed again, and told them that Eve was a copy of Adam, not a direct copy of God. She was made from Adam's rib as a biological counterpart, to facilitate a means of reproduction and to keep him company. They then ignored my statement completely and went to another part of the Bible to again (by a false logic), attempt to prove their claims, despite the Bible never saying anything that justifies the notion that God has a wife. When I refuted their next argument, they just smiled, turned away, and looked to bother somebody else. Of course, such religious people do not really care what the Bible says. They care only about what they choose to believe from it, and what they can get other people to believe from it.

This is the core of all religion and its movement: Convincing the foolish via illogical doctrine, of something which is not true, and then convincing them further to spread their poorly-founded dogma to the feeble minds around them. When presented with logic that they cannot argue against, they will run to the sanctuary of "…because the Bible says…", and they will lock themselves there so that no common sense can enter.

It is by the satanic bandwagon of such evangelism that horrendous lies are spread to societies, and it is the greed of man that capitalizes on the gullible to make money from them. Unfortunately, the devil manages (through people. Always through people) to convince people of even nonsense like "God the Mother".

The irony of Christian evangelism is that people who do not really know anything are the ones who evangelise. The people who truly know what is going on in the world are too few, and they are too far between each other. Those who know what I know are exponentially fewer in number and those who know more, are fewer still.

God has shown me and still continues to show me the realities of the world we live in, and some of them so surprising, people would never believe unless shown by God Himself. But not even I go about 'evangelising'. Although it is the truth I bring, given to me by the Holy Spirit, I understand that people must walk their own path. If it is I who must help them, then that will come to be the case. When anyone asks me a question, or for some advice I give it, and they are usually very grateful, not expecting me to have been able to advise them the way I did.

I am not preachy, and most people would not even consider me to be Christian at all, as I do not wear it on my sleeve. In fact people tend to think that I am atheist, and some would even go as far as to consider me a heathen of sorts. People are destined keep such misconceptions about me until they succumb to their beckoning curiosities and decide to ask me something that reveals to them how far from the truth their preconceptions are. I am guided by the Holy Spirit all the way, and I am in constant communication with God's angels, but I do not take the initiative to intrude upon the lives of people who did not ask me for my advice. Jesus Christ said in Matthew Chapter 7, and Verse 6: "Do not give dogs what is holy, and do not throw your pearls before pigs, lest they trample them underfoot and turn to attack you". People who do not deserve information will not receive it, because if they do, they will not be able understand or make use of it. If they ask for information, then at least they deserve some.

Most people do not appreciate good advice because good advice tends not to be in agreement with their preferred ways of life. It is because of this, and the fact that God did not appoint me as an evangelist, that I do not make a mockery of what He stands for by pretending to be a 'holy worker' on a sidewalk. The only way most evangelists can ever become successful and mainstream is through deceit and the ministering of pleasures to the masses that will accept them. This is why charismatic churches are so popular – and so rich.

The Conmen & False Prophets

If you are old enough to read this book then you are probably old enough to be aware of a consortium of televised conmen and blasphemers who go by the term: "Men of God" and "televangelists". These people are seen on multiple television channels and are associated with networks like TBN.

To the surprise of many of us (though, not many enough), the type of men and women I am about to describe are supported by millions of people – financially. A few (and I do mean, only a few) of the most famous and infamous of these people are: Benny Hinn, 'Pastor Chris', Kenneth Copeland, Robert Tilton, Mike Murdock, T.B. Joshua, and one of the newest generation: Joel Osteen.

All proven deceivers. On stage, they preach lies to millions of people, and some of the things they are documented to have said are truly shocking. But even so, it does not amaze me that these people are still in operation. Despite the overwhelming evidence against such conmen, there are too many people emotionally dependant on the lies these people preach, to be willing to see the evidence with their own eyes and to hear it with their own ears.

The fruits of religious conmen are plenty: The sick they lay hands on are never healed, they do not keep their word, they profess themselves to be messiahs, they blatantly blaspheme, they nurture selfishness in their followers, and most notably, their work revolves around money. Of all the above, Pastor Benny Hinn and his TBN buddies have been proven guilty, and their lies have been documented on film. Research them, and you will see for yourselves. These men are greedy, and power hungry deceivers. That is all they are.

It is only because the truth tastes bitter to people living a lie, that false prophets like T.B. Joshua and Benny Hinn, are so rich. They feed lies to people who want to hear them, and as a result, they live in mansions, they spend their money prodigally, and it is obvious to anyone who analyses them objectively, that they do not care about you. What they care about is your money. When Jesus said: "it is easier for a camel to go through the eye of a needle than for a rich person to enter the kingdom of God", these were the kind of rich people He was speaking about specifically.

Now, the point I am making is not that there is something wrong with being rich. We should seek to prosper in all aspects. A nice car, a beautiful house, a fancy watch, and beautiful clothes are perfectly fine. Having nice things in life is no sin, and there is no blessing in poverty. But there is especially no blessing in being spiritually poor. When you die you cannot take your money with you. All you get to take is yourself: your spirit. And if your spirit is poor, the place you wind up will reflect that.

Being wealthy materially is no sin, and there is nothing wrong with having nice things, but when you look for satisfaction solely from worldly belongings, and endlessly seek to extravagantly please yourself with deeply carnal luxuries, you are cursed just as much as a homeless man whose alcohol abuse defines him. An insatiable thirst for the "pleasures" of this world is as much a sickness, as it is to be too poor to feed or shelter yourself.

You are even more damned by your own actions, when as a pastor, you are living comfortably by no merit of your own, but rather by the generosity of millions of poverty-stricken people who naively believe you to be doing good things with the money they painstakingly send you.

But what is worst about these televised thieves, is not their emphasis on the tithe or the amount of money they steal from unknowing people. It is how they push people away from God. Liars like Pastor Chris, Benny Hinn, and

T.B. Joshua, claim to be able to heal the sick. They claim that by God's power they can cure people of cancer, arthritis, and even HIV/AIDS. They declare themselves to be "men of God", before anyone else does, and pompously act as if God has sanctioned their on-stage theatrics, when in fact there are countless untold stories of people who have been led to believe that "God will heal us by Benny Hinn's power", only to be disappointed when they return home from the church event(s). In fact, a very high number of such people have died because they refused to seek medical attention. Opting rather, to place their hopes in televangelist devils, and these devils' empty prayers.

"Men of God", televangelists, are certainly not. The people who follow them, believe that it is God who works through these priests to perform so-called "healings", but when these priests are exposed as having failed to heal, the priests say: "I am just a medium. It is God who is responsible for the healing".

As easily as that, they shift the blame onto God, and claim that it is He who has failed to heal the sick. That it is He, who has refused to perform "miracles". Such behaviour is indicative of satanism, and its agenda to try to shame God before mankind. To push people away from Him, and represent Him as a failure.

Because of these satanic conmen, many people say: "Christ has deceived us", or "God does not care", when the reality is that it is not Christ who deceives, it is the conmen who claim to be of Him that do so. The devil has achieved just what he wanted, in slowly pushing people away from God by placing liars like Mike Murdock and other television evangelists on centre stage to have them blasphemously claim to represent Christ.

satan works through deceptive priests who strut on stage, and utter all manner of indignities against God every day. And the fact that these people get away with it, is a large protruding pimple on the face of humanity's intelligence. These evil conmen lie to you, they poison you, and they blaspheme! All "in the name of God".

Worse than this, is how the atrocities of the evil spirit and the evangelizing conmen through whom it travels, are not limited to the blatant satanism of individuals like Mike Murdock. The evil spirit also worms its way into the world by means of somewhat unexpected avenues.

Now, let me tell you a little bit about satanism. satanism is not only the worshiping of satan, and the things that are of him. At its core, it is a proud sect of anti-Christianity, and many of its followers believe that Christians are lost. Yes, most satanists genuinely believe that it is they who are on the right path, and not the Christians.

Partly, they believe this because they are senseless people. But mostly, it is because the devil has enticed them with several things. In the West, most satanists are highly uninformed and foolish individuals whose thoughtlessness has allowed for them to be deceived by pseudo-spiritual new-age con-artists who tell them that satan and his demons can grant them "knowledge", and that Christians have an "incorrect" or "twisted" understanding of the devil. These people proclaim the badge of satanism upon themselves, but are not more than gullible fools who have been duped into mischaracterising devil worship to other people. They certainly do not represent satanism's true face.

Those who truly are satanists, engage in unspeakably perverse activities in the name of satan, and for the sake of things which they think they will gain. You see: A satanist's path is the ill-informed pursuit of power. A path marinated with lies and delusion and littered with the footsteps of devils. Footsteps leading to the destruction of anyone who follows them.

Through the eyes of a satanist, the devil is spreading his filth across the entire globe, and rapidly. All manner of abominations roam this Earth, and all manner of evil have managed to infest the planet with their presence. To the satanist, or a person susceptible to becoming one, this means one thing: That 'the devil is winning, and God is losing'. They see how widespread chaos and disaster are. How even in churches the devil is working, and how very few Christians know the reality of their ignorance.

People who cut through the general population to stand out, are very few and far between, and fewer still, are the people who are formidable opponents to satan and the systems in this world established in support of his agenda. It is so easy to look for evil, and so easy to join the selfish masses who work as a coherent force against the minority that is 'good'. So easy to fall into the sins of this world and be pleasured in doing so.

People of this world, (like satanists or those who would be), lust for many things, but 'Power', is the most important to them. Power, and pleasure, are the first things the devil promises to give those who might worship him: To 'sinners of the flesh'. The devil will tempt any man, to see whether the weaknesses of carnal desire are with him. After satan failed with the likes of Jesus (as described in Matthew Chapter 4, and Verses 1 to 11 for example), he found others on Earth whom he could corrupt. The descendants of those people have been ruining the world ever since. Having failed several times in history to realise their ultimate goal(s), we are now at a point again where these devils seem to be succeeding in brainwashing humankind and destroying the world. However, they will fail again.

The devil has been referred to as "the great dragon", because he is very powerful to the people of this world. By the fault of man, the devil and his legions managed to pervert the Earth such that they now have some considerable standing with demon-possessed people in the high places of politics, religion, etc., but make no mistake – the devil is a big fat joke, and the only power he has is over those who allow themselves to be deceived by him.

The weak ones are people who seek the easy way out. The devil lies to them, making them believe they can become gods, making them think that with all the riches of the world, they will be eternal rulers somewhere. It is the selfishness of an evil spirit which longs for such things, and a person susceptible, will cast aside whichever moral tethers it needs to, in order to obtain the things which devils promise.

However it is not everybody who will succumb to temptations of that nature when it is presented to them in the form of devil worship. This is where a modern branch of religious gospel known as "the prosperity gospel" comes in. The prosperity gospel, may seem a rather peculiar thing for anyone to condemn, because it appears mostly to uplift people. To make people happy, feel empowered, and eager to be successful in life. However, this 'gospel' is quite possibly one of the most sinister modern vices that has ever been conceived. And I mean that.

Firstly, let us get this straight: The 'prosperity gospel' is a misnomer, for there is no such thing. People like Joel Osteen (possibly the most well-known prosperity gospel preacher in the world) do not preach any gospel whatsoever, they only preach prosperity. I have seen his sermons, and it is very clear to me that this man, is extremely manipulative. From my analyses of him, I can honestly tell you, that he is well learned in the art of deception. He speaks the kind of lies that would impress even the best liars.

Listening to Joel Osteen is very much hazardous to your mental health, but you would not easily notice this from his sermons. He seems always to be preaching about how people are strong, how they can overcome obstacles, and how problems cannot conquer them.

Joel Osteen speaks such sweet, sweet words, and seems to know exactly how to keep everyone interested in his fantastical stories. Not only that, his tales speak of trials and tribulations that have been overcome by either himself or somebody he knows, or of fortunes that have been stumbled upon by virtue of providence of some sort. His smile is contagious, he presents himself in a beautiful light, and he knows just how to end his ridiculous tales in a manner that makes people cheer and nod their heads in approval.

Joel Osteen is one of the world's most iridescent and enthusiastic conmen. Any man who studies the methods employed by Joel Osteen in his sermons, will without a doubt conclude him to be a con artist with a large audience, and not much else. His uplifting prosperity gospel is a money-making tool that relies on people's emotions. It is so glaringly evident in every one of his stories. There are several tactics manipulative story-tellers operate by, and Joel Osteen uses them all with razor-blade sharpness to entrap his listeners. In every one of the speeches he gives, he does the following:

He leads and maintains his on-stage tales with some profound and highly inspiring words, to get people to really fall for him. In doing so, they trust him. This allows him to every now and then, subtly drop verbal suggestions that implant hedonistic world-views, and program into them, the deceptive notion that God is here to serve us (when the reality is, it is we who are here to serve Him). That is the holistic ideology preached in all of his sermons.

Unlike the likes of Benny Hinn, Mike Murdock, or 'Pastor Chris', Joel Osteen does not directly appeal to the selfishness, naivety, and greed at the core of most people. Rather, he infiltrates the various areas of insecurity in most people's minds and hearts, offers his words as a sort of crutch, and gets people to rely on him and his word for transient remedies to their need to hear something they want to hear.

What he does, is package common sense and psychological bandages in the form of 'healing' or 'good advice'. He then wraps the notion of 'God' around this package to be sold to ignorant masses. He uses the context of God to mask his psychological manipulations. Through this, he programs audiences not only into holding him in high regard as a provider of nourishing words, but also as a saviour of some sort. Like the devil, he aims for people's emotions. He targets their sensibilities in order to get to them.

Now let me be clear that Joel Osteen, and the devil are two separate entities. I am not saying that the devil directly works through him. What I am saying however, is that both the devil, and Joel Osteen, happen to work in somewhat similar ways. Joel Osteen's primary objective is to make a lot of money, and to grow his church. He does that by deceptively counselling a large audience who believe it is God who is working through him, and who have confused his motivational speeches for God-inspired sermons.

The recurring theme of Joel Osteen's messages, is that you can have **power**. That you are to seek **glory** and success. It is always about **you.** God only ever comes into the picture when He is portrayed as having something to give you. "God wants you to live **an abundant life**", he always says. But what is an "abundant life"? What does he mean by that? Well he means a life with a lot of money, and Earthly pleasures, of course. He alludes to that all the time. In addition, Joel Osteen implies constantly that we are or can be, like **Kings** of this earth.

The above highlighted words ring a bell to you I hope, because they are the very same things satan tempts man with. The very same things he tempted Jesus Christ with, and they are what people of this earth are most likely to fall for. The followers and supporters of Joel Osteen have given themselves over to a uselessness, which masquerades as a light barer.

Joel Osteen and his followers are not satanists, but they are advocating things inherent to satanism. If the devil cannot get you to worship him or the worldly things which are of him, in his name, he will try and get you to do so in the name of something else. If he cannot get you to do that either, he will try to keep you in one place and prevent you from moving forward. You can call a lump of dog faeces, "unprocessed food", or you can call it "crap". It does not matter what you call it, it is still a filthy, foul-smelling pile of disease and bacteria.

The prosperity gospel is just another fad of people telling more people things they want to hear, but this fad traps people in stagnation and a poisonous form of sedation, of which its victims are generally unaware. Instead of getting up and working for what they feel they need, followers of people like Joel Osteen sit down listening to his sermons, and expecting

God to bring them the things they desire.

"God has a plan for you", "God will do this", and "God will do that". Such a 'gospel' preaches fanciful notions, but refuses to make any mention of things like the hypocrisy and dysfunction of most Christians. This of course, is because people do not like to hear such things. They despise the truth if it means exposing the lies they have been comfortable living, but you cannot fix a problem with lies. You can only use lies to delude yourself into a happiness that avoids the central problem.

It is for the sake of this delusion that people would rather hide the truth with inspiring and uplifting tales of fiction, than work through the dirt to uncover the root cause of their problem(s). In the same way which cocaine feels good to those who use it, this 'gospel' feels good to those who want it. Although they do not see it, it does not contribute much to them.

The prosperity gospel can be likened to a devil who transforms into the most beautiful woman in the world. satan appears as an angel of light to some, and only those who pay attention to, and scrutinise the message he brings, can discern him to be the evil that he is truly is.

Joel Osteen preaches prosperity. Not the gospel. But his followers do not see this. They cannot. They are far too occupied by the overall beauty of his stories. Too busy marvelling at the woman of prosperity's voluptuous breasts, drooling over her enticing physique, and staring into her wonderful eyes, to notice the gangrene obscenities being excreted from the corners of her mouth every now and then. After all, who takes the time to check that her mouth is clean, when everything else seems so perfect? The prosperity gospel must be a very beautiful woman indeed.

But what of people like Benny Hinn? One can understand how people would fall for the clever deceptions of Pastor Joel Osteen, but one might find it difficult to see how people would fall for likes of Benny, for he is not nearly as good at lying as Joel is.

You need to understand though, that many of the Christians who believe such people to be 'men of God', are guilty of sinfully carnal desires themselves. You cannot usually support such thieves without being just like them. As 1 Timothy, Chapter 6, and Verse 9 to 12 says: "But those who want to be rich fall into temptation, a trap, and many foolish and harmful desires, which plunge people into ruin and destruction. For the love of money is a root of all kinds of evil, and by craving it, some have wandered away from the faith and pierced themselves with many pains.

But you, man of God, run from these things,

and pursue righteousness, godliness, faith,

love, endurance, and gentleness.

Fight the good fight for the faith;

take hold of eternal life

that you were called to

and have made a good confession about

in the presence of many witnesses".

The priests I have just written about are all preachers of the 'prosperity gospel', and the Bible very clearly condemns what they are doing, but still, they use it to do what they do. You shall know these false prophets by their fruits indeed, and the biggest fruits of the kind of people I have just written about, are: deception, selfishness, and greed.

I can respect Joel Osteen for one thing: he does not demand money from his followers, nor does he entice them with the prospect of "money-seed" fortunes. Rather, he cleverly coaxes them into giving it from their hearts. As for the likes of Benny Hinn, Mike Murdock, and Robert Tilton… Well, let me just say that these criminals are a very obvious cancer to the Lord's work, but they are not the only ones. There are many others I could name.

To spread some joy (or possible revulsion) to you though, I recommend that you look up 'Mike Murdock', 'Robert Tilton', or Kenneth Copeland. They are among the most hilarious manifestation of rotten, greedy, demon-possessed, televangelist evil, I have ever seen in my life. Now they are old, and do not have anything interesting to say, but watch their older videos of them ministering evils to people, and I guarantee that you will be both shocked and tickled to tears by the perversions they have uttered and endorsed.

They are as pathetic as the devils who channel through them, but nonetheless, they do succeed in their endeavours, because they exploit the weaknesses in many peoples' minds. As I have said: the people who buy into their stories are at fault as well, and the reason that is so, is how susceptible they are themselves to temptation, and false doctrines.

Religious Folly

In many modern churches, it has become common to find people doing certain types of things. For example, it is common for people to shout "Amen!" after every few words spoken by their pastor (or respective representative of a specific subject matter), and it is common for church people to nod their heads to those words.

As a child, I always thought it to be rather silly for people to be nodding their heads and shouting "amen" after very simple and seemingly irrelevant quotations of scripture were read to them by a pastor. I would see this going on every time I happened to be among an audience receiving sermons, and wondered how the pastor felt about it. I wondered, until one day I had the honour of giving a sermon of my very own.

It was a Monday morning at the high school I was attending, and as per the routine we were going to have an assembly of the school, where we were informed of important events and preached to (by anyone who felt the need, I think). Our teacher informed us on that morning that it was time for someone in our class to go up there and preach some gospel. I did not like the thought, and respectfully declined when he asked me. However our teacher was – forcefully insistent, and I wound up in the same position I had always felt the need to criticise.

I got on stage, and as I was ministering to the good people of that congregation, I saw several of them nodding their heads and saying "Amen" to themselves. As I carried on, more people began to do this, and I felt, really proud. I was quite delighted that people took my words so seriously, and that they seemed to feel my sermon to be of much value to them.

When I ended my little speech, everybody clapped, and I thought: "Ah. Now that's why priests take no issue with people shouting 'amen' regularly. It makes them feel good". The reason that people do utter "amen" as often as they do in churches, is that it has become the assigned protocol. It is what they have become conditioned to doing. The good news for anyone preaching to such a crowd, is that he/she is instantly seen as an authority figure, and the likelihood of the audience believing anything they are told, by him/her is relatively high.

The nodding of one's head and the utterances of certain words or sounds on cue, is a precursor to (or is indicative of), obedience. An audience that is obedient to you, will do certain things that you tell them to, only because you have told them to. They will trust you until you give them a conspicuous reason not to, but given that people tend to see only what they want to see, such reasons do not regularly become apparent. Where I am going with this, is that once you already have a group of people's trust, it becomes easier and easier to pull them into your agendas as you lead their minds in a certain direction. Other than through threats and fear-mongering, this is how religion is so effective at getting people to do some really stupid things.

Churches all over the world are endorsing idiocy, and embracing sacrilegious activities for the sake of liars and conmen, but in the name of God. Not long ago, I saw footage of a pastor in South Africa telling his congregation that he was a prophet, and that whatever they did in obedience to him was in obedience to God. "All things are possible with God", he would say, as he ordered his followers to strip naked, eat live snakes, eat their own hair, underwear, bras, etc. His followers would then obey, and do those things. His followers were of all ages and were mostly uneducated and impoverished people who needed something to be a part of, so they chose to be a part of foolishness.

Given the absurd nature of some of the things going on in Christian establishments, one must wonder where it all started and how Christianity wound up like this. Surely, one would not imagine that the current state of Christianity is what Jesus Christ came to die for. Indeed Jesus did not die to enslave men with religion, yet after his death, men did become enslaved by it. How so? As usual, the problem is with the shortcomings of men.

Less than 2 months after crucifixion of Jesus, some of His followers established what is now known as the Orthodox Church. The Church, being comprised of fallible human beings, was never going to be perfect, but given that Jesus Christ was no longer physically present, it was the next best thing. After all, the likes of the Apostles Paul and Peter would help (though only temporarily) to maintain His legacy.

However, almost everything changes over time and Churches are no exception. This is because Churches are comprised of people. People who sometimes have disagreements and who sometimes take it upon themselves to establish rules and practices which they believe are to the benefit of themselves and/or those around them. At times ignorance, pride, or jealousy, leads them to make the wrong decisions. It is not a matter of "good" and "evil" people, it is a matter of human beings and the varying degrees of intelligence and integrity they possess.

Good people can make bad decisions, and vice versa, but the outcome of said decisions can have long-lasting detrimental effects. An example is the Roman Catholic Church. The Orthodox Church was certainly not without its own dirt, but Roman Catholicism's split from the Church did not change things for the better.

The Roman Catholic Church slipped even further from perfection when arrogance and pride took hold of them. Such things are the beginning of corruption within an establishment. Look at how the pope is adorned from head to toe, and look at how he is worshiped and declared the foremost authority on Christ and His message.

Roman Catholicism is not all bad though. It has a long history, and the good news is that a lot of this history is good. There are also many pastors in the church who are indeed pure-hearted, and who do their part of the Lord's work in earnest and effectively.

In actuality, some of such people tend to be very powerful. The most powerful priests in the world, with God-given authority usually are highly knowledgeable priests of the Roman Catholic and Orthodox Church, because part of their spiritual practice entails ritualistic methodologies: Something all spirits (including God) respond to.

(These priests are very few and far between, and nowadays can only be found in African nations. The misinformation of religious nonsense by spiritually naïve people, and the systematic marginalization by religion, of those who hold the teachings of God's most potent principles, has turned such men into a seemingly dying race of God's 'special forces', but still they remain, and they will never die out.)

You see, at the roots of Catholicism, and what is recognised by spiritually-developed members of the clergy (the very minority of Catholic Fathers), is what modern-day laypeople would call "occultism": activities that enable communication between human beings and spirits (like God's angels, for example). Any person who denies this about Catholicism, is either ignorant or trying to mislead you.

When you call God He will respond, and when you call Him effectively, He will respond effectively. Spiritual practices are the most effective way to communicate with God, and particularly, specific forms of spiritual practices which are seldom known to people. But sometimes it is best not to reveal that to naïve and underdeveloped people who may take the idea and run with it to their oblivion.

Hebrews Chapter 5, and Verses 11 to 14 speaks to this adequately when talking about Jesus and how some things about Him cannot easily be explained: "About this we have much to say, and it is hard to explain, since you have become dull of hearing. For though by this time you ought to be teachers, you need someone to teach you again the basic principles of the oracles of God. You need milk, not solid food, for everyone who lives on milk is unskilled in the word of righteousness, since he is a child. But solid food is for the mature, for those who have their powers of discernment trained by constant practice to distinguish good from evil".

Dealing with God, His angels, or other spirits, is not something to be taken lightly. People often speak of the fear which one must have for God, but they do not know the meaning of what they speak. God is a kind and loving God, but the spirit realm has rules, and God has rules. Rules which most people are too susceptible to breaking, and which can have terrible consequences.

An example is what happened to Noah in Numbers Chapter 20, and Verses 6 to 12: "Then Moses and Aaron went from the presence of the assembly to the entrance of the tent of meeting and fell on their faces. And the glory of the Lord appeared to them, and the Lord spoke to Moses, saying, "Take the staff, and assemble the congregation, you and Aaron your brother, and tell the rock before their eyes to yield its water. So you shall bring water out of the rock for them and give drink to the congregation and their cattle." And Moses took the staff from before the Lord, as he commanded him.

Then Moses and Aaron gathered the assembly together before the rock, and he said to them, "Hear now, you rebels: shall we bring water for you out of this rock?" And Moses lifted up his hand and struck the rock with his staff twice, and water came out abundantly, and the congregation drank, and their livestock. And the Lord said to Moses and Aaron, "Because you did not believe in me, to uphold me as holy in the eyes of the people of Israel, therefore you shall not bring this assembly into the land that I have given them."". It would seem, that for the simple error of striking the rock instead of speaking to it as God had commanded, Noah was punished and denied entry into the promised land of Canaan until his death. It was no simple error though. The average man would not know it, but Noah's transgression ran deeper than his mild assault on a stone.

Spiritual things are no joke, and this is why only a very small percentage of Roman Catholic priests know the real truth about how to call on God's powers to strike thunder, how to summon His angels of war, how to banish even the most powerful demons to hellfire, etc. Roman Catholic Fathers are ranked hierarchically, because Human beings are not perfect, and not everyone who calls himself a pastor can be trusted with God's secrets. Funnily enough, these secrets are identical to the things which they themselves (as well as other Christian denominations) call "paganism" when they see Africans practicing them.

The truth is: Any Catholic priest, who in accordance with Catholicism, accepts the recognition of one's ancestors as protectors, yet simultaneously damns the spiritual practices of people who recognise individuals' descendants, is either being a hypocrite or intentionally misleading. Catholics recognise the ghosts of humans who came long before them, and even treat them as intercessors between God and mankind. Beyond that, these long-dead people are prayed to directly, and protection is asked from them directly. If Catholics want to call the prayers to one's ancestors "evil", then Catholics must recognise their activities/denomination as "evil" as well.

Catholicism, at its roots is indeed not evil, but the Catholic Church in many ways is just another label, like all denominations, behind which evil or non-evil people may reside. It is by virtue of this fact that the church has been made vulnerable to comedians and critics all over the world. The constant allegations of child molestation by Roman Catholic Fathers in the Western world (especially considering that most of their victims are young boys), are a manifestation of the sin in which the Catholic Church has drenched itself.

You see: God is no longer with the papacy in Rome, for they sinned against Him and opened their hearts to evil not long after breaking away from the Orthodox Church. The pope and the clergy who worship him, are misguided remnants of the Church of Christ from which Catholicism was born.

It has been proven that Roman Catholic priests accused of molesting children have been purposefully moved to other churches by the papacy in an effort to conceal the offending priests' misdeeds. If the fruits of the Roman Catholic Church in Europe and America are the consistent allegations and convictions about child rape by its priests, then it is by a reasonable deduction that one can assume, there is something about the Catholic Church in the Western world, which attracts and/or manufactures homosexual paedophiles. This "something" is largely spiritual.

In the absence of light, there is darkness. Just as certain animals inhabit areas naturally conducive to their existence, spirits too of certain kinds are known to inhabit certain places. They are free to migrate, but for any reason(s) good enough, they will remain in particular areas.

This is why the number of Catholic Fathers accused of sex crimes in Africa for example (where the most powerful Catholic fathers can be found), is negligible to none. Whereas the number of Catholic Fathers accused of such in the Western world is so undeniably high. The infiltration of evil by fault of the papacy, combined with a general dilution of the original spiritual practices of the Catholic Church over time, are the reasons Children are being molested in the Western world by Catholic priests, and why people are losing faith.

The Definition of Faith

"All will be well. Just have faith". People say that allot you know. But what is faith? Many people abuse this word too frequently to really know what it is and what it actually implies. The Oxford dictionary would define faith to be: "**complete trust and confidence**", but where does this trust and confidence come from, and is it a trust and confidence justified by evidence?

If you are like most people, then the answer to the last question is "No". Christians and religious people of all types claim to have faith in their beliefs, and when questioned about why they lay claim to their faith(s), the most ignorant among them will cite their Bible or their Qur'an, erroneously predicating their religious standpoint on the unjustified premise that their "holy book" is correct, first and foremost, without needing any proof whatsoever.

"What kind of proof do you expect?" you may ask. Well, the criteria is surprisingly non-extensive. There is only one major indicator of whether or not your religious text is of any good, and that is what it teaches.

Should you endeavour to perform unbiased research and discover that your book does not correspond with historical accounts, or that if it does, it does so in a manner that works against itself, then you have a clue as to whether or not you should continue to trust it. Let us very briefly analyse the Qur'an for example.

The Qur'an claims that both Jesus Christ and the so-called "Prophet" Muhammad were Prophets, but that Jesus Christ is not the Son of God, and that He did not actually die on the cross. However it acknowledges that Jesus Christ performed many miracles, whereas Muhammad performed none whatsoever. If you ask me, confessing that Muhammad was an ordinary human being who could not even cure the common cold, immediately throws Muhammad out of all competitions with Jesus: a man who raised people from the dead. However a much stronger case can be made against Islam.

Although this book primarily addresses Christianity, I wrote it to spread the truth to everyone, and not just to Christians. Considering that Islam is the second largest religion on this Earth, I must address it too, and sufficiently, so as to accurately portray the religion.

Let us start with the Qur'an. In short: It is complete nonsense. In much longer words: The Qur'an is Islam's religious book. It is composed of words, written in Arabic, which a man named Muhammad claimed were the direct words of God (Allah). The chapters and verses in the Qur'an are not written in any chronological order, and the book constantly references things which it makes no attempts to clarify. In addition, a significant portion of the Qur'an is completely unintelligible even in its modern Arabic forms, as it is riddled with incomplete sentences, chapters and verses which have no beginning or end, sentences which rhyme for no reason other than the sake of rhyming, and grammatically incoherent text. More than half of the Qur'an is nothing but repetition of the other things written in the book, and its chapters and verses are primarily devoid of context.

Because of these problems, Muslims need to refer to other texts which complement the Qur'an. These texts are called Hadiths. The Hadiths, are a very old collection of historical accounts of the life of Muhammad, his actions, his beliefs, etc. by Islam's most loyal, dedicated, and respected Muslim scholars. Everything in the Qur'an is elaborated upon and explained in the Hadiths. The Hadiths include much, much more information on the life of Muhammad and Islam, than the Qur'an could ever even begin to explore (for the Qur'an usually only mentions Muhammad to praise him alongside Allah as an equal), so the Hadiths are fundamental to Muslims. Without the Hadiths, the Qur'an makes sense to absolutely no one, despite the Qur'an repeatedly claiming to be a very clear collection of Allah's words. Islam therefore is based on the Qur'an as well as the Hadiths, and so are the Islamic laws which Muslim countries impose.

The Hadiths are as much of an authority to Muslims as the Qur'an is, because without them, it is not possible for Muslims to know anything about Islam or how to practice it. "The Five Pillars of Islam" for example (five basic rituals and practices that all Muslims must adhere to) are not found in the Qur'an, but come from Hadith texts. Without the Hadiths, the Qur'an is just a silly book filled with thoughtless chapters and verses. With the Hadiths, the Qur'an is still just a silly book with thoughtless chapters and verses, but at least it becomes a silly book whose thoughtless chapters and verses have a backstory. If you want to see for yourself how silly the Qur'an truly is, grab a copy of the book (the earliest version of it) and read all of it.

Of course, the reason the Qur'an is so nonsensical is because Muhammad made it up (Why else would the Qur'an and the Hadiths claim that the Earth is flat, that the sun sets in a pool of dirty water, that sperm cells are created between a man's ribs and backbone, that flies should be dunked in one's food to cure illnesses, that the devil lives in people's noses, etc.?), however that is not the only reason. You see, Muhammad did not write the Qur'an. He was a simple caravan trader from Mecca who could not read or write. His followers therefore, had to memorise each and every verse as it came to Muhammad, and recite those verses regularly so as not to forget them. It was only at a much later time that somebody among his companions had the bright idea to start writing some of Muhammad's 'revelations' down, and it was only twenty years after his death that his companions began piecing their individual versions of the Qur'an together.

After Muhammad's death, his companions pieced their versions of the Qur'an together, and assembled to review them. However, in addition to some chapters and verses being forgotten by them, others being completely lost with people who had died, some verses going missing, etc. there were many discrepancies. Some people had chapters and verses that differed from what others had, and some people had chapters and verses that they were not sure they should include. To resolve this problem, one among them decided they would collaborate on the compilation of some of the texts into one Qur'an, and then burn all the other versions. The chapters in the Qur'an were then arranged in order of their lengths, and not by any other criteria. Today's Qur'an therefore is a mess of incomplete chapters and verses, and unintelligible information. This, despite the Muslims' claims that it has been perfectly preserved by Allah. If you want proof of the Qur'an's poor preservation, you need not look anywhere but the Islamic sources themselves, which confirm all that I have just told you. 99% of Muslims do not know these things, because 99% of Muslims do not read their texts, and consequently, know next to nothing about their religion. Some Hadith references which reveal how poorly preserved the Qur'an is, are as follows:

- *Sahih al-Bukhari Volume 6, Book 61, 509*
- *Sahih al-Bukhari Volume 6, Book 61, 510*
- *Sahih al-Bukhari Volume 6, Book 61, 527*
- *Sahih al-Muslim #2286*
- *Sunan Ibn Majah #1944*
- *Jami at-Tirmidhi #3104*

Aside from the Qur'an being mostly unintelligible, jam-packed with repetition, poorly preserved, etc. there are hundreds of problems with the parts that do manage to convey some information. And the problems are such that the Qur'an completely discredits itself. I will single out one of these problems specifically, because I believe it to be the most detrimental to the Qur'an, to "Allah", to Muhammad, and to Islam. Let us begin by looking at some verses of the Qur'an.

Qur'an 3:3: "He has sent down upon you, the Book in truth, confirming what was before it. And He revealed the Torah and the Gospel"

Qur'an 5:44: "Indeed We sent down the Torah, in which was guidance and light. The prophets who submitted (to Allah) judged by it for the Jews, as did the rabbis and scholars by that with which they were entrusted of the scripture of Allah, and they were witnesses thereto. So do not fear the people, but fear Me, and do not exchange my verses for a small price. And whoever does not judge by what Allah has revealed – then it is those who are the disbelievers"

Qur'an 5:46: "And we sent, following their footsteps, Jesus, the son of Mary, confirming that which came before him in the Torah; and we gave him the Gospel, in which was guidance and light and confirming that which preceded it of the Torah as guidance and instruction for the righteous"

Qur'an 6:114: "(Say), "Then is it other than Allah I should seek as judge while it is He who has revealed to you the Book explained in detail?" And those to whom we (previously) gave the Scripture know that it is sent down from your Lord in truth, so never be among the doubters"

Qur'an 6:115: "And the word of your Lord has been fulfilled in truth, and in Justice. None can alter His words, and He is the hearing, the knowing"

Note: The "Book" the Qur'an refers to, is in fact the Bible.

Qur'an 3:3 claims that Allah is the one who revealed both the Torah and the Gospel to Jews and Christians, and Qur'an 5:44 commands Muslims to judge by what both the Torah and Gospel contain, for the Torah and the Gospel are both from Allah. Any Muslim who denies the Torah and the Gospel is a disbeliever, according to the Qur'an. Qur'an 5:46 then says that Allah is the one who sent Jesus to this Earth to confirm the Torah, and that Allah is the one who gave Jesus the Gospel.

So, according to the Qur'an: the Gospel and the Torah are Allah's words. Qur'an 6:114 further commands Muslims never to doubt the Bible because it is Allah who revealed it, and Qur'an 6:115 proclaims that **no one** can alter Allah's words. No one at all. The men who hear Allah's words cannot corrupt them, and the men who write Allah's words cannot corrupt them.

That is a very bold claim. Allah does also claim to be God though, and it is not unreasonable for a God to make His words incorruptible. Unfortunately for Allah, his claims present a serious problem. You see, when you read the Bible you will find that it contradicts the Qur'an. The Qur'an denies that Jesus is the Son of God, that He died on the cross, and that He rose from the dead, but the Bible completely contradicts the Qur'an on this. The Qur'an claims that Muhammad is the "seal of the Prophets" and insinuates again and again, that Muhammad is to be praised alongside Allah as an equal. The Bible however, confirms Muhammad as an antichrist and reveals the true identity of "Allah" to be none other than satan himself (I will explain that later). Aside from those things there is the serious matter of how the Qur'an says many hundreds of things which directly contradict itself and the Bible.

Muslims are commanded in the Qur'an to read the Bible, but when they do, they see that it discredits their religion and proclaims the opposite of what Islam proclaims. Muslims therefore, are forced to say the Bible has been corrupted. The Qur'an certainly does not ever say the Bible has been corrupted. Rather, it affirms the Bible as divine words from Allah, and commands Muslims to read and obey it. Furthermore, the Qur'an says: "None can alter His (Allah's) words"! If the Bible has indeed been corrupted, then whichever man corrupted it, is more powerful than Allah. As you can see, Muslims are in a serious debacle. But it gets worse:

The Qur'an says that Allah revealed the Bible and that none can change His words, yet the Bible condemns Muhammad and contradicts the Qur'an. As I am about to show you, the seriousness of this is catastrophic to Islam.

You see, there are only two possibilities about the Bible for Muslims: Either the Bible tells the truth, or it does not. If the Bible tells the truth, then Islam is a lie, because the Bible contradicts the Qur'an. If the Bible does not tell the truth though… then Islam is still a lie, because the Qur'an claims the Bible to be true and delivered by Allah (whose words are unchangeable). Either way you look at it, **Islam cannot possibly be from God. Islam is a lie.**

Just like that, the Qur'an has discredited itself and torn Islam asunder. Of course there is much more (much, much more) in the Qur'an that can be investigated to reveal Islam as a bed of lies, but the above dilemma is amongst the most damaging.

So now that you know a few things about the Qur'an, let us move on to the evaluation of Islam's 'prophet' Muhammad. Although the Qur'an claims that Jesus Christ did not die on the cross (even though historical evidence proves otherwise), it acknowledges that His body is not on this planet, for it is with God. If Muhammad is held most high next to God Himself (as constantly expressed in the Qur'an), then why is his dead and decayed body lying somewhere in a grave in Medina today? I am about to tell you.

The answers, are again in Islam's holy texts, and the evidence within these texts which condemn Muhammad and Islam itself is so great in quantity, a book four times the volume of this one would have to be written to reveal them all. So I will briefly list only some of the evidence here with references to the Islamic texts themselves, so that you may investigate them more deeply, and uncover even more evidence on your own. Again: the following are from authentic Islamic sources, i.e. the Qur'an and the Hadiths, which are authorities to Muslims. I have also included references to the oldest and most authentic biographies on the life of Muhammad. So in no particular order of the severity of the incriminating evidence, let us begin:

Muhammad believed he was demon-possessed and tried to commit suicide multiple times

After being terribly assaulted by a spirit in a cave (the spirit Muhammad later claimed to receive revelations from), Muhammad believed he had encountered a demon, and that he was demonically possessed. He then tried to commit suicide by jumping from a cliff but failed to do so, and ran home to his wife Khadija and her cousin Waraka, who in desperation then tried to comfort Muhammad and prevent him from killing himself, by telling him that the spirit he encountered must have been the angel Gabriel, and not a demon. **Ibn Ishaq's "Sirat Rasul Allah", page 106**

Khadija's cousin did add though, that he was afraid the spirit Muhammad encountered could be a demon that would drive Muhammad crazy and corrupt him. As you are soon about to find out, Waraka was not wrong. **Ibn kathir's "Al-Sira al-Nabawiyya", Volume 1, page 296**

Later on in Muhammad's life, the so-called 'revelations' he was receiving from the spirit he first encountered in the cave stopped for some time. During this time, Muhammad became so distraught he attempted to commit suicide on several occasions. **Sahih al-Bukhari #6982**

Muhammad uttered satanic verses by his own admission, and then later claimed that the devil tricked him

When Muhammad first started to spread Islam, it was very difficult for him to gain followers. Mainly because everyone at the time was pagan, and was not interested in the sayings of someone who seemed to have invented a new monotheistic religion that he then tried to convert people to. Secondly, the things he was saying were being directly challenged by people who claimed they could speak in the same so-called "prophetic" manner that Muhammad claimed.

Desperate to find something that would finally convince people to follow him as a prophet, Muhammad decided to attribute to some of the pagan 'Gods' that the people around him worshiped, in an effort to gain the people's acceptance. One day as he was preaching in Mecca and saw that people were not taking him seriously, he decided to name three pagan 'Goddesses', and claim that Allah recognised them as intercessors between the people and Allah. Muhammad then bowed down in honour of these 'Goddesses'. The people, pleased that Muhammad just acknowledged their 'Gods', bowed down as well, as Muhammad claimed that the words acknowledging the pagan 'Gods' were a revelation from Allah. ***Ibn Ishaq's "Sirat Rasul Allah", page 165***

However, Muhammad later returned to the people and said that the revelations were not from Allah, but were from satan. That he was unable to tell the difference between words from satan and words from Allah, as acknowledged in ***Qur'an 22:52***.

This is such an embarrassing event that early Muslims who pieced the many different versions of the Qur'an together, removed much of it from the version of the Qur'an most commonly known today. This is why chapter 22, and verses 52 to 53, much like many other passages in the Qur'an, make no sense at all without the supporting Hadith documentation.

Muhammad got engaged to a six-year-old girl, but was forced to wait until she was at least nine-years-old to have sex with her

Around Five years after the death of Muhammad's first wife, and not long after marrying his second wife, he began looking for a wife in Medina, where he had migrated from Mecca. He eventually found and settled for a six-year-old girl named A'isha (his closest friend's daughter), whom he got engaged to. ***Sahih al-Bukhari Volume 5, Book 58, #234***

A'isha's father was reluctant at first to allow the marriage of his child to a man in his 50's, but Muhammad was given special privileges because he claimed to be a prophet of Islam. *Sahih al-Bukhari Volume 7, Book 62, #18*

Unfortunately for Muhammad, A'isha was just too young, so Muhammad had to wait three years before he could have sex with her. She had not yet reached puberty when Muhammad penetrated her, and would have been deemed too young for anyone to have sex with at age nine. Muhammad was allowed to engage in what people even at that time would have seen as paedophilia, only because he claimed to be a prophet.

Muhammad was known to suck on the tongues of other males

Muhammad was seen sucking the tongue of a young boy. *Al-Adab al-Mufrad, Al-Bukhari #1183*

He was also seen sucking on the tongue of a man. *Musnad Ahmad #16245*

Muhammad admitted that he was a victim of witchcraft

At one point in Muhammad's life, a Jewish magician had placed a spell on him, after acquiring some hair from a comb which Muhammad had used. The extent of the curse was such that Muhammad would have hallucinations of himself having sex with his wives. One day Muhammad heard a conversation between two men regarding this, so he went to tell one of his wives about how he had been bewitched. *Sahih al-Bukhari #5765*

Muhammad was a cruel, and vengeful man, who tortured and killed many people for poorly justified reasons

The list of atrocities committed by Muhammad in this regard is extensive, but I only need to reveal a few of them to you, to show you the kind of person Muhammad was.

1) **Muhammad murdered a woman because she spoke out against his murder of another person**

After the unjust execution of a certain elderly man by Muhammad's orders, a woman by the name Asma bint Marwan became disturbed, and one day expressed her disapproval of Muhammad to some of his companions. Because of this and the fact that she had written some poetry criticising him, he sought her execution.

The man Muhammad had given the task to, crept into her home in the dead of night to slay her, but Asma was a mother of five children, and one of her infants was still feeding on her breast. The man then pulled the infant from her and stabbed her until the knife pierced her back. **Ibn Sad's "Kitab al-Tabaqat al-Kabir", Volume 2, page 30**

The man who did this terrible thing felt bad about what he had done, and when he asked Muhammad whether or not he (the man) would have to bear any ill will for his actions, Muhammad said: "No. Two goats won't butt their heads about her". **Ibn Ishaq's "Sirat Rasul Allah", page 675**

2) **When one of Muhammad's scribes discovered Muhammad was making the Qur'an up, Muhammad tried to kill him**

Because Muhammad was illiterate, he needed other people to write the Qur'an for him. One of these people was a man named Abdullah Ibn Sa'd Ibn Abi Sarh. Abi Sarh would sit with Muhammad and write down the Qur'anic verses that Muhammad spoke. However, Abi Sarh would often make improvements to the things Muhammad would say, and he would even make additions of his very own to the Qur'an. Muhammad would say one thing, and Abi Sarh would add something to it, as a suggestion. Muhammad would then say: "Yes, write it down".

It did not take long for Abi Sarh to realise that if he was writing things down in the Qur'an, the Qur'an could not possibly be the "eternal uncreated word of God" that it claims to be. This prompted him to apostatise from Islam, and move back to his village in Mecca, where he told people of how he would manipulate Muhammad to include things in the Qur'an, and how Muhammad allowed him to make his own additions to the Qur'an. *Al Sira Al Halabiya, Chapter 3, page 90*

Of course Abi Sarh's apostasy outraged Muhammad. Not only did Abi Sarh leave Muhammad's side, Muhammad knew that Abi Sarh's existence was a serious threat to the credibility of the Qur'an, and the credibility of Muhammad as a prophet. This is why Muhammad came up with *Qur'an 22:52,* which is actually referring specifically to Abi Sarh.

When Muhammad conquered Mecca, his instruction to his army was to kill only those who fought them, with the exception of a list of people Muhammad did not like. Abi Sarh was one of these men. *Ibn Sad's "Kitab al-Tabaqat al-Kabir", Volume 2, page 168*

Knowing this, he (Abi Sarh) went to hide with one of Muhammad's closest friends: Uthman b. Affan. Uthman was Abi Sarh's half-brother, so he later went with Abi Sarh to Muhammad, and asked for Abi Sarh to be pardoned. Muhammad said nothing, and stared at Abi Sarh for a long time. Abi Sarh took that to be a pardon, and went on his way. After Abi Sarh had left, Muhammad scolded his men, telling them that they should have killed Abi Sarh right then and there without Muhammad needing to give the order. Of course the presence of Uthman is the only thing that saved Abi Sarh's life, as Muhammad would not have liked to offend his very good friend by killing Abi Sarh. *Ibn Hisham's "Al Sira Al Nabawiya", Chapter 4, page 58*

3) **Muhammad brutally tortured and killed people as an act of vengeance**

Muhammad was a highly vengeful person, and was known to kill people who said anything that offended him. On one particular occasion though, the people who had wronged him did more than just insult him. They had killed a Shepard of Muhammad's, apostatised from Islam, and drove away some camels.

Muhammad chased them down, and after catching them, he had their hands and feet cut off. He then burned their eyes out with hot nails, and left them in the desert sun to die the most painful and horrible death he could have imagined at the time. **Sahih al-Bukhari Volume 2, Book 24, #577**

Incidentally, these men had earlier asked Muhammad for assistance with some illnesses they were having. Muhammad then told them to cure themselves by drinking the milk and urine of some camels. I suspect the camel urine had an adverse effect on their minds.

4) **Muhammad looked for, and murdered people who had offended him, years after they offended him**

Muhammad spent thirteen years in Mecca trying to convince people of his new religion, but he was so unconvincing that he had only managed to gain about 150 followers during that time. Muhammad Then left for Medina, and after amassing an army there (by enticing people with the bounty they would earn from villages they raided and caravans they robbed), he returned to Mecca eight years later.

Upon his arrival, he gave his army a list of at least six people to be killed. These were mostly people who had offended him when he was still in Mecca. When one of those people heard that Muhammad had returned to Mecca, he ran away to the Kaaba (a place built in honour of useless, pre-Islamic Arab 'gods', but naively worshiped by ignorant Muslims around the world today as something Holy from Allah) and tied himself up in the Kaaba, expecting Muhammad not to kill him in such a Holy place. Of course Muhammad wasted no time murdering him in the Kaaba, because the sanctity of God's establishments is irrelevant to Muhammad when he has a personal grudge to settle. **Ibn Hisham's "Al Sira Al Nabawiya", Chapter 4, page 58**

5) **Muhammad tortured a man to extract money from him**

When Muhammad led his army to underhandedly conquer the unsuspecting Jewish settlement of Khaibar, he captured their leader: Kinana ibn al-Rabi. Kinana was the keeper of a treasure Muhammad sought, and was threatened with death if he did not reveal the treasure's location.

Kinana led Muhammad to the treasure's location, but not all of it was there. When he refused to comply with Muhammad any further, Muhammad gave orders for Kinana to be tortured until he revealed the location of the remaining treasure. A stick was set alight, and placed on Kinana's chest until he was nearly dead, and after that, he was handed to one of Muhammad's companions, who then cut his head off. **A. Guillaume's "The Life of Muhammad", page 515**

Now Kinana was dead, but he still had a wife (Safiya bint Huyai) whom he had widowed. She was captured in the war, and when presented before Muhammad, he wasted no time in taking her and marrying her to himself. **Sahih al-Bukhari Volume 5, Book 59, #522**

Muhammad wasted no time in marrying Safiya, but only after finding out that she was the wife of Kinana. His initial intention was to give her to somebody as a slave before it was mentioned to him who she was. **Sahih al-Bukhari Volume 1, Book 8, #367**

Throughout his life as a demon-possessed and self-appointed "prophet", Muhammad had done far worse than the things I have just listed, and so have his companions. On the occasions that his companions would commit terrible deeds of their own accord, Muhammad would never even bat an eyelid. However, anyone who had anything unflattering to say about him, he would have slaughtered.

Muhammad and his companions would rape women

Muhammad was involved in several military missions where they would conquer small villages, and take the women in those villages captive. Usually they would kill those women's fathers, husbands, uncles, etc. and therefore Muhammad's companions were deemed able to rape these women.

However on one occasion, both the men and the women were captured alive by Muhammad and his companions, so it was apparent that the women were still married to these men. Muhammad's companions, unsure of whether or not they could have sex with these women in the presence of their husbands, went to Muhammad for guidance. After explaining to Muhammad the situation, Muhammad then received a "revelation" from Allah (*Qur'an 4:24*) which allowed the rape of these women despite their husbands being alive, as long as a waiting period had passed (to ensure the women were not pregnant). **Sunan Abu Dawud #2150**

Muhammad advocated prostitution

During the period of Muhammad's and his companions' military excursions, they did not always have female captives. Therefore Muhammad's companions often felt sexual frustrations. One day they voiced this to Muhammad, and he told them that they could alleviate themselves by finding a woman and temporarily marrying her for a short period of time (a day, or even an hour), and in return give her a garment. **Sahih al-Bukhari Volume 6, Book 60, #139**

Muhammad then received the 'revelation' of *Qur'an 5:87*, and claimed that temporary marriage (prostitution) was not unlawful. This, among other things (like Muhammad's sexual relations with a prepubescent girl) has ramifications even today, as in Islamic nations people are selling and renting their very young daughters out to old men for sexual purposes on the basis that Muhammad authorised such transactions.

Muhammad married his own adopted son's wife after causing the divorce between them

Muhammad had an adopted son named Zayd, whom he had acquired as a son from his first wife: Khadija bint Khuwaylid. Zayd was married to an attractive woman named Zaynab bint Jash: Muhammad's own cousin. So attractive she was though, that Muhammad desired her for himself. With much pain in his heart, Zayd was eventually forced by Muhammad to tell his wife that Muhammad wanted to marry her. ***Sahih Muslim, Book 008, #3330***

"Why would Muhammad do such a thing?"? Well, he was sexually perverse. His heart turned for Zaynab when one day he walked into her room expecting to find Zayd, but instead found Zaynab lying on her bed, and partially naked. Zaynab stood up quickly and clothed herself, and as Muhammad walked away he said: "Glory be to God the Almighty! Glory be to God, who causes hearts to turn". His attraction to her became evident to Zaynab, and so she went and told Zayd. ***The History of al-Tabari, Volume 9, Page 2***

Now, when Zayd first discovered that Muhammad was secretly sexually aroused by Zaynab, Zayd approached Muhammad to offer her to him because he knew Muhammad was the kind of person who would stop at nothing to get what he wanted. However Muhammad declined the offer, telling Zayd that he could keep his wife. Unfortunately for Zayd and his wife, Muhammad soon received the revelation of ***Qur'an 33:37*** which claimed that Allah wanted Muhammad to marry Zaynab, that Muhammad had no right to conceal his desire for Zaynab and thereafter decline Zayd's offer of her, and that the purpose of Allah wanting Muhammad to marry

Zaynab was so that other Muslims could marry the wives of their adopted sons without issue. *Sahih al-Bukhari Volume 9, Book 93, #516*

Despite Allah's approval of Muhammad's actions, the people in the village were shocked that a so-called "prophet of God" could do such a thing. This became a source of embarrassment to Muhammad, and so much so that he later received the revelations of **Qur'an 33:4** and **Qur'an 33:5**, which declared one's adopted sons not to be one's true sons, and abolished the practice of adoption all together. To this day, Islam forbids adoption because of the two aforementioned Qur'anic verses.

After Muhammad got to commit his incestuous crime, it became impossible for Muslims to marry the wives of their adopted sons because Muslims cannot adopt. **Qur'an 33:37** therefore, is a worthless verse like all the others, and only exists so that it can be used against Muhammad to show that he was as a false prophet plagued by sexual perversion.

Muhammad would break his oaths, and 'revelations' often occurred to him only to please his own desires

By now it should be apparent to anyone that Muhammad was a man who loved to have sex, and that Allah was a "God" who loved for Muhammad to have sex. This is why Muhammad had many wives and sexual partners. It is known that he had nine wives when he died, but he once had at least 11 at a time. This, in spite of the Qur'an only allowing each Muslim up to four wives. Each Muslim except Muhammad of course, who received a special 'revelation' (**Qur'an 33:50**) telling him he could have as many wives as he wanted.

Now, certain days were allocated to each one of his wives, and it is supposed that he would have intercourse with them regularly. However, all those wives were not enough for him. You see, Muhammad's wife Hafsa, had a domestic servant (Mariyah the Copt) whom Muhammad fancied having sex with, and he eventually succumbed to his desire to commit adultery with her. *Sunan An-Nasa'i #3411*

When Hafsa caught him having sex with Mariyah on Hafsa's own bed, he swore to Hafsa never to do it again so that she would not go and tell the other wives. Naturally, she went and told the other wives anyway. Muhammad's wives then became angry with him and he felt much shame. Unfortunately for his wives, Muhammad soon thereafter received the revelation of *Qur'an 66:1* from Allah, which forbid Muhammad from refusing to sleep with his wife's maid. *Tafsir al-Jalalayn 66:1*

He also received *Qur'an 66:2* (which allowed Muhammad to break the oath he made), *Qur'an 66:3*, *Qur'an 66:4*, and *Qur'an 66:5*, and withdrew from his wives for a month. In the three aforementioned verses, Allah admonished Muhammad's wives for taking issue with the fact that Muhammad was committing adultery with Mariyah. *Sahih al-Bukhari Volume 3, Book 43, #648*

He then continued sleeping with Mariyah, and she eventually gave birth to a bastard son called Ibrahim, who then died at the age of around two years old. Interestingly, all three of the biological sons Muhammad ever had, died at around age two. I suspect that had something to do with the demon he was diseased with, and its desire for the blood of infant boys. *Sahih al-Bukhari Volume 8, Book 73, #214*

The second Muhammad wants anything, a 'revelation from Allah', will descend upon him so that he can have it. "The Qur'an is Allah's eternal and uncreated word" Muslims say, and yet Allah seems to have nothing better to do than ensure Muhammad can indulge every perversion that comes to his mind. His wife A'isha, made mention of this when she complained of Muhammad's inability to treat his wives fairly. *Sahih al-Bukhari Volume 6, Book 60, #311*

Muhammad was disgraced by God in his death. His death was perhaps the most humiliating death in all of history

It all begins with a revelation Muhammad claimed to have received one day as he declared himself a prophet of God. He said that if indeed he was a false prophet, God would sever his aorta (the human body's main artery) **Qur'an 69:44.** In fact this is something he would say over and over again for years as he preached in Mecca. Nevertheless it won him few followers, for it was quite apparent to people even in his time, that any man who has to say: "If I am not a prophet, God will strike me down", or things of that nature, is usually not a prophet.

One day though, this ridiculous claim to Muhammad's divinity was finally going to be put the test. On that day, Muhammad had slaughtered the family of a woman during one of his raids, and kept her captive. Vengeful at the actions of Muhammad, the woman prepared food for him, but put poison in the food as a test of Muhammad's divinity. The poison was noticeable by Muhammad's companions as well as by himself, so they confronted her about it. She then told Muhammad that she had poisoned the food, and that if indeed he was a prophet of God, the poison would not have an effect. Muhammad then said Allah would never allow for the poison to kill him. **Sahih Muslim #5430**

Unfortunately, not only did the poison indeed kill him, it killed him very slowly and painfully, as the course of his suffering spanned years. In his last days he could not even walk, and had to be dragged by his feet by his companions. **Sahih al-Bukhari #2588**

During Muhammad's last moments, in which the poison finally claimed his life, he would complain to his wife in whose bed he lay stricken, that he could still feel the effects of the poison he ate those years ago, and that he felt as if his aorta was being severed. **Sahih al-Bukhari #4428**

Muhammad uttered the most self-condemning words he could have ever spoken. He forgot how he once used to say that if he was a false prophet, God would sever his aorta. Muhammad died in the exact same unusual manner he said he would die if he was a false prophet, and I have not ever heard of anyone dying in such a strange and particular fashion except Muhammad. "Coincidence?" No.

In addition to the nature of his demise, Muhammad's utterance of the satanic verses that had him mention three pagan 'Goddesses' in the name of God, makes him a false prophet according to the Bible. Deuteronomy Chapter 18, and Verse 20: "But the prophet who presumes to speak a word in my name that I have not commanded him to speak, or who speaks in the name of other gods, that same prophet shall die" His admission that these verses came from the devil, is as well proof that he is a false prophet. Although, in his defence: Allah and the devil are not unlike each other. The Qur'an confirms this.

Qur'an 3:54: "And they (the unbelievers) planned to deceive, and Allah planned to deceive (the unbelievers), and Allah is the best of deceivers"

Qur'an 7:99: "Are they then safe from Allah's deception? No one feels safe from Allah's deception except those that shall perish"

Qur'an 8:30: "And (remember) when the unbelievers plotted deception against you (O Muhammad), to imprison you, or kill you, or expel you. They plotted deception, but Allah also plotted deception; and Allah is the best of deceivers."

According to the Qur'an Allah is the best of deceivers. There is **no one** who can deceive better than Allah can. What does the Bible say though, about the best of deceivers? Deuteronomy Chapter 8, and Verse 44: "You are of your father the devil, and your will is to do your father's desires. He was a murderer from the beginning, and does not stand in the truth, because there is no truth in him. When he lies, he speaks out of his own character, for he is a liar and the father of lies". According to the Bible, satan is the father of lies. The Qur'an therefore, exposes "Allah" as being none other than the devil himself.

Several English translations of the Qur'an have adulterated its texts in order to try and hide the true face of Islam, the harsh nature of its texts, and the absurdity of some of its declarations. Among many of these adulterations is the replacement of the word "deceive" with "plan" in the Qur'anic verses I have just quoted. The Arabic word "Makr" used in the Arabic versions of the Qur'anic verses above, means "to deceive". Not "to plan".

Muslims often try to excuse the myriad of problems with the Qur'an by citing that the Qur'an has to be read in Arabic. For once, I agree with them (as far as seeing what the Qur'an actually says, is concerned). If you want to see the true face of Islam, look for the most authentic Arabic Qur'an you can find, and read it. Doing so will in fact strengthen the arguments against the Qur'an, and will only degrade your perception of Islam.

Lastly, the Qur'an's denial of the fact that Jesus is the divine Son of God, that Jesus died on the cross for our sins, and that He rose from the dead, convicts Muhammad as an antichrist according to the Bible which the Qur'an affirms as truth. 1 John, Chapter 2, and Verse 22: "Who is the liar but he who denies that Jesus is the Christ? This is the antichrist, he who denies the Father and the Son. No one who denies the Son has the Father. Whoever confesses the Son has the Father also".

- Jesus is the divine Son of God
- Jesus died on the cross for our sins
- Jesus rose from the dead

Those three facts are the central message of the Gospel, and among other objectives, it is the focus of demonic entities to attack that message. Anyone who denies the three things above, and yet claims to be a Prophet of God, is an antichrist. Muhammad's denial that Christ is the Son of God, is due to the demonic possession that plagued him, but the myriad of other errors and logical fallacies in the Qur'an are due to the fact that Muhammad was an uneducated man who only knew as much about Christianity, Judaism, science, and the world, as he had heard from the stories and opinions circulating in his time. He inserted the stories he had heard into the Qur'an, and although some of them were true, most of them were half-truths and lies. Should you read the Qur'an, and then investigate its texts in the Hadiths, it will become quite apparent to you that Muhammad made the Qur'an up as he preached it. This is why the scope and depth of the Qur'an go no further than what we would expect an illiterate seventh-century caravan trader from Mecca, to have known and understood at the time.

So that is most of what you need to know about Muhammad. He was a deceptive, demon-possessed, suicidal, child-molesting, murderer, who used to idea of being a "Prophet" to indulge his perversions.

Knowing all these things, you might be wondering why anybody in his/her right mind would be Muslim. The reason is simple: The vast majority of Muslims do not know these things, because they do not read their holy texts. In fact they are discouraged by their imams (Islamic leaders) from reading their texts, and it is claimed by their imams, that this is because only they (the imams) can accurately interpret the texts. The Qur'an itself in chapter 5, and verses 101 to 102 outright forbids Muslims from questioning anything about Islam that would cause them concern (like the myriad of atrocious and disgustingly evil acts Muhammad committed, and the various logical fallacies, inconsistencies, incoherent garbage, and absolute lies in the Qur'an) lest the Muslim then lose faith in the religion.

There are some very (very) small groups of Muslims who, having encountered the truth about Muhammad's evil and revolting nature in the Hadiths, claim that the Hadiths are not required for one to be a Muslim, and that the Hadiths are lies. Of course if they were to publicly say these things in Muslim countries, they might very well be executed, but in free countries like the U.S., and public forums like the internet, they can claim these absurd things. Ask these people basic questions about what many of the Qur'anic chapters and verses are referring to however, the context behind the verses, or anything at all about Muhammad, and these people will not be able to tell you a single thing without first enquiring from a Hadith, or from someone who has read a Hadith.

Any Muslim who claims Islam's most treasured Hadiths to be lies, or who says that revered Islamic scholars like Muhammad al-Bukhari are liars, are people in desperate denial who typically reside outside of Islamic nations, and therefore can think a little outside of the box of Islam to twist and construe the basics of the religion to suit what they wish was true. These are people happy to live a lie, and displeased at the notion of questioning things. As the Qur'an says: "A people before you indeed asked such questions, and then became disbelievers on account of them".

To call 'Muslims highly ignorant of their religion' would be quite the understatement. Not only do Muslims not read their own texts, they are told that should they ever question 'Allah' and his 'prophet', they will go to hell. Of course that is a nonsensical claim. Islamic leaders know very well that should most Muslims be made aware of the true nature of Islam and the deeds of their "prophet", they would apostatise from the religion (as many Muslims already have). At least in their hearts, and not outwardly. I will tell you more about Islam, and why exactly a Muslim would fear outward apostasy, later.

For now, let us look at Christianity too and how blind faith has enabled its problematic divisions. There are many different Christian churches with very contradicting world views and interpretations of the Bible, all claiming to represent one God. But how can one Bible give rise to so many different perspectives?

You see: the problem not only lies with the contradictory nature of the book, it also lies with **religious interpretation**. As I have indicated before in this book (and will do so again), the Holy Spirit of God is a bringer of truth. It deals only with the truth, because it offers us a direct connection to God. The Holy Spirit cannot manifest itself through people who choose to believe lies for the purpose of their desires, and it cannot live inside people who cannot tolerate the truth. People who do not have the Holy Spirit cannot be led to truth by it, and when such people who lack the means to adequately interpret and comprehend biblical text, read the Bible, their conclusions on many occasions are not going to match up with what the text actually meant or what its writer intended to portray.

Where there is a symbolic meaning in what Jesus is quoted as saying, the religious mind will take it literally. And where there is a literal meaning in what Jesus is quoted as saying, the religious mind will only understand it metaphorically. Jesus Christ primarily speaks in parables, but men and women who lack understanding cannot discern this for themselves.

When people who do not possess either the intellectual competence or the spiritual guidance to study the Bible, read the Bible, they spread their incorrect interpretations of the texts to others, and consequently there is a problem. That is how all these churches came about with their ridiculous dogma.

Of course another manner in which different kinds of churches' doctrines spring up, is the deliberate misinterpretation of Biblical texts by people who seek to gain a following of ignorant and naïve sheep in order to expand on popularity or to make money.

People who adamantly and vehemently stick to their religious beliefs without logic, tend not to have the Holy Spirit with them. Those who have and act in accordance with the Holy Spirit, apply reason and have a justified theology by which they seek to understand things in and out of this world.

People with the Holy Spirit will be led to the truth, and it is their responsibility to either accept it or not when it confronts them, but they for a fact will typically find the truth, and something inside them will know it when they come across it.

Religious people that you will meet on the street ministering lies like that of "God the Mother" or the Jehovah's Witness theology, are people who have been misled by a spirit of rigid religion and deception.

These are the kinds of people who will claim to have the Holy Spirit when in reality, no such spirit dwells within them. In fact, they are incompatible with the Holy Spirit, because what they campaign and are willing to accept is in direct contradiction to the reality of things. In direct contradiction to God.

Notorious campaigners of misinformation wrapped in the context of religion as referenced above, can easily be spotted by several key characteristics. For example: Such people may approach you on a street, and attempt to program their doctrine into you ordinarily by quoting scripture or by having you read it, and then through a series of invalidly interpreted and declared logic, make an argument for their case.

Let me just say that from a psychological perspective, they prefer for you to read it out loud, so that you are more easily fooled into accepting the lies they will try and lead you to believe. It is an old technique, employed by hypnotists and scammers to create an association between yourself, the texts you are reading (as it is you who reads and speaks them), and the logic that the evangelist will attribute to the text.

They will pick a single paragraph or sentence, interpret it out of context, and bait your mind to the jaws of whatever nonsense that they are trying to get you to agree with. They will point to some highlighted words and say: "Read this". Once you have done so, they will dictate to you what it means or ask you questions in a manner which attempts to sway you in their direction.

With their recent dictations in your mind, they then move onto another body of text, which they will again isolate and explain to justify their beliefs. The verse (or even the sentence) which directly follows or precedes the one(s) they had you read, might refute everything they are about to tell you, but in the minds of the people who originally fooled them and their kind, you do not need to know that, and neither do their evangelising minions. This technique works well on people who do not possess the knowledge or the mental ability to guard against it. i.e.: the ignorant or the unintelligent.

Of course reasonably intelligent people can be fooled also, as long as they fall prey to the manipulative stereotypical smiles and seemingly free-spirited dispositions of any deluded man or woman who claims to minister "the truth of God's word". This is why, when an evangelist knocks on your door, I advise that you do not answer, and when he/she preaches doctrine to you, I advise that you do not listen.

When they ask you not to shake your head at their doctrine because "it's rude", continue to shake your head, and when they try to dodge criticism by telling you not to "judge" them, stand firm in your ability to reason, and spot their doctrine for what it is: nonsense.

Anybody who is open-minded to information is very likely to accept it, so conmen in all professions seek to take advantage of your emotional responses, and the premise of you having "an open mind" to invite themselves into a room you probably do not want them messing around in. Being closed-minded to the truth is definitely a bad thing, but I can assure you that being closed-minded to deception is good for your health. If you open the door to a thief, the thief will march right in, and the thief will rob you. In this case, the plunderer will do so while he/she sweet-talks you into allowing it to happen.

Do not confuse the typical evangelist church personnel who says "Read this" for a hypnotist or scammer of some kind however, for they are only doing what they have been told to do. They would not know hypnotism if it jabbed them in the throat, and that is precisely why and how they have come to be fooled into the false doctrine that they preach in the first place.

But you might be wondering: "If indeed the Bible in other parts, makes clarifications contrary to that of the door-to-door evangelists' teachings, why do deceived religious people like these remain deceived?" You see, the human mind is such that once an idea has been engrained within it to an extent (not much of an extent in many cases), the mind will seek to justify the notion whenever the opportunity presents itself.

This means: When someone happens to believe that "God has a wife" for example (as is the case with some of the religious sheep wondering the streets of my neighbourhood), whenever he/she encounters information in the Bible that speaks of a "bride", a "wife", or alludes to marriage in any vague spiritual contexts, that reader will be inclined to interpret it in a fashion that suits his/her preconception(s) that God is married. It is foolish human nature, and it is by virtue of this nature that religion thrives.

A mind as described above can for example: see a sentence which reads: "Our heavenly caregiver", as one which alludes to 'a spiritual mother' because he/she has learnt somewhere that "mothers take care of their children". A rational mind knows that anyone or anything can be a caregiver, and in the case of Biblical contexts which only ever make mention of a male God, that caregiver will definitely be a male God. But a mind indoctrinated with the notion of "God the Mother" (and the idea that Jesus Christ was recently reborn as a South Korean Asian man), in spite of the Bible never (ever) mentioning it, is not a rational mind.

The illogicality of such a mind can be due to more than just psychological manipulation. It is not only from a psychological dimension that deceived evangelists endeavour to corrupt others (knowingly or unknowingly), because convincing somebody of something blatantly illogical requires tactics of many dimensions. You see, anybody who goes about spreading a message of "God the Mother", or 'Jesus the 20th Century South Korean (as the aforementioned Church actually believes)', are people who in one way or another are being used by evil to perpetuate delusion amongst societies. The spirits that lead these people to your doorstep or your side of the street can be very dangerous.

If you could see the things that walk alongside such evangelists, you might never want to speak to them again. I have seen these things and can confirm that they are not pretty. Worms that seek to breed ignorance into the human race is what they are. The primary mechanism of evil and its transmission is human beings, and deluded evangelists are such human beings. Believe it or not, as a misguided religious evangelist ministers to you the words of their "truth", if it is a spirit that drives him/her, it will attempt to become a part of you just as it has wormed its way into its current host. This fails to have effect a majority of the time, but whenever it happens to work, the number of misled religious human beings among us definitely increases by '1'. There is some good news however, for these people are not difficult to point out.

Evangelists in tune with a deceptive religious spirit can easily be discerned by the fact that they typically will not accept any logic or reason, and only have "The Bible says" to present as an argument. Never mind the fact that even when considering what the Bible says, it does not say what they have twisted its scripture to mean.

Furthermore, the snake that has deluded these people into preaching garbage, often rears its head in the form of an attempt by them to belittle or subvert any objections you may have by saying "But Jesus says…", "Do you not believe in Jesus?", and "Do you not trust Him or His word?", etc.

Religiously indoctrinated evangelists will constantly shift the root of their false doctrine to Jesus Christ or what the Bible says, claiming that it is not they who have come to tell you what they are telling you, but instead Jesus

Christ or God, through the Bible. They are as manipulative as the snakes that often lead them, and regularly abuse the authority given to the name "Jesus Christ" in order to get you to side with them.

The irony, is that these people will always reveal themselves as not being of God, by their very own actions. If they do not do so immediately, at some point very soon you will see it, for they are masters at discrediting themselves. Often their actions, statements, and behaviours will be in direct accordance with what Jesus Christ very clearly in the Bible said **not** to do. The Bible may not be the word of God, but it is still an asset of knowledge and wisdom captured on paper, and these kinds of people cannot coherently abide by any of it.

When you ask these brainwashed evangelists questions they do not have the answers to, they usually respond with questions that question your Christianity or your loyalties. They are ridiculous. The reason they assume such tactics will work (and unfortunately, it seems that sometimes they do), is the fact that religious people worship mostly the Bible. They do not worship God. They treat the Bible as if it were God Himself, yet simultaneously, sort and choose what they want to believe from it, and completely ignore that which they do not.

Take the time to argue with these evangelising people, and you will see that they do not really care about you or your "salvation" nearly as much as they care about being right or getting you to join their denomination/cult. Some may indeed have good intentions, but good intentions are useless when they do not help anyone.

These people will call themselves "faithful" and "Godly", but rarely will you find one amongst them that even has proof of their own that their God exists. They discuss God as if they know Him, and impudently confine His infinite word and wisdom to a small book, yet most likely have never seen any works by Him.

They preach all sorts of garbage and mix their garbage with statements about God being "a loving God", "a kind God", or how His Son "died for our sins", but how do they know? Of course, they do not. They operate on a basis of blind faith, and I have discussed before how dangerous that is. Their closed-minded approach to life is living proof of the dangers of such a faith. If you have observed no evidence for what you believe in, then at the very best you are only hopeful.

I have personally seen and experienced the things which I communicate in this book, so when I say "There is God, there is Jesus Christ, and there is His Holy Spirit", I have every authority to. Most Christians can only pretend to know what they are saying when they speak of "the devil" or "evil spirits", because they have no experience with such things beyond the superficial discussions they sometimes have with one another.

Religious Christians typically do not really understand what the Bible means when it speaks about faith, and its ability to crumble the walls of Jericho. You see, faith is the result of an affirmation contingent upon the realization that **God is** and that **He will**. Such a realization is only grasped by those who know without a doubt that they have reason to.

Allow me to digress for a moment, to explain this briefly. You see, I have a considerable amount of direct, hands-on experience with the spirit realm, and its physical associations. So I know for a fact that the world unseen (unseen by most anyway) is there, and that it affects people every day. My faith therefore is not a blind one. When I pray to God, I have my prayers answered because I know that He will respond. Of course, I do not pray for foolish things, and neither should you. A just spirit will request from God what it needs, not that which it does not. Prayers for things like "a big house", is something that false prophets and conmen feed to greedy and gullible people, but the God of Isaac and Abraham is not known to entertain such nonsense. The day He does, it might only be to teach you a lesson of how unimportant some of these things really are.

Anyone who seeks to establish a genuine relationship with God, will slowly come to know Him, for we can only connect with God spiritually. Unless we go through spiritual practices, our spiritual levels cannot increase. Even the basic ritual of kneeling down in prayer is an example of spiritual practice, and when done so honestly by an individual, his/her connection to God will become stronger. The key is the strength with which a person uses his/her will to effect the changes he/she seeks to see.

Your connection to God will correlate with your spiritual level, and the application of your faith will be in accordance. If God does not personally reveal Himself to you the way He did to Moses for example, then it is you who will need to reach out to Him. The reason being: That Adam's descendants (not all of humanity) were spiritually severed from God in a sense, when he and his wife betrayed Him. That is partially why most people do not naturally have a palpable connection to Him.

Be that as it may, each and every human being (not just Adam's descendants) on this Earth is covered by the sacrifice that Jesus Christ made, for His death was for the sake of peoples' souls no longer being excluded from the kingdom of heaven. This means the arguments of Christian denominations like the Church of God (Seventh-day Adventist), in their claim to the Passover ritual, are invalid. People who are not "saved", are people who have discounted themselves by their behaviours and the contents of their hearts.

(Be warned however: that although every man, woman, and child is automatically covered by God's sacrifice, those who hear of Jesus and then choose to reject Him after being informed, put themselves in significant danger of spiritual consequences. In rejecting Jesus and/or His sacrifice, you are throwing away something precious which God has granted you from birth.

A historical analysis of Christianity and the relatively few documents available could easily lead a person to believe that Jesus did not do for mankind what the Bible claims He did. However, I must tell you, that although the Bible has misinformed many a person on many other matters, on the matter of Jesus' sacrifice for mankind, there is truth. It is a truth which God has allowed me to see for myself.)

Now, look: because it is your spiritual level which allows you to channel God's power through prayer and faith, people who lack the spiritual level, typically lack the faith. This is why not just anybody can raise his hand and declare himself a spiritual healer or a "miracle worker".

Churches across the globe are filled with spiritually underdeveloped people who regularly claim that by faith, they can heal you, when they do not have the power or authority to do so, and it is stereotypical of such naïve children to walk with their egos inflated, thinking themselves "Holy". Take care not to follow in the footsteps of such individuals, for the pride that is apparent in them has been the downfall of many men.

Because it is commonplace for such self-important and presumptuous frauds to fail in their attempts to heal, they often resort to excuses. They say "you are healed" in the hopes that their empty affirmations will convince you to deceive yourself, but when failure is apparent even to their intended sheep they will shift the blame onto anything and everything. The suffering individual's "lack of faith" or "sinful nature" are the first options, but when those are untenable, these frauds will dare to say it is "in God's plan".

There has been for a long time, the consensus by a considerable number of people, that God is responsible for everything, and that everything that happens is in accordance with His will. "It is God's plan", they believe, but I am here to tell you that is a lie.

As I have written earlier, we all have free will. The freedom to do literally anything that we want to. Free will is responsible for most of what happens on this planet today, but I have come to find that religious people would rather use the argument of "God's plan" to validate inconsistencies in the Bible or to justify their own shortcomings in life. When such people fail to get a job or when they encounter some sort of problem in life, they say "Well, God must have not wanted that for me. Maybe He has something better in store for my life". When "something better" does not eventually come along, they inevitably become upset with God as if it is His responsibility to do for them what they could do for themselves. They would rather not acknowledge it was their own fault that the job interview did not go so well, or that it was their carelessness that lost them something they thought to be important.

The biggest problem with the ruse of "God's plan" though, is not the delusions of men and women who seek not to take responsibility for their lives. The biggest problem is the fact that when people say that something is "in accordance with God's plan", what they are in effect doing is saying: "God is responsible, so He is to blame if the outcome is not as desired". This can be a very dangerous claim, as it is used not only when people survive accidents, it is used as a reason when people die.

Sometimes the reason for a person being told "It was his/her time to be taken by God" can be in the hopes of consolation at the loss of a loved one, but it tends only to create the impression that God destroys the things we love with little regard for our emotional wellbeing or even our safety. Some people ask: "God, why did you take my brother away from me?", while others say: "God never gives us more than we can handle". They attribute the aforementioned and highly misused interpretation of scripture to their suffering, as if it is God who sends evil to afflict all mankind. As if He is responsible for all the murders, rapes, poverty, witchcraft, robbery, car accidents, diseases, famine, demonic-oppression, and depression going on in the world. The religious idea that "everything happens according to God's plan" is an idea of satan's own devising, so that God can take the blame for the evils in this world.

There are many people alive today who are angry at God that they have lost a loved one. They have been falsely led to believe that events such as peoples' deaths are in His plan, and that it is His doing when a loved one passes away. These are accusations of murder against God, and such accusations are very serious. God does not just kill people. The excuse that "it is God who did it", is exactly the kind of thing the devil likes to hear. After all, a benevolent God would never allow murderers, who commit unspeakable acts, to run free while innocent and very good people die continuously.

The nature and purpose of this thing we call "life", and God's association with it, are things which the Bible, in its state of such imperfection, has very much mischaracterised for humanity. Many people wind up saying: "If there is a God, then He doesn't care", or "…He must not be bothered by evil", because Christians are cherry-picking from their flawed and man-made agenda-driven Bibles, and mixing their cherry-pickings with erroneous preconceptions about God and life. They then advertise their misconceptions to other people. Many of whom become indoctrinated, and many of whom are pushed away. While doing this, religious Christians are also eradicating the very things which God has left with us for our wellbeing and protection. Things I will clarify in the final stages of the last chapter.

(The vast majority of atheists will point to all the inconsistencies in religious' peoples' claims of God being a certain kind of Person, and they will use such misunderstandings to declare that there must be no God. They do this because they lack the ability to separate such things from the matter of whether or not there is a God. The nature of God is a theological matter. Whether or not there is a God, is something else entirely, and it is something the evidence clearly demonstrates.)

This is why it is very dangerous for people to be deceived into believing that the Bible is the word of God. The concept of the Bible being the word of God, is a fabrication by manipulative people whose intent is to dictate to others how they are meant to live their lives, and to take advantage of said others.

(Atheism is largely the same thing. It is the substitution of one 'God' with another. It is for this reason, that many atheists seem very much to throw all manner of sense and logic away when discussing their atheism or when condemning the belief in God)

When a conman presents religious people with the declaration that the Bible is the word of God, and demands that they therefore follow him and his interpretations of Biblical text, he can get his followers to do anything. As long as he has shown to them that it is what the Bible says, they will do it, because they therefore think it is what God says. Religious institutions and the religious people harboured within them are easily swayed from side to side by deceptive evil spirits, because evil spirits love the idea of God's word, being declared to be where it is not.

When a Bible is believed to be the word of God by naïve people, the consequences of their acceptance of the scripture as such can be very damaging. To such religious people, the Bible is all the truth they need. They do not care about searching for the truth, because they believe God's infinite word can be limited to a small book. Notorious religious cults like

"The Branch Dividians", "Heavens Gate", "The Peoples Temple", "The Unification temple", "The Westboro Baptist Church". etc. are very good examples of some of the things that the devil aims to do with religious people and how the evil spirit tries to move through them.

It is common to see similarities between the ridiculous behaviour of cult members and those of similarly religious people who claim to be "working for The Lord", because it is the nature of evil made manifest in the form of religious dogma, to do and say ridiculous things. There are many churches which advocate beliefs in such a dogmatic fashion, and although most of them are not as extreme as those named above, they are all of the same religious mind-set of bigotry. I am glad that some of them have been imprudent enough to put themselves on television for all to see, so that people may be made aware of the caution which one should take before joining some churches.

Religious people and the cult leaders/fraudsters who deceive them, are under no contract with The Lord whatsoever, but they will claim that they are. How come? When you do not know anything about God how can you claim to know His will? The trickery of people who say they bring God's word, is the sole reason for the existence of religions like Islam.

Muslims believe Muhammad was a prophet only because he said he was, yet historical facts refute Muhammad's teachings and cast some undeniably serious doubt on his title as a prophet of any kind. The likes of David Koresh, L. Ron Hubbard (the creator of scientology), Jim Jones, Joseph Smith, and even Adolf Hitler, all share similarities with Muhammad in that they declared themselves to be some sort of God-ordained "prophet" or "messiah", yet have not been able to prophesy a single event, nor were they able to perform a single miracle other than the fact that they found people to follow them.

To this day there are people from around the world who are claiming to be the reincarnation of Jesus Christ, and to this day there are people around the world who follow and believe them. The primary determining factor for the acceptance of such false prophets by their followers is a lack of understanding of who Jesus Christ was, and who the Son of God was.

A person who can follow a delusional (or clever) conman who calls himself Jesus Christ is someone who has made the mistake of worshiping Jesus Christ **the man**, instead of **God** who incarnated Himself in the human form of Jesus Christ. When a criminal claims to be a prophet of God or a "chosen one", and when he finds people to believe him, he can (and he will) create all sorts of trouble.

Even Adolf Hitler, like all the many false prophets and evil-doers before and after him, found a way to use Christianity to justify his motives and actions, and there are many other people/organizations throughout history who have successfully used to the Bible to advocate the foolishness of things such as white supremacy. As a result, even in this day and age, there are people who believe that "only white people go to heaven".

If a creature as vile as a white supremacist "KKK" member, can get away with using the Bible to validate his stupidity, then anyone can use the Bible to do anything, and they will claim that it is God who sent them. That it is "in God's plan", or in "His will".

When the so-called "prophet" Muhammad left the cave and therefore the presence of what Muslims believe to be an angel, he was convinced that he had seen a demon. Not only that. He also believed himself to be demon-possessed and subsequently attempted to commit suicide more than twice. Any Muslim who endeavours to find out the truth about Islam will no doubt denounce their Islamic faith.

Do not make the mistake of believing religious Christians to be any different from religious Muslims though, because they are both religious, and they both have no valid reasons for believing in what they do, other than the fact that somebody has told them to believe. When you ask a religious Christian what proof he has that God exists or that his beliefs are sound he/she will point to the Bible and say, "Because the Bible says…", As if to imply that they are right simply because they say they are, and other people just have to agree.

The nature of religion is to strip people of logic and of sense, and a discussion or debate with any religious person will prove this to you. I am sure you have had such debates before, so I am also sure you have all the proof you need.

I once spoke to somebody who told me he used to be Christian, and that his parents raised him in a Christian home. However he said Christianity lost its appeal to him when one day he asked his uncle why it took God seven days to create the universe, and his uncle responded by calmly reprimanding him for the question in saying: "We do not ask such questions".

"That day, he destroyed all my faith bro, and at that point, I left Christianity alone and thought I might try Buddhism", he told me.

This highlights the main problem with all religion. It does not want you asking questions, especially the ones that it cannot answer. However it will, without much proof, expect you to believe the stories it has to tell you. In order to ensure people maintain their faith in these stories, religion tends to rely on fear and other forms of psychological manipulation to keep its followers loyal. Fortunately though, such tactics are not impervious to intelligent analyses.

This is why it is crucial to your wellbeing that you investigate the claims of any religion that is brought to you, and endeavour to dig into what it really teaches. If most evangelising, and religious Christians (like the Jehovah's Witnesses) questioned and properly tested the origins of their church doctrine, they would leave their churches in an instant. Fortunately and unfortunately, this can be seen happening in places all over the world, in the form of people who saw the ridiculous nature of religious dogma, and left Christianity for good, often embracing a new faith: atheism.

Only a few, are informed enough or intuitively know to make the distinction between religious Christianity, and the Christianity of Jesus Christ. This is because religion works hard to suppress people, mislead them, enslave them, and get them to spread their garbage to those around them. If it does not succeed in doing that, then through its oppressive and misleading ways, it tends to succeed in its other purpose: to build bitterness towards religion, build misplaced bitterness towards God, and push people away.

I mention religion as if to say it is alive, but it is obviously not a living organism or entity in the literal sense. Religion is merely a tool through which an individual or group of individuals, control people. It is the politics of blind faith personified, and designed only to pour delusions into the minds of its captives.

But then again, these delusions are oftentimes created by the captives themselves, in order to justify and rationalise their beliefs. This is not unusual, because anyone who does not actually understand what he/she chooses to believe, has to come up with some sort of explanation for it. And in the case of the religiously indoctrinated: some of these explanations are fear-driven. For example: the fear of "God".

The fear of punishment by God or not living "a proper life" is typically found in religious people with debilitating insecurities. People who feel guilty or pressured, for some reason into a religious lifestyle tend to be men and women who evidently, are unhappy with themselves.

I have seen so many people go through the torment of living life as a rigid rod, and therefore, isolating themselves from a life of happiness, naively believing they are only on this Earth to do what they claim is "worshiping God". To live in accordance with the Bible's every word, and to do so in a manner that starves them of a fruitful life. They forget that God allowed us to be born in the flesh for much more than that.

I have also seen that the majority of the kinds of people who go through extra pains to be religious are either the worst of people, or the most confused. Practitioners of witchcraft, for example go to church more than anyone else, and they tend to pray an awful lot when in the view of others. Straining their faces in an attempt to seem righteous or holy.

However people who have judged themselves to be unworthy or who believe that they are sinners, and struggle to forgive themselves of past deeds, as well are commonly found to be the most religious. The lowest common denominator between most religious people is fear. Fear that they will disappoint their parents, fear that they will disappoint their church, or fear that they will disappoint their "God".

Do not become afraid and seek to start living a highly strict lifestyle just because you feel you must be on "the right path". Remember: the spirit of deception capitalises on fear, and fear is a large part of what religion is all about. Speak to God, receive the Holy Spirit, and truth will gradually make itself known to you.

Understand that being a good person (a good person, not a naïve one) and living life to the best of your ability are things that will reward you. God understands why many people claim not to believe or why they believe in the wrong God. Jehovah is a fair God, so you will be judged according to your situation and your life's decisions.

Do not pressure yourself into a religious lifestyle of unproductiveness and servitude to a power men have conceived for you, because when your life is over and you see for yourself what lies in wait for you on the other side, you will regret having wasted your opportunities here on Earth to do something meaningful. A wasteful manner is how religions like Islam expect people to experience their lives, so it is no surprise that a lot of Muslims (particularly those who do not reside in Islamic nations), are only Muslim by name and not by practice.

This is because most Muslims recognise that Islam is not doing anything of notability for them. They do not see any miracles, they are not being satisfied in accordance with Islam's claims, and it offers no proof that "Allah" even has the right to be held in any high regard. Christians on the other hand frequently report miracles. Even when neglecting the liars and the religiously immature, you will find that the number of miracles with proof and witnesses, testified by Christians is many times more than the number of such claims by Muslims.

Muslims say that Islam is the fastest-growing religion in the world, and will attempt to use such a claim as a testament to its validity, but in fact Islam is only growing because many Muslim nations are third-world countries, where birth rates are high. Not only that, but Islam allows Muslims to subscribe to polygamy, so more children are born to Muslim households than would be the case if every Muslim was in a monogamous relationship. Also, most Islamic nations are persecuting and restricting anyone who is non-Muslim in their countries. No one is allowed to share or openly display any religious beliefs apart from those that are Islamic, in Islamic nations. Other nations on the other hand, allow Muslims and anyone of any faith to spread within them freely.

Ironically, Muslim people generally do not desire to stay in Islamic nations. Why? Well, because the manner in which Islamic nations are governed more or less reflects a slightly watered down manner in which Muhammad would have liked the nations to be governed. Needless to say, this slightly watered down manner is still a highly potently oppressive one. Even to Muslims. This is why more people are migrating from places like Saudi Arabia, than those who are migrating to it.

The only people to move to Islamic nations are foreign workers who need money, and are willing to risk their well-being for it.

Under the Islamic law of Muslim nations like Saudi Arabia (where Islam is practiced most authentically), leaving Islam results in the death penalty by public beheading, and any kind of 'blasphemy' against the religion leads to the same punishment. A more gruesome fate awaits perpetrators of "lesser" crimes, however. Adultery for example, leads to one being publically stoned to death. Uttering even a single sentence against the religion will easily get you killed, and the oppression is worse for women in Islam.

Islam teaches that women are like domestic animals (The History of al-Tabari Volume 9, and Number 1754), that a woman is not different from a dog or a donkey (Sahih al-Bukhari, Volume 1, Book 9, and Number 490), that men are in charge of women, and that men can beat their wives (Qur'an 4:34). Islam also teaches that women are deficient in intellect, are morally inferior to men, and are more likely to go to hell than men (Sahih al-Bukhari, Volume 1, Book 6, and Number 301). Women in Islam are by far the most oppressed women in the world, but the ever-present danger of public execution is surprisingly good at preventing criticism by them, let alone apostasy. It is no wonder that the number of Muslims defecting from Islamic nations is so high.

When Muslims arrive in parts of the world like the United States of America, where they can practice Islam as they wish (i.e. not as Muhammad intended), they do so. Most of them do not wear their traditional clothes, the women do not hide their bodies with cloth, they make friends with non-Muslims, etc. After a generation or so living in the U.S., being allowed to abandon much of their religion in practice, and doing their best to forget about their oppressive religion, some Muslims might try and convert a few people by living peacefully with non-Muslims and deceiving their new friends by claiming Islam is peaceful. After a very small number of Americans have converted to Islam, Muslims will then say "You see? People are being converted".

Before I rebuke the quoted statement above, think about the following for a second: Islam is so oppressive and inherently repulsive, that countries which impose its laws (Sharia laws), are inadvertently forcing Muslims to leave them and go to places where they finally have the free will to twist the doctrine of Islam in order to be able to practice it both with a clean conscience and with the ability to spread lies about Islam being peaceful, which then leads to the unlikely but still real possibility of other people converting to Islam.

Muslim women have to leave Islamic nations just so they no longer have to hide their faces, and just so that they can finally drive a car or be romantically involved with a non-Muslim man. They have to leave the system of Islamic governance just so they never have to live in fear of being punished (beaten) by the courts or killed by members of society, for being the "defiled" victims of rape by one or more men.

Upon arrival in countries like the U.S. where "liberals" can side with the erroneous notion that "Islam is peace", and a small number of people therefore can become converts, it is funny that in spite of the aid from mainstream media lies, Islam largely fails to take off amongst people. You see: about 75% of all the converts to Islam in the U.S. leave the religion within three years.

This is because in Western civilizations people have the basic human right of questioning religious doctrine. When you mix such a human right with the access to things like the Qur'an and the Hadiths, the end-result is a rejection of Islam and its evil. The only Muslims outside of Islamic nations who are not being forced to be Muslim, are those who seem content with the religious label, but do not concern themselves any further with anything related to the religion. They therefore do not practice the religion, or bother to know what the Qur'an and Hadiths say.

When you tell most Muslim women in the U.S. that Islam oppresses women, they will deny it. After you show them the proof, they will still probably deny it and then proceed to say "the Qur'an must be read in Arabic instead of English". When you tell Muslim women in Islamic nations that Islam oppresses women, they will commonly defend their oppression by citing how inferior they are to men, how men are smarter than them, how men provide for the family, etc.

Fundamentally, Islam is growing because the religion oppresses non-

Muslims in its nations and threatens all who would dare leave, with death. Islam is also growing because many people are being born in Muslim households. Compounding this is the fact that in Islamic nations, non-Muslim women who marry Muslim men are being forced to convert to Islam, whereas Muslim women who are even seen with a man of another faith are killed. As I have said: the number of people who are leaving Islam very far outweighs the number of misled members of the human race who are converting to it.

To further ridicule the claim that "Islam is the fastest growing religion, so it is the most valid religion", is the fact that although Islam is growing due to the factors I have mentioned, the rate at which people are being born as Muslims is far less than the rate at which people are being born as non-Muslims. For there are many more non-Muslims on the planet than there are Muslims. Therefore, with every passing year, the percentage of Muslim people on this Earth is getting smaller and smaller. The number is growing, but the global percentage is shrinking. Islam… is shrinking.

Even within the demographic of people who are considered Muslim by birth or through forceful conversion, there is a very (very) high number of individuals who reject Islam. In the Western parts of the world these people refrain from declaring their apostasy primarily because of ostracism by family, friends, and their society. In conformity to the nature of Islam, many Muslims will disown their children and cut ties with them for leaving the religion. In Arab nations however, where Islam is practiced more closely to the way it was intended by Muhammad, all Ex-Muslims are killed for their betrayal. Ostracism is the least of many Muslims' concerns.

Even in Western civilizations there are many, many unreported cases of people being killed by their family members for leaving Islam. Whether the apostate is a middle-aged man or a teenage girl, he/she must be put to death, according to Islamic law. The truth is: there are many millions of Muslims who have secretly apostatised from the religion, because it is easy to see that Islam exists to oppress and to kill. Not to bring peace to anyone.

In fact, "Islam" and "peace" are things which are diametrically opposed to each other, and anybody who takes the time to carefully study both the Qur'an and the Hadiths, will not be able to deny that Islam is a big lie, wrapped around some nonsense, and coated in sparsely distributed truths. They will know that Islam can never be seen as a religion of peace, for the "God" of the Qur'an is a satanic tyrant, and in accordance with the nature of a satanic tyrant, he promotes hatred, slavery, death, and ignorance.

Having said that, let me make something clear: There is a big difference between most Muslims, and the kind of people that their religion would like them to be. The religion of Islam is of an immensely diabolical and controlling nature, but the Muslim people I have met, were all for the most part well-mannered and respectful people.

However, this is not because those Muslim people were of Islam. You see: most Muslim people, are not of Islam. A very (very) high percentage of Muslims know almost nothing about their religion. They were born in Muslim households, and that is good enough reason for them to continue to claim to be Muslim.

They are good people, but as long as they are good people, they can never be of Islam. Rather, they will be practicing a different religion which they have created for themselves. Those who follow Islam as it was intended, are the ones of whom we hear committing horrible crimes against innocent people, beheading "non-believers", abusing women, and blowing themselves up for seventy-two virgins. The "prophet" Muhammad's history is a history that all good Muslims are surprisingly ignorant of, because most Muslims believe for the sake of believing, just as ignorant religious Christians do. They are spiritually numb, and lost in a forest of lies.

As Yusuf al-Qaradawi (one of the Middle-East's most prominent Islamic leaders) said: 'Were it not for the fact that leaving Islam is punishable by death, the religion would not exist today'.

Chapter Five: A MATTER OF UNDERSTANDING

Cause, Effect and Our Spirituality

After many pages, this is where it becomes important that you have understood what the meaning of life is. As I have shown you, purpose is inherent to all things in the world around us, for it is the central metaphysical principle around which all things, both animate and inanimate are based. This is an integral component of what constitutes the spiritual dimension, and once you understand this one thing, you can begin to understand a lot more of what occurs around you.

"Purpose" pertains to the action something performs. However when that something is attributed to anything with the ability to think, "intent" becomes its precursor. For example: when a stone flies across a field, its purpose is that very action, but if it was a human being who threw that stone, the stone's purpose was an intent beforehand.

In the spirit realm, intent can effect a purpose as well, because the physical world is built around spiritual dynamics. When God created the universe, it was His intent that brought everything into being. His energy manifested everything we see in our physical universe in the spiritual sense first, and therefore the universe can be seen as a 'mirror image' of what exists in the spiritual realm.

All things in existence are energy. What is seen, as well as what is not. So we too are beings composed of energy. The difference between us and a grain of sand, is that we have the ability to manipulate the energy around us and have it serve a purpose in accordance with our intents, as we are cognizant. In a sense, we can do some of what God does, but on a somewhat infinitely smaller scale in comparison. This is because God is a sentient being, and His ability to think and manipulate is an ability given to all other sentient beings to various extents.

Now it is a fact that you cannot get something from nothing. When energy is detected in one form (for example: heat), it must first have been in another form, and before that, another form, and a form before that, until traced to the beginning of time, where it can be seen that the primal source of all energy in the universe is God: its Creator.

All things exist in the spirit first, before they do materially. The ability to change spiritual energy into such a form that it manifests physically, requires a lot of power, and given what we have around us, you can easily see why God will forever hold the title as the most powerful.

The fact that God has the ability to create via His intent, means so can we. God is a spirit, and He operates on certain principles, some of which we as well do. In the spirit realm our intentions hold a lot more power than in the physical world, because things in this physical dimension are generally in a state that could have only come into being by meeting and/or exceeding certain energy or activity thresholds.

Remember that nothing can be gained from nothing, and that all energy merely changes form from one to another. For God to create a tangible universe, He first does so in the spirit, as He is a spiritual being. Because he has enough power and technical expertise, he can establish a physical realm of existence where all things operating or existing within a given spectrum of constraints reside.

Creation is very much a science, and God is the ultimate scientist. He is no magician. His abilities are such that they fall very far outside of our ability to comprehend as spirits created by Him, but He is highly methodical in the things He does, and these things can all be explained scientifically.

Luckily for us, what we are capable of understanding is sufficient to influence the world around us both spiritually and physically. In the spirit realm, our intents effect a purpose, and if the energy attributed to our intents is significant enough, this purpose can manifest physically and objectively. Belief and intent are two components of a person's spiritual ability without which, no purpose can be effected by him/her.

Our beliefs are responsible for many things, and potentially have the power to cause certain events or even prevent said events from taking place. The saying: "Just believe it will work", has origins in this realization, and the mechanism behind the 'placebo effect' is this very fact also.

Our ability to manifest our intents is why people who merely believe they would get better or well while suffering from an ailment, stand a much higher chance of healing, and of doing so more quickly, than those inclined to pessimism or those who seem indifferent.

We are our own minds, and the power of our minds dictates the power of our selves. Part of the reason that most people are spiritually weak, is that they are mentally weak as well. The brain and the mind are separate things. The brain is a biological support system for, and a facilitator of, the mind, but it is the mind that accepts reason. Even if said reason was falsely derived by the brain. You can think of it this way: the brain is computer hardware constituting an architecture such that computer programs can be executed by its means.

The brain is also a system that manages these programs, as the brain allows us to store and manipulate data from a physiological standpoint for the means of a world dependant on physicality. The mind is more closely linked to spiritualism. Most people are cut off from the spiritual aspects of their existence, but only as much as their ability to recognise their spirituality goes unnoticed by them.

The intelligence of an individual dictates his/her capacity to identify and distinguish spiritual things from 'ordinary' ones in a given time frame, as well as to explain them. In our bodies there are several mechanics at work, and many of them are non-physical. People who can uncover this fact, are people who endeavoured to explore to that effect, or those who subconsciously have recognised these things.

Remember that 'reality' is a term for the world around us relative to our perceptions, and because everyone sees things from their own mind, reality is not absolute. Everyone has their own world, and this is why a person's ability to explain something which has been personalised, to another person (particularly if these things are not ordinarily perceived objectively), corresponds to his/her intelligence.

In my experience (and those of many other people, I am sure), most people just lack the insight and understanding to be able to explain and adequately illustrate phenomena they believe to be specific to their realities, especially if these phenomena are detected from a more subconscious apprehension.

This is why many things of the spirit realm and those pertaining to individuals and their discoveries cannot usually be easily explained by said individuals in a manner that makes it clear and easily replicable. Everyone has a different experience and interpretation of life as well as the spirit realm. The best way for anyone to learn and self-actualise, is by seeing things through their own eyes, and not attempting to comprehend them mainly through the eyes of other people.

There are people who go to universities without really thinking about what they are doing, and some of them battle all sorts of adversities amidst their attempts to make it in the academic world, but most of these people do not genuinely have an interest in the things which universities were actually built for, and they see universities as a means of achieving something else (like money). Their incentives are disconnected from the original purpose of academic institutions, and this is why there is a large number of university graduates in various faculties who do not actually possess the competency that is required of them in their respective fields. In fact, the vast majority of university graduates obtain their degrees while having learnt nearly nothing, apart from the ability to copy and regurgitate information.

The problems associated with the mentality of people who venture into a field of study for reasons other than genuine interest, are in some ways the very same problems many people face when they hope for something, or even when they pray to God. When we pray to God, our intentions matter a great deal more than the words we use. If our spoken words do not correspond with our intentions, the prayer can become invalidated in several respects.

For example: People tend to go through life clinging onto misbeliefs about "righteousness", "humility" and "what it means to be a good person", which they have absorbed through films and other media. These misbeliefs are contrary to what many people know to be true at the subconscious and spiritual level. A person's prayers, when influenced by such things will not reflect what his/her spirit wishes to say, but rather will reflect what he/she thinks people of this world would accept or resonate with.

As mentioned earlier: our intents carry with them, energy. This is how spirits can communicate with each other without the need for an artificial language. When people express themselves in an audible language, they tend to be expressing intentions in the spiritual sense as well. A spoken sentence in an artificial language is only an encapsulation of a message intended to be decoded by the recipient, and may or may not contain information that relates to the true intentions of the sender.

However in the spirit realm, our intentions are almost always conveyed clearly, regardless of what exactly we say in the form of an audible language. Some people are aware of this in the form of certain feelings or energy signals they perceive to be radiated when communicating with other people. These signals are themselves energy signatures which may contain very exact information about a person's intentions.

Potentially, energy is matter, and this is why as spiritual beings, our ability to manipulate spiritual information and energy, means we have the ability to create. In relation to our metaphysical constituencies, and their bearing on reality, I have shown (in The Meaning of Life section) that every one of our thoughts and conceptions, however intangible, is something which exists.

It may not exist in our objective reality until it meets the criteria of the various constraints pertaining to our world, but it will still exist, and by virtue of this, as well as the fact that our realities are subjective, there are many other realities in existence.

These realities are dimensions of which there is an infinite number, and many are dramatically different from what any of us have ever seen before. However there are also worlds which serve as almost exact replicas of our physical universe, with attributes just as similar.

In the science of theoretical physics there have been some rather unnerving and sometimes controversial discoveries pertaining to this, and several other facts. This is because 'science' is composed of the recognition and analyses of relational information, so as also to be able to predict possible outcomes of their interactions based on given data. There are various scientific models for interpreting phenomena in our known universe, because different things have different rules. There is no one-size-fits-all scientific model for anything.

For example: the science of geography is different from the science of physics and mathematics, but they are interlinked with each other and additional sciences to constitute an entire system of properties and mechanisms inherent to our world. Modern science has a lot of work to do before it can begin to explain certain spiritual things, for it has a lot of work to do before it even comes close to being able to define most of what constitutes our physical universe.

So far, most of us can only scientifically explain spiritual things that have something to do with our objective reality and universe. For example: ghosts needing to meet standards within a spectrum of perceptibility in order to affect our world to varying degrees, or in order to be seen.

You see, for an entity to exist in a given world, it must abide by its rules, for it is these very rules that create and define the world. The parameters of what constitutes a world cannot be contravened, so even when something appears to most people as "magic" or "impossible", it really is not. This is why I say there is no such thing as 'the supernatural'. There is an explanation for everything, no matter how complex or simple.

Our world is made up of spiritual components, and is host to the dynamics that pertain to them, so it must be understood that there are correlations between the physical and the spiritual. Things in the spirit realm do affect things in the physical realm, and we are in fact affected everyday by occurrences in the world which are unseen by most people.

For example: I am sure you are familiar with the term 'intuition': The acquisition of information by somebody, apparently without having gone through the cognitive process of its derivation. Our intuitions and various other sensations can in large part be due to our spiritual awareness.

That strange feeling people get when they walk into an area not otherwise unusual, the arbitrary sensation of being watched that a person can sometimes acquire, the "bad/good vibe" about a person that can be felt by someone else, and even the spontaneous or unexplained predictions of some future events, are all examples of our spiritual senses allowing for the transfer of information to us.

It is your sensitivities that will govern the severity of such experiences. Of course, there are psychological factors to which many instances and experiences of "feeling strange" can be solely attributed, but unless you are regularly paranoid, or prone to delusion, these experiences are more than just in your mind.

We are all to some extent, spiritually aware whether we believe that to be the case or not. This means we all have the potential to be psychic or clairvoyant, and anyone who practices certain facets of their "mysticism" (as some people call it), will advance their capabilities. The more sensitive to, and aware of, spiritualism a person is, the greater his/her ease of being able to perceive such things.

I must remind you that being a good person has nothing to do with your ability to utilize your spirituality. Even when one's spiritual abilities are predicated upon a power source whose description confines it to being either good or evil, such things are generally a non-factor.

This is why there are witches. Our abilities as spiritual beings can be likened to guns: Just as it is not the gun that kills, but rather the person who uses it, it is not the spiritual ability that does good or bad, but the person by whom it is manipulated.

The ability to prophesy for example, is something which both good and bad people can practice. One of the reasons that venturing into spiritualism and its various sectors is dangerous, especially to the poorly informed, is that even the devil can predict what is going to happen, or grant you the ability to do the same.

Demons can prophesy as well as any other spirit can, so it is not every soothsayer who should be trusted merely because they have told you some truth about the future. And in that same sense, people who use Ouija boards and encounter spirits that claim to be whoever they may claim to be, ought not be doing such things.

Using those kinds of tools and attempting to contact spirits has been the cause of many terrible things in many homes. Hauntings tend to begin by interactions between naïve people and the spirits who would attempt to exploit them. People who lack the jurisdiction to be exploring the spirit realm in such a manner tend to find out the hard way, that most of the entities residing on "the other side" do not cater to anyone's interests but their own.

While on the topic of not catering to anyone else's interests, let me also tell you that there are thousands of scam artists and conmen claiming to have the gifts of precognition or psychic ability. So much so, that they very far outnumber the people who really do have these abilities. You see, psychologically, people tend to believe only what they want to believe, and this is why the nuisance of the horoscope scam for example, is so popular.

There has not been one single valid test of a horoscope's accuracy which has been passed, but still there are millions of people who have been tricked into believing there is divinity in the arbitrary transmission of mass-produced messages that claim to be personalised to individuals. Such naivety by innocent people just looking for something to believe, or hope for, is the reason the business of fake palm readers and 'psychic' charlatans is so lucrative.

It is a fact that everything in the universe is connected somehow. This connection is such that certain events are dependent on others, and the properties of specific things can be used to make predictions about them. A person's name, birthday, gender, etc. are of spiritual significances, but the mass-produced nature of horoscopes and the fact that they take only a person's month of birth into account, makes them completely fraudulent.

And unfortunately, even amongst the population of people who do have powers of precognition, and can inform you about spiritualism, there are criminals. Some soothsayers are evil doers, and mostly use their abilities to benefit only themselves. It is common to find that these people have employed the abilities and powers of an evil spirit in order to do what they do.

Sometimes, when you visit such people, you leave their presence more damaged than you were before you sought their counsel, for it is the nature of evil to destroy. When you go to tell them you are having a "run of bad luck", they might make your luck worse, while claiming to have helped you (for a fee of course), and when you return to them to tell them how things have not changed for the better, they will keep you as a ready source of income by lying to you about how a certain amount of visits are required before they can remove your curses, or how you need to pay a certain fee for whatever reason they will give you.

These people can place curses on you or replace your current problems with different ones, just so you will keep seeing them. Sometimes the evil spirits which trouble them, they will try and pass onto you in order to be rid of such spirits. So be careful of fortune tellers and soothsayers, because most are charlatans (especially in the Western world, where 99.9% are crooks), and some are just evil people who happen to have spiritual abilities. Those who are good, usually have good reputations. So if you can, enquire with other people about their experiences.

There are many good practitioners of the 'spiritual arts' who help people and do not operate by a source of evil, but there are also those who do operate through evil spirits, so you must be careful as to whose help you would enlist for the purposes of spiritual healing or inquiry. Some people become cursed because they sought help from devils who promised them "riches" or "victory" over their enemies.

One of the many possible reasons people encounter misfortune in their lives is the influence of a curse. To clarify what exactly a curse is: it is the act of wishing harm upon somebody. When someone says "I hope", he/she expresses an intention, and if this intent has enough momentum, it can have an effect.

Our ability to create through intent means we can have a wide range of affects. Because everything in existence is composed of energy, our thoughts and intentions are energy forms as well. This means that theoretically, we can create almost anything with them. The easiest things to manifest are those things which are abstract in nature, because our thoughts are abstract in origin.

When you seek vengeance and wish harm upon anyone for whatever reason, you generate an energy form that may or may not have an effect, depending on many things, and if it does not affect the individual, the energy must still go somewhere. Generally, it will come back to you, and as if having built momentum along the way, it will hit harder.

Our beliefs can manifest many things, and this is why it is important that you be a head-strong individual. There are a lot of lies floating around, and unless you know the differences – the facts – you can fall victim to all sorts of things. I have heard people say "If you stand for nothing, you will fall for everything".

Misapprehensions of a New Generation

Jesus said in John, Verse 3, and Chapter 12: "If I have told you earthly things and you do not believe, how can you believe if I tell you heavenly things?", yet the pompous religious conmen disguised as leaders, and the naïve people who follow them, dare to say that the Bible is the only source of truth. And beyond that, they claim the Bible to be the source of **all** truth because it is "God's word".

Misinformation is very common, and the fact that it masquerades as the truth, means people who do not test it become deceived. Anybody can claim to be anybody, and say anything, expecting you to believe them because they have told you so.

The problem, is that the concept of the Bible being "the word of God", is a grand deception by people who work by means of an abusive, misleading entity called religion, which seeks control through trickery and dogma. It does not serve the interests of anyone other than the people who made it up and spread it.

The Holy Spirit may have inspired most of the concepts and ideas in the Bible, but the men who shared what the various concepts and ideas in Biblical text, under the influence of the Holy Spirit were human, just as you are. Anyone who has the Holy Spirit dwelling within them, will receive subtle communications by it, telling him/her whether something is wrong or right, or guiding him/her in other ways.

The words I have written in this book have been given to me by the Holy Spirit, and my experiences have been afforded to me by the Holy Spirit, so my words are truth and inspired by God. However my words are not God's words. No one speaks the words of the Almighty but the Almighty Himself.

People who say that the Bible is the word of God because the Holy Spirit has inspired it, are implying that they themselves do not have the Holy Spirit in them to inspire them to speak truth. The Holy Spirit does not discriminate, but religious people are clearly of the opinion that it does.

Religious people think they know everything because they have read the Bible, but if they had to be placed in an examination room and quizzed by truth personified, they would all score abysmally low. The Bible does not hold or contain within it, any significant fraction of the real truth out there. It is a book which serves as a reliable (for the most part) historical documentation of events that occurred on our planet, and it is a book which serves a socio-political control mechanism. Much more than that, the Bible is not. It contains some very important information, but if the Bible was all we needed, God would have stopped communicating with us after its numerous publications.

Quite a few of the Old Testament's authors were themselves aware that it is not everything they could share in their texts. There are things in the Bible which to this day, puzzle scholars, priests, and laypeople alike because they were not sufficiently revealed. This is because some things are best left for individuals to stumble upon on their own, while others should never be made known. There are large bodies of information which God has shown me, that I could never share, merely because it would be more detrimental to people than it would be beneficial. Also there many things I cannot share here merely because 'time' is constraint I adhere to.

Now you are likely to already know, that religious Christian people are in the habit of advocating certain ideas, because they believe the Bible to be in insinuated agreement with them. Statements like: "God did not make any aliens", and "The Earth is only 6000 years old", they believe to be true because "The Bible does not mention Aliens", or "The Bible says so" (even though it does not).

However, the Bible does not mention microwave ovens or children's jumping castles either, yet these things are in existence, and to no one's amazement. "The Bible does not speak of (insert phenomenon or object here)" religious people say, and to that, any sensible person would respond: "So what?" There are many things happening in the world today that most Christians would not believe, even if God Himself were to tell them, only because these things go against what they have been led to believe all their lives.

The spirit realm for example, is not as many Christians believe. Many of them will die, only to be disappointed that there is no heaven for them. There is in fact a heaven, but most people will not be able to enter such a kingdom because they will not be qualified. They think going to church, paying their tithes, or performing The Annual Passover ritual, will guarantee the gates of Heaven open for them, but a massive surprise is waiting to greet such people.

This does not mean they will go to hell, as hell is a place reserved for abominable creatures (some of whom are behind the British monarchy and the U.S. presidency), but it does mean that they will be going to places other than heaven. There is a place for every kind of person, and largely the spirit realms are open for spirits to travel through at whim. Hell is there, and it waits for those who deserve it.

Something else people are quite misinformed about is God. People think that they understand God. That they know Him. But no one has ever seen God the Father except God the Son. Not any angel, not any demon, and not any demigod. Yet religious men and women confine God to their ignorance, and hold Him to a standard of their limited capacity for reason by thinking they have Him all figured out. They love to keep God right where they are comfortable putting Him: in a box of their own misunderstandings and fabrications.

Naïve religious people may take scripture like this: "If you had known me, you would have known my Father also. From now on you do know him and have seen him (in John Chapter 14, and Verse 7)", and declare that it means the people literally saw and knew God, when it is clear that Jesus was merely stating that He and God the Father are one.

In seeing and knowing Jesus Christ, His disciples came to know an aspect of God, because Jesus Christ represents Him. Jesus is God, because God the Father, God the Son, and God the Holy Spirit, are a coherent entity representing one Eternal Creator. The above-statement's meaning is analogous to how we as God's creations, are composed of both a soul and a spirit. Without your soul, you cannot be. And neither can you be, without your spirit. You are your soul as well as your spirit, so if a person saw your soul they would not have seen you, but they would have seen an aspect of you. Just as your spirit and your soul are distinct from one another and yet constitute the same being, God the Father, God the Son, and God the Holy Spirit, are the three distinct aspects of God the Creator.

Because God is so greatly misunderstood by the religious mind, it is also a commonly held religious belief that once upon a time there was God, all by himself when suddenly, He thought "Hey, let me create many solar systems, galaxies, this enormous universe, and on only one little planet, shall I create life". Furthermore, the tendency is to believe that He did this all in only six Earth days.

What proponents of the aforementioned belief seem not understand, is that God is infinite beyond our comprehension, and there are countless things that even the first angels do not know. The story of God and Creation is inconceivably complex and immense. God's day, represents an age: A long passage of time. It is not an Earth-day, for an Earth-day is the time measured in hours of 24 units that the Earth takes to revolve once about its axis. Days on other planets are very different. One day on Jupiter for example, is more than 4 330 Earth-days.

Our time is not God's time, because in the spirit realm there is not really such a thing as time. Time is a construct pertaining to physical existentialism, and is exclusive to physical existentialism. The Bible does not say so, but it is true. The Book of Genesis' account of creation is flawed and cannot be taken literally. The history of our planet alone (never mind the universe) is far deeper than what the Bible could ever even begin to cover.

You cannot compress something as vast as the history of all mankind and planet Earth, into a book as small as The Bible. Studies of Earth's Geology indicate that the Earth is very old indeed, and that it has been through a lot of changes. Yes, the method of finding the ages of fossils and rocks by radiometric dating is indeed a highly flawed and often very inaccurate one, and results in wild and sensational conclusions by people who do not know as much as they wish they did. And yes, the Earth **is not** millions of years old (which is why soft tissue has been found in dinosaur bones), but claims of rocks being many tens of thousands of years old are not nearly as removed from the truth as some Christian fundamentalists believe.

As alluded to in my previous mentions of Adam and Eve: the history of mankind as well, is not all detailed in the Bible. People speak of Adam and Eve as being the first human beings ever to walk to Earth, but they were not. In fact, the Bible contradicts itself to reveal that Adam and Eve were not the first human beings ever created. When Cain killed his brother Abel (Adam's and Eve's only other son) and found himself banished, he expressed to God concern that other people would see the mark He put on him, and that they would try to kill him too. God however, assured Cain that no one would kill him, and Cain subsequently left His presence to settle in the land of Nod, where he met his wife, who bore him a son they called Enoch.

Genesis Chapter 4, and Verses 1 to 17: "Now Adam knew Eve his wife, and she conceived and bore Cain, saying, "I have gotten a man with the help of the Lord." And again, she bore his brother Abel. Now Abel was a keeper of sheep, and Cain a worker of the ground. In the course of time Cain brought to the Lord an offering of the fruit of the ground, and Abel also brought of the firstborn of his flock and of their fat portions. And the Lord had regard for Abel and his offering, but for Cain and his offering he had no regard. So Cain was very angry, and his face fell. The Lord said to Cain, "Why are you angry, and why has your face fallen? If you do well, will you not be accepted? And if you do not do well, sin is crouching at the door. Its desire is for you, but you must rule over it." Cain spoke to Abel his brother. And when they were in the field, Cain rose up against his brother Abel and killed him. Then the Lord said to Cain, "Where is Abel your brother?" He said, "I do not know; am I my brother's keeper?" And the Lord said, "What have you done? The voice of your brother's blood is crying to me from the ground. And now you are cursed from the ground, which has opened its mouth to receive your brother's blood from your hand. When you work the ground, it shall no longer yield to you its strength. You shall be a fugitive and a wanderer on the earth." Cain said to the Lord, "My punishment is greater than I can bear. Behold, you have driven me today away from the ground, and from your face I shall be hidden. I shall be a fugitive and a wanderer on the earth, and whoever finds me will kill me." Then the Lord said to him, "Not so! If anyone kills Cain, vengeance shall be taken on him sevenfold." And the Lord put a mark on Cain, lest any who found him should attack him. Then Cain went away from the presence of the Lord and settled in the land of Nod, east of Eden. Cain knew his wife, and she conceived and bore Enoch. When he built a city, he called the name of the city after the name of his son, Enoch".

If Adam, Eve, Cain, and Abel were the only human beings around, where did the other people come from? In attempts to try and hide the contradictory nature of Genesis, some Christians (of the few who are aware of it) make claims that Cain slept with his sister or niece in order to give birth to Enoch. This claim of course does not answer the question of which other people Cain was referring to when God put the mark on him, but it is also invalidated by the fact that it is just a claim.

The Bible does not say or even indicate that Cain slept with his sister, but because some Christians are desperate to cling onto things they have been led to believe their whole lives (e.g. that Adam and Eve were the first humans), they feel that they must find a way by all means to reconcile any and all contradictions they find in the Bible by making things up.

God did in fact create people before He made Adam and Eve, but Adam and Eve were the first of a different generation of human beings. A generation whose existence was necessitated by, and proceeded, the fall of Lucifer and some of the things he got up to since then.

Before Adam's creation, the devil was found guilty of impersonating God before men, and receiving worship from them as if he were God. Consequentially, satan was demoted from his appointed position in the heavens, and the bitterness of this defeat never left him. So he endeavoured to ruin much of what God had created. When Eve encountered satan in the Garden of Eden, the meeting presented itself as another opportunity to tarnish something God had made, and the devil seized the opportunity to convince Eve, who then convinced Adam to eat the apple God had forbidden them from consuming.

As I am sure you know, before the Bible's interjection into Africa, the indigenous people had spiritual practices of their own. There were beings whom they prayed to, and from time to time they would perform various ceremonies in honour of these spirits. However, the arrival of the West saw most of that destroyed and replaced with the teachings of Christianity. The Westerners taught the people they were colonising that what the people were doing was wrong, and that they were committing crimes against God. Their "juju"/"voodoo" items were encouraged to be destroyed, and many of them were convinced by the Christian converts among them to cease their practices.

Ultimately, this wound up doing far more damage than good, and is the reason witchcraft is now a common thing in Africa. You see, as I have pointed out: religious people are spiritually ignorant and naïve. They do not operate on fact, and in spite of personal experience indicating to them the unfruitfulness of their beliefs, they defy logic over and over again by refusing to learn.

It is the nature of religion to nullify intellect, and it is the nature of religious people to act in accordance with such a nullification. This is the reason witches and warlocks have such an advantage over most religious people. Demons lie all the time, but when it comes to teaching someone how to destroy, they tell the truth. You cannot destroy something effectively if you do not have the facts about it.

People who practice witchcraft and consult with evil spirits know enough about the spirit realm to be able to do the things that they do. They have the facts. They understand the dynamics involved and they know what it takes to manipulate something spiritually. Most Christians on the other hand do not seem to know anything about anything, and their ignorance is a representation of their shallow understanding in Christianity.

Spiritualism, is something which has been severely misrepresented to most people by religion, and because people do not understand the spiritual dimensions of our existence or the nature of spirits, they are not aware of how to protect themselves spiritually. Not anymore, at least.

Most people do not seem to fully understand that **God does not forsake His people**. Despite your average Christian's readiness to utter and accept that highlighted statement, your average Christian does not know that before the Bible's introduction, God was still with his creations in Africa, as well as other parts of the world. Still watching over them and monitoring their activities.

Please do not think for even the slightest significant lapse of time, that because God favours only his European creations, He blessed them with a Bible and ordered them to enslave and torture innocent people in other nations so that they too may have a book called the Bible. Such an idea is ridiculous, and it is the very idea insinuated by anyone who says "Without the Bible, you cannot be saved". It is an idea of the devil's.

An infinitely kind and just God would not leave a portion of the men and women He created in His very own image to suffer eternal damnation by virtue of the fact that they were not born with a Bible around them. If the God you believe in would do just that, then I must inform you that your God does not exist.

God was with humanity before the Bible, in many ways. As I have discussed before, an aspect of the nature of spirituality and of God, is the act of performing rituals. This is why the ritual of Jesus Christ's sacrifice had to be performed in order to free humanity from sin and its imprisonment. In chemistry, when you react element/compound 'A' with element/compound 'B', there is an effect.

The aforementioned reaction will yield a specific result because there are properties inherent to each element or compound specifically, such that when mixed together in a certain way there is a certain outcome. Remember that objects in the physical realm have spiritual properties and such properties are unique to them, as everything exists in the spiritual sense first.

Different types of plants or rocks have different spiritual attributes, for example. When you mix certain things together and under specific conditions, the result of their mixture is manifested in the spiritual realm as well as the physical, and the spiritual consequences can be good or bad depending on its intended use. This is the basis of rituals and their purpose.

In John, Chapter 9, and Verses 1 to 7, Jesus performed a ritual that would cure a man of his blindness: "he saw a man blind from birth. And his disciples asked him, "Rabbi, who sinned, this man or his parents, that he was born blind?" Jesus answered,

It was not that this man sinned, or his parents, but that the works of God might be displayed in him. We must work the works of him who sent me while it is day; night is coming, when no one can work. As long as I am in the world, I am the light of the world

Having said these things, he **spit on the ground** and **made mud with the saliva**. Then he **anointed the man's eyes with the mud** and said to him, "Go, **wash in the pool** of Siloam". So he went and washed and came back seeing".

The act of combining His saliva with mud, and having him go wash his face in the pool of Siloam is what resulted in the man being able to see again, and Jesus knew exactly why He needed to do that in order to heal the man. The science of rituals cannot easily be understood or comprehended by most people, but it is still a science.

In today's time, if an African man, adorned in traditional garments, were to cure someone else of blindness in the same fashion as Jesus Christ did, people would call him a practitioner of black magic or a demon-affiliated witchdoctor of some sort. Never mind the fact that he just cured someone of a disability and blessed him with health. Something an evil spirit will never (ever) do.

(Now, think about how people would react if a European man did the same thing. I guarantee that people certainly would not accuse him of witchcraft, in fact they would welcome the idea that "the Lord sent him")

Jesus Christ Himself only started performing miracles after John (the Baptist) baptised Him. He needed to undergo the ritual of baptism before the Holy Spirit descended upon Him in the form of a dove, because rituals are a vital aspect of spiritualism that God responds to. There are many things that simply cannot be done without the necessary rites or ceremonies.

Now I will tell you how all this relates to this thing which people call "paganism" and how God was with men before the Bible came to them: In regions of Earth such as Africa, before the Bible was ever known by their inhabitants, there were spirits with whom the people lived, and they were of different kinds. Some of them good, some of them bad, and some of them somewhat inconsequentially neutral.

Some of these spirits were (and they still are) very powerful, and could manifest themselves materially for any reasons particular to them. The natives of such places had a close relationship with these beings, and some were referred to as "Elders", "gods", or "demigods".

The connections between these spirits and the people who recognised them was dynamic, and the people would offer certain things to the spirits in return for favours such as the protection of their livelihoods. Many of these spirits and their activities were sanctioned by God Himself, as they were helping the people, providing protection for them, and informing them of matters they sought to enquire about.

God's angels exist to extend His reach this way. Traditional healers relied on these spirits and the information they would give them in order to perform the necessary rituals that could heal the sick or protect the village. It was known by the people that these spirits were not God Almighty, and that they could only act in accordance with the jurisdiction He gave them.

Many of the rituals performed were to pass through God first before the other spirits, so there was a common understanding between people of that time that there was one God the creator, (and also that He was composed of three parts), but beyond that, most of them did not know many things which would relate to Christianity. This was not paganism. Pagans are people who believe in multiple Gods. Multiple universal creators. African spirituality does not conform to that delusion, but religious people will tell you otherwise.

Now, the people were being taken care of and they were good people. The villagers had morals and rules. The community was united, and they knew the difference between right and wrong long before the Bible ever came to them. There was communication with not only the aforementioned spirits, but with human spirits as well. The people knew how to contact their deceased, and they regularly did so. Many of their ancestors were themselves spirituality developed, wise, and powerful by the time they died, so even in the spirit realms they were great assets to those who still lived. This is why Roman Catholics too, pray to human ancestors. Catholicism recognises spirits who have power to help them. The mother of Jesus Christ for example, is no ordinary spirit. The spirits of Saint Paul, Saint Ninian, the archangel Michael, etc. are entities who are experienced and powerful enough to be of great aid.

Now, keep in mind though that a spirit is a spirit, and what differentiates one from another is its temperament. Spirits who were in service to God and those who sought to do good deeds, were not the only kinds who affiliated themselves with human beings. Evil spirits did as well, and to this day, they still do, which is why we have the ever-present problem of satanism and witchcraft.

In the old days of "paganism", some of the spirits that people dealt with were not at all 'good', and in fact could care less about God or the benefit of mankind. These are the kinds of spirits who would grant people powers to destroy and bewitch others. Most of these creatures were demons, and believe it or not, the introduction of Christianity helped give them gain leverage over people.

You see: The arrival of the West's religious indoctrination of Africans, advocated the notion that all the indigenous peoples' way of life was sinful. That the natives were to cease their traditional practices and throw their traditional objects away in order to please God.

When Christianity was being used to show that African traditions were wrong, and to encourage people to destroy their ritual items, the only people who actually did get rid of their items and forsake their practices, were the people who wanted to do good. The people whom the slavers had convinced that indeed what they were doing was wrong. Being good people already, they desired to do what they thought was right and slowly began to abandon their culture.

This means that the good spirits who were helping these native people of the land, were no longer being supported by the people, so many of these spirits left. However, those who were practicing witchcraft would never forsake the demons that they felt gave them power over other people. They would not sacrifice their practices for a religion that claimed to bring goodness. And certainly not, when those who brought this religion, were the very same human beings attacking and molesting other people.

"Love your enemies and pray for those who persecute you (Matthew

Chapter 5 and Verse 44)", is a laughable notion to any witch. Do you think devil worshipers do not know that what they are doing is wrong? You do not need to present a Bible to a witch for her to know she is committing sin. She knows very well that what she is doing is wrong. You cannot minister the Bible to a group of demon-worshipers, and expect them to change. **THEY WILL NOT!** They know the Bible, and they go to church every Sunday to read it.

The difference between the paganism of those who worshiped Baal in biblical times, and the witchcraft of those who worship demons and other such evil 'gods' today, is the fact that Baal did nothing for the people who believed in him. The evil spirits of witchcraft that people cling onto today however, deliver on their promises of power that people can use to cause destruction. Albeit only to stab the humans who consort with them in the back later on in life (usually on the very last day of their lives).

Elijah had demonstrated to the worshipers of Baal, that Baal was no 'God' by testing him against God Himself. When God caused fire to evidence Himself, in the absence of Baal's ability to do the same, the pagans realised that Baal was a false 'God'. It is because they saw evidence of God, that they forsook Baal and acknowledged God the Creator.

1 Kings, Chapter 18, and Verses 24 to 39: "And you call upon the name of your god, and I will call upon the name of the Lord, and the God who answers by fire, he is God." And all the people answered, "It is well spoken." Then Elijah said to the prophets of Baal, "Choose for yourselves one bull and prepare it first, for you are many, and call upon the name of your god, but put no fire to it." And they took the bull that was given them, and they prepared it and called upon the name of Baal from morning until noon, saying, "O Baal, answer us!" But there was no voice, and no one answered. And they limped around the altar that they had made. And at noon Elijah mocked

them, saying, "Cry aloud, for he is a god. Either he is musing, or he is relieving himself, or he is on a journey, or perhaps he is asleep and must be awakened." And they cried aloud and cut themselves after their custom with swords and lances, until the blood gushed out upon them. And as midday passed, they raved on until the time of the offering of the oblation, but there was no voice. No one answered; no one paid attention.

Then Elijah said to all the people, "Come near to me." And all the people came near to him. And he repaired the altar of the Lord that had been thrown down. Elijah took twelve stones, according to the number of the tribes of the sons of Jacob, to whom the word of the Lord came, saying, "Israel shall be your name," and with the stones he built an altar in the name of the Lord. And he made a trench about the altar, as great as would contain two seahs of seed. And he put the wood in order and cut the bull in pieces and laid it on the wood. And he said, "Fill four jars with water and pour it on the burnt offering and on the wood." And he said, "Do it a second time." And they did it a second time. And he said, "Do it a third time." And they did it a third time. And the water ran around the altar and filled the trench also with water.

And at the time of the offering of the oblation, Elijah the prophet came near and said, "O Lord, God of Abraham, Isaac, and Israel, let it be known this day that you are God in Israel, and that I am your servant, and that I have done all these things at your word. Answer me, O Lord, answer me, that this people may know that you, O Lord, are God, and that you have turned their hearts back." Then the fire of the Lord fell and consumed the burnt offering and the wood and the stones and the dust, and licked up the water that was in the trench. And when all the people saw it, they fell on their faces and said, "The

Lord, he is God; the Lord, he is God"".

Notice the ritual which Elijah had to perform before God's fire devoured the sacrificed animal, and drank the water around the offering: "Then Elijah said to all the people, "Come near to me." And all the people came near to him. And he repaired the altar of the Lord that had been thrown down. Elijah **took twelve stones, according to the number of the tribes of the sons of Jacob**, to whom the word of the Lord came, saying, "Israel shall be your name," and **with the stones he built an altar in the name of the Lord**. And he **made a trench about the altar, as great as would contain** two seahs of seed. And he **put the wood in order and cut the bull in pieces and laid it on the wood**. And he said, **"Fill four jars with water** and **pour it on the burnt offering and on the wood**." And he said, "**Do it a second time**." And they did it a second time. And he said, "**Do it a third time**." And they did it a third time. And the water ran around the altar and filled the trench also with water".

Elijah had to perform the above ritual before God would strike the offering with fire. If Elijah had only called for God to prove His existence, God would have stayed just as silent as Baal did. Just as silent as He is in many churches today. Elijah performed the same kind of ritual which would get Africans condemned as "pagans", and yet **that is what he had to do**. Had he not done that, God would not have responded.

When the West brought religion, all they did was declare their beliefs and state that their Bible (which at the time they claimed, gave them permission to enslave men and women), was representative of God. They did not evidence this in any manner whatsoever. No miracles were ever performed, and there was no proof that they were even telling the truth. Unfortunately though, systematic slavery, colonialism, and the brainwashing of a peoples' children with religious dogma will shift the peoples' mind-sets over time.

Just like Islam's "prophet" Muhammad, and Mormonism's Joseph Smith, the colonialists and their Christian missionaries were not sent by God, but they claimed to be. Evil that comes in God's name always fails to prove God's power because God does not support the fabrications of manipulative conmen and devils. Even so, people who do not know any better fall prey to these deceptions, so the devil has absolutely no shame in deceiving people with the name "Jesus", and he loves to use the Bible and the notion of God to justify his crimes. The devil knew very well that in order to get people to abandon what was helping them, he would have to trick them into believing they were being sinful. It is only good people that care about "doing the right thing". When Religion succeeded in convincing good people that the spirits protecting them were evil, those spirits (not being the type to try and force anyone into doing what they do not want to do) left, leaving good people unprotected, while witches decided to keep their devils with them.

However, quite a few people (particularly in West Africa) only claimed to abandon their spiritual practices. They not only kept their things of "divination", they used them to make money by establishing churches and performing miracles before people. These people condemn African spirituality, and yet secretly use the same kinds of things they condemn, to heal people and to speak prophecies. No, I am not referring to the likes of "prophet" T.B. Joshua. He is just a manipulative conman who bribes and enchants people to bear false witness with ludicrous acts on television, and who preys on the minds, the hopes, and the dreams, of susceptible, brainwashed, and gullible laypeople (and who has been caught several times bribing journalists and church-goers).

What is particularly strange and hypocritical about Christianity's condemnation of "divination" and "fortune-telling" with the Bible, is how such things are eagerly sought after by Christians today, and exist even in the first Church of Christ. Now, just so we are clear on the meanings of "divination" and "fortune-telling", let me give you the Oxford Dictionary descriptions. A fortune-teller is: "a person who tells people's fortunes". Divination is: "the practice of divining or seeking knowledge by supernatural means".

Deuteronomy Chapter 18, and Verses 10 to 12 says: "There shall not be found among you anyone who burns his son or his daughter as an offering, anyone who practices divination or tells fortunes or interprets omens, or a sorcerer or a charmer or a medium or a necromancer or one who inquires of the dead, for whoever does these things is an abomination to the Lord".

Leviticus Chapter 19, and Verse 31 says: "Do not turn to mediums or necromancers; do not seek them out, and so make yourselves unclean by them: I am the Lord your God".

Leviticus Chapter 20, and Verse 27 says: "A man or a woman who is a medium or a necromancer shall surely be put to death. They shall be stoned with stones; their blood shall be upon them".

Revelation Chapter 21, and Verse 8 says: "But as for the cowardly, the faithless, the detestable, as for murderers, the sexually immoral, sorcerers, idolaters, and all liars, their portion will be in the lake that burns with fire and sulfur, which is the second death".

Acts Chapter 16 and Verses 16 to 18 says: "As we were going to the place of prayer, we were met by a slave girl who had a spirit of divination and brought her owners much gain by fortune-telling. She followed Paul and us, crying out, "These men are servants of the Most High God, who proclaim to you the way of salvation." And this she kept doing for many days. Paul, having become greatly annoyed, turned and said to the spirit, "I command you in the name of Jesus Christ to come out of her." And it came out that very hour".

The above verses clearly condemn the kinds of things which charlatans like T.B. Joshua and his ilk are doing, yet these conmen attract religious Christians in hoards. People (particularly Africans) are abandoning the things of their ancestors: the things of true God-given spiritual power – for the useless things of conmen and false prophets. They run to the likes of T.B. Joshua (a man who cannot foresee the collapse of his own buildings), for his supposed powers of divination, and yet they avoid (or claim to avoid) their African traditions because the Bible condemns divination. Ironic, no? T.B. Joshua is just another avenue through which the evil spirit of religion divides and captures humanity with immense foolishness and the deification of ridiculous conmen. Like Benny Hinn and the rest, he is no man of God.

Furthermore: Many of T.B. Joshua's followers are guilty of worshiping him, for they praise and revere him blindly, and frequently dub him "the messiah", "the saviour", etc. with no reprimand whatsoever from Mr. Joshua who very clearly enjoys to hear them say such things, and whose organization does its best to advertise such misconceptions to his deceived masses of idolaters who know relatively little about what the Bible actually says.

From what the Bible has to say about divination and fortune-telling, it is quite clear that it condemns anyone who seeks knowledge through divine means. Anyone who claims to have had a dream about someone's future, or who intends to warn someone about impending danger that he/she was informed of in a dream for example, would be committing sin, according to the Bible. According to the Bible, if you see something in a dream, and it happens, or if you have the gift of fortune-telling, then there is something wrong with you and you are probably possessed by a bad spirit.

The implications of the afore-quoted Bible texts are highly nonsensical when one examines what occurs in reality. You see: In reality, there are some people who are natural psychics, and there are others who can see ghosts. These people have spiritual abilities which they maintained from birth, or received as gifts from angels or other spirits. These are gifts, and they are not evil. These gifts are the things which many people are in fact born with. Many infants can see ghosts and foretell the future, but slowly lose their spiritual senses as they grow. The fact that there are some people who maintain their senses, does not make them "abominations to the Lord".

What is ironic, is that the Bible condones fortune-telling and divination whenever it feels like it and whenever it suits a particular narrative. For example: Genesis Chapter 37, and Verses 1 to 27, talks about how a boy named Joseph had dreams and told fortunes which his family did not like. He would tell them that one day they would bow down to him. He would also say he had dreams of the sun and eleven stars bowing down to him. This contributed to his brothers' envy of him, and because of this envy, they sold him to Midianite traders. Of course Joseph's dreams turned out to be true and his brothers did indeed wind up bowing down to him years later. Despite this, the Bible never called him an abomination to God.

What is even more ironic is that the people who compiled the Bible in accordance with their agendas, practice the things which they condemn Africans for. The Catholic Church prays to the ancestors of men. They pray to Saint Ninian, Saint Catherine, Saint Genesius, Saint Thomas, etc. In fact, the church performs rituals (e.g. feast days) in honour of the human spirits they pray to.

Yet they frown upon Africans doing the same things, or praying to their ancestors. Why? Why must Africans neglect the things of their ancestors in substitution for the things of Europeans' ancestors? Should people pray to Saint Ninian because he is white? If the colour of his skin is not the reason, then on what basis do the Europeans oblige people to pray to people who are human ghosts of European descent, and not to people of African descent who are also human ghosts?

I will not pray to this European man called Ninian, nor the other people whom naïve Catholics would like for me pray to. I do not know them, and they have not done anything for me. The people to whom I will pray, are my forefathers, God, and His angels. Were it not for my ancestors, and the spirits who protect the village to which I was born, I would not be alive today. Had I been praying to the likes of Saint Ninian or Catherine, I would not be alive today. Had I forsaken the things God gave me, for the things of man and slavery, I would not be alive today.

It is not that the recognition of one's ancestors are exclusive to Africans, nor is it that the spiritual practices which Africans are typically associated with are exclusive to them. Such things have been practiced by people all over the world, and Europeans constitute a high percentage of those who do. The evil of Witchcraft, (Again: I am not referring to Wicca), as well as the blessed things which are in compliance with God, are closely-guarded secrets for many of them.

In high-school I used to know a girl who said she was atheist and did not believe in God. I met her again seven years later, and in conversation I remembered what she used to think of "God". I asked her if she was still an atheist and she told me that she now believes in God. I then asked her if she had seen anything to justify her apostasy from atheism, and she said: "My late grandfather, protects three generations of the women in our family". "I see", I said.

My father once told me of what he saw when we had a problem with the plumbing in our home one day. When the plumber came over (a middle-aged European man), my father could see a host spirits with the man. Spirits of various kinds. These were not evil spirits, and my father wondered where the man got those things. He would have asked the man, if not for his shyness. All those spiritual abilities, and yet this man was content with being a common plumber. Indeed, such is a sign of a humble soul who obtains his joy from within himself, because plumbers do not make much money at all where we live.

I will say again: Do not think for even the slightest significant lapse of time, that because God favours only his European creations, He blessed them with a Bible and ordered them to enslave and torture innocent people in other nations so that the people of those nations may also have a book called the Bible. Such an idea is ridiculous, and it is the very idea insinuated by anyone who says "Without the Bible, you cannot be saved". It is an idea of the devil.

The Holy Spirit is the spirit of truth. It is God's spirit, and it is available to everyone whim whom the Spirit is compatible. God's energy echoes throughout this universe, and every man/woman who is righteous has it with him/her. Jesus Christ died for all of us, and not only for the "white people" or the religious fanatics. Jesus did not die for "Christians", he died for the human race.

Religious lies are the reason Christianity is now not doing much for people, and church attendance serves only to satisfy most peoples' weekly quotas. Peoples' ability to navigate the world as spirit beings encased in flesh, has been drowned out by religious indoctrination, peoples' ability to communicate with God and His angels at a spiritual level has been muted by religious indoctrination, and peoples' ability to think and to reason, has been repressed by religious indoctrination.

As Christianity loses its significance and the spiritual practices of people die out, people begin to see Christianity as another useless religion filled with charlatans and thieving religious leaders. When that happens, more people start becoming neutral on the topic of spirituality, and when that happens, more people start converting to atheism. The notion of God then becomes increasingly ridiculous over time. Things of spirituality, angels, demons, ghosts, and the contacting of dead relatives, then become things of legend and folklore after religion has banned them to extinction before shortly-after banning itself. When that has happened, only a very sparsely distributed few will possess the secrets of some of these "magical" things which people once took for granted, while the rest of the world falls faster into the delusion of "naturalism", spiritual bankruptcy, and helplessness. Religion will then be reborn in the much more apparent image of satan, and it will be to the narcoleptic slaves of the new world, as if God never visited us. That is what is slowly happening in the Western world, and that is what the forces conspiring in the shadows there, are striving hard to make happen across the globe. They will not succeed, but nevertheless, they are tying.

In many parts of Africa, people know of these spiritual things and they have had first-hand experiences with them, but religious Christianity's condemnation of African spirituality is being accepted by people who have been raked in by fear and threats of hell-fire against them. They abandon the things which God has given their people because a Bible whose texts were hand-picked by men with an agenda, condemns their things.

As with what is already happening in Western countries: when the original and spiritual things of a people die out and decades pass by, people will begin rejecting Christianity and the moral infrastructure of their society will decay and transform into something the devil has envisioned for them. Africans will only tolerate the ineffectiveness of "church and prayer" for a certain amount of time, and they will not turn a blind eye to the evils of deceptive priests for ever. If nothing is done to bring the truth to them, their ancestors' things will be wiped out completely by the time religion turns their faces away from God.

Religion has gone far in separating Europeans from God already (evidenced by the hundreds of churches in Europe which are now empty and about to be auctioned), but Religion must not be allowed to do the same to Africa. The inevitable consequence of religion is the separation of people from their spirituality, but I do not want that to happen. I know that it will not happen. I have written this book to help make sure the devil falls flat on his face once again, and that those "world-dominating" people who hide themselves and strive for the world's destruction are left with nothing but humiliation and disappointment. They will certainly fail again.

The West invaded Africa, plundered its resources, and then left Africans religiously indoctrinated and destitute. Now, the West is rapidly converting to atheism, advertising deceptions and perversion through their media sources, and painting the countries whom they have enslaved with religion as being "religiously indoctrinated", "unsophisticated", and "backward".

This is not by accident. You see, the European colonisers needed a way to separate Africans from what unified them. Their spiritual practices, and the effect those practices had on their cultural practices, were a wall the Europeans had to overcome if they were to be successful at stealing from the countries they visited with relative ease and turning the slaves into willing participants of their oppressive regimes (in whatever capacity that was possible).

While many of them used Biblical passages to promote amongst themselves the idea that only white people go to heaven, the colonialists were accompanied by Christian missionaries to promote meekness and a mentality of servitude amongst the people of the nations they would abuse. In the lands they invaded, the missionaries would typically target the young by befriending many of them, and using the schools they would build to encourage the children to break away from the traditions of their parents and their grandparents. The unique colour of the invaders' skins particularly was used to leverage their relationships with natives, and contributed greatly to the cause of colonialism and the mass brainwashing of people with

Christianity.

Christian missionaries would often use the Bible to convince the youth to whom they ministered, that being rich and prosperous was a "bad" and "Earthly" thing. That suffering on this Earth was worth it for the treasures they would receive in heaven. Missionaries said this to the people from whom the missionaries' people were stealing natural resources and to whom the missionaries' people were forcing into slave labour for the enrichment of Western civilization.

As any good historian will tell you: one of many examples of the massive role religion played in the theft and exploitation of Africa's people can be seen in the resulting chaos from the Colonization of Central Africa's Congo, and King Leopold II's invasion of the land. With support from the Roman Catholic Church, The Belgian King brutalised the people of his so-called "Congo Free State", cut off the hands of men, women, and children, and forced them into slave labour for the growing rubber industry. The Roman Catholic Church knew of his atrocities, but remained silent until the news of what was going on became too big to handle. Below is a letter supposedly from King Leopold II himself to the missionaries of the Congo Free State in the late 1800s.

"Reverends, Fathers and Dear Compatriots: The task that is given to fulfill is very delicate and requires much tact. You will go certainly to evangelize, but your evangelization must inspire above all Belgium interests. Your principal objective in our mission in the Congo is never to teach the niggers to know God, this they know already. They speak and submit to a Mungu, one Nzambi, one Nzakomba, and what else I don't know. They know that to kill, to sleep with someone else's wife, to lie and to insult is bad. Have courage to admit it; you are not going to teach them what they know already. Your essential role is to facilitate the task of administrators and industrials, which means you will go to interpret the gospel in the way it will be the best to protect your interests in that

part of the world. For these things, you have to keep watch on disinteresting our savages from the richness that is plenty [in their underground. To avoid that, they get interested in it, and make you murderous] competition and dream one day to overthrow you.

Your knowledge of the gospel will allow you to find texts ordering, and encouraging your followers to love poverty, like "Happier are the poor because they will inherit the heaven" and, "It's very difficult for the rich to enter the kingdom of God." You have to detach from them and make them disrespect everything which gives courage to affront us. I make reference to their Mystic System and their war fetish-warfare protection- which they pretend not to want to abandon, and you must do everything in your power to make it disappear.

Your action will be directed essentially to the younger ones, for they won't revolt when the recommendation of the priest is contradictory to their parent's teachings. The children have to learn to obey what the missionary recommends, who is the father of their soul. You must singularly insist on their total submission and obedience, avoid developing the spirit in the schools, teach students to read and not to reason. There, dear patriots, are some of the principles that you must apply. You will find many other books, which will be given to you at the end of this conference. Evangelize the niggers so that they stay forever in submission to the white colonialists, so they never revolt against the restraints they are undergoing. Recite every day-"Happy are those who are weeping because the kingdom of God is for them."

Convert always the blacks by using the whip. Keep their women in nine months of submission to work freely for us. Force them to pay you in sign of recognition -goats, chicken or eggs- every time you visit their villages. And make sure that niggers never become rich. Sing every day that it's impossible for the rich to enter heaven. Make them pay tax each week at Sunday mass. Use the money supposed for the poor, to build flourishing business centers. Institute a confessional system, which allows you to be good detectives denouncing any black that has a different consciousness contrary to that of the decision-maker. Teach the niggers to forget their heroes and to adore only ours. Never present a chair to a black that comes to visit you. Don't give him more than one cigarette. Never invite him for dinner even if he gives you a chicken every time you arrive at his house".

It is claimed that a Congolese man (Mr. Moukouani Bukoko), found the above letter in a second-hand Bible which he bought from a Belgian priest who had forgotten the letter in the Bible. Now there is not enough evidence for me to believe Leopold wrote that letter, but the letter's contents certainly do fit quite perfectly, the rhyme of what in fact has occurred in Congo, and every African country whose cultures have been wiped out and replaced with the things their colonial masters desired for them, so I have included it as evidence.

Before colonialism divided the African continent into separate pieces of land to be shared among European conquerors, Christianity was introduced to West Central Africa in the 15th century by Portuguese explorers, and was adopted by a king of the area for political purposes (particularly, the benefit of trade with the Portuguese). Because the people in West Central Africa already believed in one universal Creator, Christianity was portrayed as only being supplementary to the existing beliefs and practices of the people, rather than being a different set of beliefs. The translation of the Bible into the peoples' language as well was done so that no one would see Christianity as being different from what was already known to the people. This certainly contributed greatly to Christian missionaries' ability to turn Congolese people (and other Africans) into practitioners of a religion belonging to people who enslaved them.

Religious Christianity, racism, and slavery are very closely tied. This is why the very first ship to bring African slaves onto U.S. soil was named after Jesus Christ Himself ("Jesus of Lubeck", to be specific), and this is why the infamous and racially-motivated "KKK" is a religious Christian group. This is also why Jesus Christ is deceptively portrayed to people as being a long-haired, fair-skinned, European man, when in fact it is quite impossible for Him to have ever taken such an appearance.

The Muslims who occupy Egypt today, are descendants of Arabs who invaded the nation and conquered it, in the 7th century. They are not of the original Egyptians. Likewise, the Jews who occupy the country called "Israel" today, are not of the Israelites who were led out of Egypt by Moses. All the historical evidence points indisputably in the following direction: That the ancient Egyptians were black Africans, that the original Jews were black Africans, and that the man whom people know today as "Jesus Christ", was a black African.

In fact: The oldest images in the world which depict the most prominent Biblical characters, depict them all as black Africans. Such images are recognised as authentic by the Catholic Church and prayed to directly by the papacy. An example is the "Black Madonna". Old sculptures and paintings of the Virgin Mary and Jesus Christ which portray them very clearly as black Africans. The papacy has been praying directly to the Virgin Mary and Jesus Christ in this form for hundreds of years now, and in many other places around the world as well, these original sculptures and paintings are recognised as accurately depicting Christ and His mother (as far ethnicity is concerned). The paintings and sculptures many people have seen of a European Mary and her Son Jesus, have all been deceptive forgeries and tools of white-supremacist propaganda.

Furthermore, the historical evidence indicates very clearly, the highly unfortunate and tremendously disgusting fact that Europeans have intentionally destroyed and defaced ancient artefacts of the Negro race, cunningly contaminated the truth of African civilizations, and systematically white-washed history with lies to paint themselves as superior, and to hide from the world, the fact that the arts, mathematics, philosophy, medicine, the sciences, and even speech, were in actuality all originated by Africans. The idea that Europeans pioneered these things is amongst the most ludicrous large-scale lies in history, and this is no secret. It is a very well documented and well-known fact to all the world's most renowned and well-researched historians.

It is common knowledge to many people now, the blatant European cover-ups of African history, the large-scale European conspiratorial defamation of the Negro race in order to justify the slave trade, and the one-sided lies being told in most school history books in favour of 'the white man' and against the African people, but the Europeans who sought to have themselves worshiped, continue to misrepresent all that is good in this world in their likeness, including Jesus Christ.

Some people will say "It doesn't matter what colour Jesus was", but if that was true, the Europeans who brought their colonized nations the Deity of Christ would never have tampered with His appearance in the first place. They obviously felt it mattered, and the fact that a European Jesus is being universally worshipped today, means it still matters to them. After all, why would they want to worship a "black" God?

Now understand: that my point has nothing to do with advancing the notion that 'white people are evil' or anything of that ridiculous nature. We are one human race of brothers and sisters, and God is for us all equally. Likewise: the evil spirit is against us all. Brown, beige, purple, or blue, a man is a man, a woman is a woman, a child is a child, and a devil is a devil. Skin colour means nothing. To the types of Europeans specifically discussed above, skin colour is justification for racism and other evils, but that is all satan ever needs: justification. To the evil spirit, it does not matter what exactly is used to justify evil, and it does not matter through whom the evil works, as long as the act of evil is carried out.

The point I am making for you is that those who conspired to rob a certain group of people of their land, their culture, their natural resources, their spiritual beliefs, and their strengths, are groups of people who continue to steal from the people whose homes they broke into long ago. Most of their victims are willingly handing the goods over to the thieves robbing them. Africa is certainly not the only land which devils have exploited, but it is by far the most exploited.

The vast majority of Africans who practice Christianity today are remnants of European slavery, and their overwhelming poverty crisis is a remnant of

European slavery also. They might not know it, but they remain servants of their white-supremacist controllers. In the Western world, most Africans do not even know where they come from, and they have lost themselves. In Africa, they are in the process of losing themselves. Africa has been looted by devils, and it is still being looted by them because people are allowing it.

Luke Chapter 6, and Verses 20 to 26: ""Blessed are you who are poor, for yours is the kingdom of God. "Blessed are you who are hungry now, for you shall be satisfied. "Blessed are you who weep now, for you shall laugh. "Blessed are you when people hate you and when they exclude you and revile you and spurn your name as evil, on account of the Son of Man! Rejoice in that day, and leap for joy, for behold, your reward is great in heaven; for so their fathers did to the prophets. Jesus Pronounces Woes "But woe to you who are rich, for you have received your consolation. "Woe to you who are full now, for you shall be hungry. "Woe to you who laugh now, for you shall mourn and weep. "Woe to you, when all people speak well of you, for so their fathers did to the false prophets"".

Ephesians Chapter 1, and Verses 5 to 7: "Slaves, obey your earthly masters with respect and fear, and with sincerity of heart, just as you would obey Christ. Obey them not only to win their favor when their eye is on you, but as slaves of Christ, doing the will of God from your heart. Serve wholeheartedly, as if you were serving the Lord, not people". Indeed these are the kinds of messages white-supremacists love for their dark-skinned slaves to be hearing every day.

Religion is evil, and it comes only to destroy and enslave. In the wake of religious Christianity's indoctrination of Africa, witchcraft has become prevalent and a very big problem, as most of the spirits who offered protection and help are no longer protecting and helping, for the people have abandoned them. The demons who tried to establish themselves have not left, and they maintain their hold on entire generations of families who keep passing the evil spirits on to their offspring.

You see: when you convince good people to throw their guns away, you only empower the evil ones. The enemy's goal is to strip us of our spiritual guns, so that evil-doers will have free-reign over whom they choose to shoot at. This is unfortunate, because witchcraft is really not that powerful. It is an immensely weak weapon in comparison to God's things.

It is a shame, that religious Christians are not aware enough of spiritualism to defend themselves, and that those among them who try to think outside of religion's box are usually assailed by their religiously enslaved brethren and the evil spirits of fear and guilt who work in tandem with religion to dissuade individuals from that which is truth.

Note that the problem is not Christianity, because Jesus Christ did in fact die for all of mankind. However when religion claims to represent Christ, we have a problem. Witches are going to church every Sunday, and are preying on helplessly simple religious sheep who think tithing makes them of God. Even the devil knows the Bible. If you want salvation you need God, but the evil spirit that brings religion, turns people to the Bible for salvation instead of turning them to God. You see, if you can convince people to trust in a small book and tell them that is where God is, you have made them quite powerless. Especially when you misinterpret the contents of that book to them.

So evil-doers go to churches and they pretend very well to be like worshipers of Christ. While people pray, these evil people are praying alongside them, but not to the same end. Remember that witches tend to be very jealous individuals, and seek only to destroy what is good in this world. This means impeding their peers and associates from success in any way that they can. When witches go to church, they use it not only to fit in as Christians, but to curse the people around them. They listen in on other people's prayers, and they pray against them to the best of their abilities.

People's lives have become more difficult, illnesses are more common, and witchcraft is killing people, because peoples' souls are lost in a religion that is not helping them. The God of Isaac and Abraham is not the same God that religious Christians know today, for they worship a God who wants your money and exists only to serve, or to be praised aimlessly for the sake of religion. Religious Christianity, like Islam, Mormonism, scientology, and any other useless religion, does not represent the will of God. It represents the will of man, his quest for control, and the devil's manipulation.

The fact that this world is saturated with so many evil people means you should practice caution when befriending people or telling them things about your life, because not everyone in this world, would like to see you prosper. Especially in many parts of Africa where witchcraft has become a plague upon the people. Do not become paranoid when things in your life do not go according to plan though, because everyone has his/her own challenges in life. It is only the fighters that overcome their hurdles. Make sure to never stop fighting, and whenever useful information (such as what is contained in this book) crosses your path, do the best that you can with it.

We all have problems. Some of us more than others. I myself have been through some terrible things, and a majority of my real world battles were amidst the backdrop of a spiritual war unbeknownst to anyone else. Some people have to worry about paying bills, and others complain about their day being ruined by a rude customer. While some of us have to deal with angels who visit us arbitrarily, evil spirits who invade our homes almost nightly, and of course, the annoyances of everyday life in addition. But we who fight, come out on top. Those who only complain, stay right where they are, and then usually fall backward.

Whether you are going to the gym to combat laziness and fat, whether you are trying to develop and sell the best electronic devices to maintain market share and profit, or whether you are crawling yourself from the pits of a crime-ridden suburban ghetto in search of a better life – life is a struggle. Some struggle more than others, but one thing is true for everyone: when the battles stop, it is probably because you have given up.

For of course, even your enemies are fighting. When they attack you they are fighting, and for them to attack you, they must have been fighting long before they ever took action. Jealousy for example, pits people against you only because it defeats them, and it causes war within them. In addition, your enemies have troubles in life besides those that they associate with you, just as you too have difficulties in life that are unrelated to them.

To the good people on this planet who have envious people trying to hinder their progress, remember that the people who envy you for your successes have long been defeated, for they have no peace in their hearts, and every moment they spend thinking about you brings only pain to them. The evil that works through them to attack and destroy the good they see in other people is the very same evil that is rotting their insides, feeding on their life energy, and turning them into diseased corpses of failure and shame. People who trespass against others so as to curse and sabotage their triumphs will reap the rewards for their sins tenfold.

Blessed are people who refuse to harbour hatred and evil in their hearts by the reminiscence of their enemies' sins against them, for they have inner peace. Their enemies have no such peace. Jesus Christ was able to forgive those who trespassed against Him, because He was free from the jaws of vengeance and angst that drove his enemies.

Life is a battle, but battles are the only way to become stronger. We must push and pull weights in order to increase in size and strength, and we must train until we gasp for breath in order to increase our stamina. When you become stronger, the battles become less and less of a challenge – but they do not stop.

The irony of your enemies' attempt to thwart your goal-kicks, and ruin your objectives, is that in doing so, they only provide an opportunity to make you stronger and more experienced. They dig a deeper hole for themselves. The greatest people among us have gone through some pretty tough times, for it is these times that will strengthen and mould people into warriors of prestigious repute.

Remember that even in heaven a war broke out, and battles were fought. If a war can break out in heaven of all places, it can break out anywhere. The angels who defeated Lucifer have won that fight, but that fight was not their first, nor was it their last.

An angel once told me: "There is not a single place you can go, where there will not be someone to watch out for". Even the birds, gifted with the ability to fly, are only as free as they allow themselves to be, because they as well have problems.

Every living creature manages its way through life, and faces challenges as it grows. There is not a single man the devil fears, who has not had to combat and triumph over him. satan is a joke, and only those who have fought him know this for sure.

As you become successful in life, the envious nature of mankind will only become more apparent to you, but the frequency of the rapid downfall of such people too, will become more apparent. Be very watchful of the company you keep, because when they fall behind, they will try to drag you down with them.

The devil does not bother people who are no threat to him, and just as my enemies know very well how much of a threat I am to them, your enemies too, know how much of a threat you are. The people who are least attacked by evil, are the people who the devil does not need to worry about. Evil only attacks that which threatens to expose it and/or that which will grow to become powerful against it.

The devil fears God, and he fears people who are of God, because people who are of God, have the truth. The truth is the greatest enemy of any evil. The toughest of us fight the toughest battles, and the toughest of us get to enjoy victory, in spite of the men and women who envy us, and very often, in plain view of their unfortunate demise.

I guarantee you, that every one of your enemies: those who have attempted to bewitch you, those who have attempted to spoil you, and those who have attempted to shame you unjustly, are digging a gutter for themselves. You will one day walk past them, and witness the sorrowful sight of their decaying bodies lying in the very gutters they have dug. The devil consumes all his puppets. People of the devil and of the evil spirit, create problems in their own lives more than they do, the lives of others. There is no need to worry yourself about them.

And I cannot say enough, how important it is for you to understand that you usually cannot blame the devil for everything that goes wrong in your life. You are in charge of your life, and the power your enemies have over you, is only what you allow them. Live life well (that means fun, as well as responsible), always strive to learn, and help people along the way. You can never have all the answers, but you can keep amassing your database, and there is no such thing as too much knowledge. Not really, anyway. Be strong, and keep climbing your mountain, because every mountain has a top, from which you can see the magnificence of the world around you.

I myself have been dragged up some extraordinarily steep mountains on course to the places I have reached. I have had many encounters with demons and with witches, but that is not what is extraordinary. What is extraordinary about my battles, is that all these encounters stemmed from within my own family. Specifically: my grandmother.

Let me explain this to you: You see, my father's mother is a witch… but not just any witch. Through an immensely sad and unfortunate set of circumstances, my father was born to a woman whose home is the headquarters of all the witchcraft that exists in my hometown. A woman, who through the most perverse of evils, had been made 'queen' of the evil spirits in that area. The most pathetic form of 'queen' there is.

My father has told me of how, when he was a child, he used to see large snakes wrapped around his mother's body in the evenings. As soon as the lights were turned off for bedtime, the snakes would appear, slithering around her, and they would glow green, on and off.

He has told me of how as a child, he used to have strange dreams of his mother holding him by the leg and attempting to butcher him with a cutlass, only to be saved by an angel at the last minute. And how angels would come to him in dreams, give him a bow and arrow, point it at a grotesque creature he knew to be his mother, and ask him to shoot. He lacked the inner strength to do it, and always wound up lowering the weapon to the ground. The angel would shake his head in disappointment, before flying away.

He did not know at the time, but having foreseen all the horrors she would later commit against him, against his family, against her own brothers and sisters, and against many others, God gave him an opportunity to end her and the streak of atrocities associated with her mother's line of witchcraft. You see, it was not the angels' place to remove her, but God afforded my father the opportunity to do so. It is only a shame that he knew not what was going on. That the creature he called his "mother" was no such thing to him, for her being ceased to be human a long time ago.

Some pastors would warn him to stop sleeping at home, or tell him that there is a great evil they could see in his household, but it was not until he turned 19, and God forcefully began awakening his spiritual abilities, that along with the otherworldly entities he was perceiving, he saw the truth about what his mother was.

My father had been gifted by God to see and do things in the spirit realms, and somewhat hereditarily, I too can see and do things in the spirit realms, so I saw my grandmother in the spirit for the first time myself, when one night she came to me in a dream, along with one of her daughters. I was quite young, and had never met or heard of my grandmother before, but when she came, I knew very well who she was. In the spirit I saw her for what she really was. I perceived beyond the flesh to see that her core was rotten. That her entire spirit had been morphed into a twisted abomination, the likes of which cannot ever be redeemed. She had thrown herself so deep into satan's pit, it permanently corrupted the very entity that used to define her.

She is the vilest and most disgusting of all the creatures I have faced in the spirit realms, and she is the vilest and most disgusting of all the 'human beings' I have ever met. A few years after my father was born, his mother tried repeatedly to kill him, and sacrifice him to demons as part of the arrangements demons have with the witches they possess. And for the sake of destruction and evil, she has tried repeatedly, to kill me for many years.

However she is fated to never accomplish those goals.

You see: Because the devil has her soul captive, he is using her as a means to destroy all that is good around her. People who affiliate themselves with such evil, and to the extent she has, stop being human beings. They turn into revolting creatures, diseased with perverse insanities, and their minds become like those of the demons they are affiliated with. Witches become a means to monitor human beings more closely, and to attempt to destroy or sabotage those whose future accomplishments are to the benefit of mankind or to the detriment of demonic forces, to any extent.

Which is why my grandmother has destroyed many people's lives already, and why she has done everything in her power to sabotage me, and to stop me from achieving the very great things her demon filth have foreseen. To stop me from eventually growing to do things such as the writing of this very book for example. My inevitable successes were apparent to my grandmother, so she worked tirelessly to ruin me from my infancy.

From the age of about 15 the real battles began. The assault of demonic forces started with various forms of illness, and over the course of seven years developed into attacks so extensive and multidimensional, I was being approached by witches everywhere I went. In schools I would see them, in my neighbourhood I would see them. Even in churches, I would see them. A lot of them I would see in churches. My grandmother underwent an awful lot of deals with demons to attack myself and my family, and I could sense it every time she did.

I knew all too well how angry it made demonic forces that I was writing this book, and I knew all too well the kind of damage my written revelations were going to do to their establishments, so despite the persistent demonic attacks, I continued to write this book day-in and day-out. I continued to develop myself spiritually, and were it not for that, I certainly would not have lived for much longer.

Night after night, I had to contend with evil spirits, and sometimes even in broad daylight I had to fight them. I felt my soul being poisoned, my mind being eroded, my whole body ached, I was exhausted, and I had a persistent headache that would become much worse whenever I dared to go to places that the spirits could see would be beneficial to my life. These illnesses went on for many years, and prevented me from being able to study even in the least, for examinations or do any of my school work. Any attempts to do academic work (or any work at all) would result in, among many other things, my skin crawling unbearably, and my mind slipping to a reality pain.

The things I suffered were of a highly sophisticated and tremendously destructive nature. It is after completing my final year of a specialized high school which offered the 1st-year-university equivalent of a final high school year (to accommodate my frequent grade-skipping), that I soon turned 15, and almost as soon as I did, my woes began. I spent the next six years failing to enter university, and ended up just going to a part-time college to try and pass time. While there, I decided to write a university entrance examination on the off chance that my efforts would not be thwarted once again, but it seemed that I would again be disappointed, as I got no acceptance letter.

One day though, I was visited by an angel who revealed to me that witches had stolen my acceptance letter, but that he (the angel) had gone to take it back from them. About a month after the angel informed me, the acceptance letter arrived in my mail and I managed to get into my engineering degree course, albeit only to continue to face problems even there.

It could never have occurred to anyone on my university campus that I was going through wars, because everyone could see that I was happy and full of jokes. I could not afford to be outgoing at night (for obvious reasons), but I had much life in me, and people saw me as a bit of a crazy character. My classmates knew me for my severe "laziness" and unwillingness to do any school work, and they knew me for my supposedly remarkable ability to pass even the "difficult" subjects in spite of this. People would have been extremely shocked if they were to discover that in actual fact, I was battling both spiritually and physically, every single moment of every single day, and had been suffering like that for years.

This was because I knew I could not tell people such things. Firstly, I have seen things that the average person need not ever be told about. Secondly, most people already assumed me to be atheist because I never spoke 'typically' of things like religion. I did not want to have to explain anything about spirituality to them, for there was an awful lot that would need to be covered. Also, my life's stories would scare the life out of many of them. I did not think it was any of their business to know anything about such things, and I was comfortable that everyone was in the dark about my life.

In the day I battled sicknesses, and in the evenings I faced the threat of spirits who would try and take my soul. Spirits would come to me as I slept, pull my spirit out of my body, and often take me to very distant, and very foreign, realms. However, the fact that I was already spiritually developed to an extent, and was an immensely fast learner meant that when they came to take my spirit away, I was able to fight back.

I found a way to travel as they do, and take myself to dimensions that they could not keep up with me to follow. At a point, I learned to depart my body at whim, and therefore, was able to face the spirits that came head on. They started leaving my apartment as battered and bruised as they intended for me to be.

God did not abandon me either, for the Holy Spirit provided me with strength, and would warn me of looming dangers both during the day and in the evenings. The Lord never forsake me, and in fact, did everything I humbly requested of Him. Sometimes to surprisingly exact specifications…

I remember when one day I asked God to sever the hands of the spirits who would often come to torment me. When those spirits came the following occasion, a pair of immensely hard and strong hands came to me, lifted me from my body, and teleported me to a place where two fire-breathing dragons were waiting. It was a planet of sorts, with a large sun in the sky, but this planet was in a spirit realm.

After I was transported, I found myself lying down with my eyes still closed. I then opened my eyes to the sight of a massive dragon eclipsing the sun as it flew past it. I then looked down, and was surprised to see only a pair of hands holding my arms firmly. Just as I had asked, God severed the malevolent spirits from their hands, and in their defiance, it was just the pair of hands that could come.

In the distance I saw a second dragon approaching me quickly. It opened its mouth wide as it approached, and at that moment I immediately took myself away from that place. I took myself back to my apartment, but the hands that had taken me away, maintained their grasp on me. I could not get them to release me, but I knew that an effective way to get away from them would be for me to enter my physical body again, and encase myself within it so that any contact those hands had with me would be rendered useless. I managed to do so successfully, and upon animating my body, the first thing I asked, was for God to destroy those very spirits completely. Hands and all.

Such experiences continued, and kept escalating in severity, until one day, when a last-ditch haymaker of an attempt was made on my grandmother's part to take my life, I made every effort to reach my forefathers in the spirit realm, and the ancient spirits from the place which I descend. I got hold of them, and at the very last minute, I gained access to the things I would use to defeat her and to remind her of satan's absolute inferiority to God.

She has since not been the same, and lives a life of humiliation before her fellow witches and her demon masters, to whom she made promises of mine and my father's death. It is only because she fears death so much herself, that her defeat did not also result in her immediate departure from this world. After being warned repeatedly of the consequences of her incessant attacks on my life, she found the ticking clock on the chance at keeping her own, near zero. My angels refrained from killing her because she promised to cease her witchcraft against me and remove herself from the quest to destroy my father's family. So, in the stead of ensuring her demise, the angels seemed to open her eyes. She now appears to regret all that she has done, and spends every day in pain because of it. Calling regularly to ask for forgiveness, and to apologise. Unprecedented behaviour for the likes of her. If it is forgiveness from us she seeks, she has it. We hold no hatred in our hearts. It seems though, that is all she has. Indeed, punishment comes in many forms, and unfortunately for her, it is only the beginning.

Because of the devil's persistent attacks on my existence, I went through many years of nothing but pain and spiritual battles, but I am grateful for all I have learned. I am bigger and stronger because of it, and not because I sat around waiting for God to do something, but because I used the things God has given me to keep fighting. I am much more accomplished than what even the demons could foresee, and at the time of writing this, I regret only that my grandmother's remaining witch of a daughter is still around, and is continuing to ruin the lives of other people.

Both she and her mother are wretched souls, and soon they will meet miserable ends. Like her mother, she does not have much time left, and the place she is headed when her time on Earth runs out, is a very terrible place. Of this, I am sure that she, like most witches, is aware.

The irony in all her and my grandmother's wickedness, is that they are taking the lives of people now, when my grandmother's was spared many years ago from a fate similar to that which she is now inflicting upon people. You see, when she was younger, she nearly lost her life to spiritual attacks which were targeted at her by someone who for one reason or another, wanted her dead. Her father, being a powerful man in the spirit himself, managed to summon powers that overcame the devils attacking her, and saved her life.

Unfortunately her mother was a witch, and although she (her mother) took care not to use any of her witchcraft when my grandmother's father was alive (lest she regret it for the rest of her days), she passed her evil onto my grandmother. My grandmother, then passed that evil onto her daughters. One of whom refused to accept it and was killed, another of whom began to reject the evil after some time and was also killed, and one of whom accepted the evil to become as wicked as her filthy scum-of-the-earth mother, and became an accomplice in the murder of her siblings.

However, my grandmother had also given birth to my father: A person who quickly became a threat to her, and a person she has repeatedly failed to kill since the day her demons saw his potential. At a very young age his natural openness to the spirit world allowed him to learn the secrets of how to summon the angels of God to him. They stayed with him, gifted him powers of the Holy Spirit, and wanted him to become a pastor.

This posed some problems. You see: God, angels, and the spirit realm, are drastically different from the mainstream and religious consensus about them. All that religious people know of angels or the spirit realm is the nonsense they have seen in movies or read in fantasy books. In reality, angels can be difficult to deal with for they are creatures of such purity, they are not compatible with most people.

The angels God sent to my father were very strict. They wanted him to be 100% pure and without any error whatsoever in order to stay with him and for God to use him. The slightest misjudgement on his part would often lead to being punished. Of course they would first warn him before/when he did something wrong, for they know no man is without sin, but angels are not very tolerant of peoples' subsequent transgressions. In fact, they are not even that tolerant of things which most human beings would not consider transgressions. Something as simple as becoming furious at another person, will prompt the angels to query you about why you got so angry, and they will advise you against such emotions. In order to co-exist with God's most awesomely powerful angels, one must adhere strictly to certain protocols.

My father once told me of how he was singing a song one day, when an angel abruptly told him: "Stop". The reason being that the people who wrote that song were evil satanic cult members masquerading as Christ-like church people. The angels despised their kind, and even a song composed by them was filthy. The song was about love and happiness, but nevertheless it came from the hearts of disingenuous devils and was devoid of value. So my father opted rather to sing another song which praised Jesus, and the angels took no issue. It is not that he opted rather to sing a song about Jesus that was the point, but that he ceased to sing the song which came from the Godless devils. Had they composed a song about Jesus, it would still be worthless and equally (perhaps more) revolting to the angels of God. And had my father continued to sing the song composed by the evil-doers after being told to stop, he surely would have been penalised.

God gave my father much spiritual power, and he became more and more spiritually developed as time went on, but at one point he stopped performing the rituals that God had intended for him to be made more powerful. You see: Having received these things from God at a very young age (his mid-teens), my father very frequently would encounter battles with demons. When you stand out as unique, you draw the attention of evil spirits who will try and suppress you, but when you have the potential to be great, you draw their attention in large numbers. For a time, no evil could stand him. However, the imperfections of man, exposed him to certain dangers.

You see: If God warns you not to do something, and you then go and do it, you will learn why he told you not to. In my father's case, he had erred in judgment at one point and did something the angels had warned him against. Angered, some of the angels left him temporarily. This is how he became more vulnerable to the devils' attacks.

The constant battles from the many witches he would encounter even when walking past them on the street, as well as the things originating from his mother, became too much for him. In addition: the angels' process of transforming him was one which required a great deal of mental strength, and bravery. So challenging it was, that he felt he would go mad. Given his young age, this scared him, and he stopped.

The time he stopped developing himself, is the time his mother became more of a nuisance in his life, and things pretty much went downhill for him from there. His refusal to accept the traditional spiritual practices of his home-town (because the Bible had portrayed those things as "evil") augmented the problems, as it prevented him from getting help. He suffered terrible sickness for years.

Eventually he was near death and preparing for his own burial, when the talk of seeking help from the elders in his village was brought up to him one last time. My father knew he would not last more than a few days anyway, so he agreed to seek help from them. He was taken to a man who enquired with all the spirits he knew, about what to do to save my father's life. Only two of the man's spirits said they could help. In return, they asked for three simple things:

- Two bars of soap
- One 5 cent coin (a coin not worth anything, even to the poor)

They did not ask for any money, they did not ask for any ritual sacrifice of an animal, and they did not ask for libation to be poured for them. They asked just for those three items, and only because they needed to use them to cure my father. The items were brought to them, and after saying some prayers for him, the process was complete. He had been skinny to the bone for months, but immediately saw all his flesh return to him the instant they finished saying the prayers. As easily as that, he had been saved from death, and his mother's third, of several, ill-fated major attempts on his life was thwarted.

Her ceaseless attempts on mine and my father's life were due to the fact that my father was not an ordinary human being. His purpose on this Earth was a very serious threat to demonic forces, and the devils knew that his bloodline also, would constitute a severe problem for them. The devil tried to kill my parents and wipe out my father's bloodline so that the devil's grander plans would not go undisturbed, but **he has failed**. It is not the devil who has gifted us with life, nor has he sacrificed his own begotten son for us. It is not he who has sanctioned our presence on this Earth, so it is not he who will ever remove us from it.

I follow in the footsteps of no man. I set my own.

Bibliography

100huntley. (2009, 02 10). *African American History: Joel Freeman 1/3* . Retrieved from Youtube.com: https://www.youtube.com/watch?v=McOhv3MSKqs

100huntley. (2009, 02 10). *African American History: Joel Freeman 2/3* . Retrieved from Youtube.com: https://www.youtube.com/watch?v=1V7hgEyeW6c

100huntley. (2009, 02 10). *African American History: Joel Freeman 3/3* . Retrieved from Youtube.com: https://www.youtube.com/watch?v=Uph9a-FZK3g

A Moore. (2014, 09 19). *10 Images of Europeans Praying to Black Madonna and Black Jesus*. Retrieved from Atlantablackstar.com: http://atlantablackstar.com/2014/09/19/10-images-of-europeans-praying-to-black-madonna-and-black-jesus/

AAP. (2015, 05 24). *'Victims weren't made a priority': Convicted priest reveals Catholic Church leaders 'buried their heads in the sand' over abuse of children and should have put clergy like himself last and victims first*. Retrieved from Dailymail.co.uk: http://www.dailymail.co.uk/news/article-3094903/Priest-claims-Catholic-Church-protects-sex-offending-clergymen.html

Abbot, J., Armstrong, J. S., Bolt, A., Carter, R., Darwall, R., Delingpole, J., . . . Moran, A. (2010). *Climate Change: The Facts*. Stockade Books.

Acts17Apologetics. (2014, 03 30). *50 Reasons Muhammad Was Not a Prophet (in Under Five Minutes)* . Retrieved from Youtube.com: https://www.youtube.com/watch?v=4Q3f15NXrLI

Admirath. (2012, 07 1). *What Many Kids Saw at Toronto's Pride Parade 2012*. Retrieved from Blogwrath.com: http://www.blogwrath.com/gay-issues/what-many-kids-saw-at-torontos-pride-parade-2012/3103/

AIDS ACTION COMMITTEE. (2005). *Little Black Book: V 2.0 Queer in the 21st Century*.

Akbari, D., & Tetreault, P. (2014). *Honor Killing: A Professional's Guide to Sexual Relations and Ghayra Violence from the Islamic Sources*. Authorhouse.

Alexis, J. E. (2014). Aleister Crowley, Rosaleen Norton, Harry Hay, and the Gay Movement (Part 1). *Veterans Today*.

Al-Khattab, H., & Al-Khattab , N. (2012). *English Translation of Musnad Imam Ahmad Bin Hanbal Volume 1 to 3*. DAR-US-SALAM.

Allen, L. (Director). (2006). *The Case for a Creator: A Journalist Investigates Scientific Evidence That Points Toward God* [Motion Picture].

al-Nasā'ī, A. (2007). *English Translation of Sunan An-Nasa'i (6 Books)*. Darussalam .

Alston, S. (Director). (2004). *Return to Glory: The Powerful Stirring of the Black Man* [Motion Picture].

American Museum of Natural History. (2011, 03 15). *2011 Isaac Asimov Memorial Debate: The Theory of Everything*. Retrieved from Youtube.com: https://www.youtube.com/watch?v=lYeN66CSQhg

Asara, J. M., Schweitzer, M. H., Freimark, L. M., Phillips, M., & Cantly, L. C. (2007). Protein Sequences from Mastodon and Tyrannosaurus Rex Revealed by Mass Spectrometry. *Journal Science*.

At-Tirmidhi, M. i. (2007). *Jami At-Tirmidhi Volume 1 to 6*. DARUSSALAM.

Bailey , J. M., & Pillard , R. C. (1991). A genetic study of male sexual orientation. *Archives of general psychiatry*.

Barnes, T. (2011). *Constantine: Dynasty, Religion and Power in the Later Roman Empire*. Wiley-Blackwell.

Barnett, A. (2003, 08 17). *Vatican told bishops to cover up sex abuse*. Retrieved from Theguardian.com: http://www.theguardian.com/world/2003/aug/17/religion.childprotection

Batty, D. (2004, 07 30). *Sex changes are not effective, say researchers* . Retrieved from Theguardian.com: http://www.theguardian.com/society/2004/jul/30/health.mentalhealth

Bauval, R. (2011). *Black Genesis: The Prehistoric Origins of Ancient Egypt*. Bear & Company.

Bearman , P. S., & Brueckner, H. (2002). Opposite-sex twins and adolescent same-sex . *American Journal of Sociology*.

Behe, M. J. (2006). *Darwin's Black Box: The Biochemical Challenge to Evolution*. Free Press.

Benscoter, D. (2013). *Shoes of a Servant: My Unconditional Devotion to A Lie*. Lucky Bat Books.

Berger, L. R. (2000). *In the Footsteps of Eve: The Mystery of Human Origins*. National Geographic.

Berger, L. R. (2002). *The Official Field Guide to the Cradle of Humankind: Sterkfontein, Swartkrans, Kromdraai and Environs World Heritage Site*. Struik Publishers .

Berger, L. R., Churchill, S. E., De klerk, B., & Quinn, R. L. (2008). Small-Bodied Humans from Palau, Micronesia. *PLoS ONE*.

Bermas, J. (Director). (2010). *Invisible Empire: A New World Order Defined* [Motion Picture].

BirtherReportDotCom. (2013, 04 28). *Activist Admits True Purpose Of Battle Is To Destroy Marriage*. Retrieved from Youtube: https://www.youtube.com/watch?v=tmGBtTZUna0

Bjerknes, C. J. (2002). *Albert Einstein: The Incorrigible Plagiarist*. Xtx Inc.

Black history of Egypt. (2013, 10 01). *The Pope praying to a Black Jesus and mary* . Retrieved from Youtube.com: https://www.youtube.com/watch?v=DZe4N6VtOtE

Bowden, M. (1982). *Rise of the Evolution Fraud*. Master Books.

Bradford, P. V., & Blume , H. (1992). *Ota Benga: The Pygmy in the Zoo*. St Martins Pr.

Brinkmann, S. (2004). *The Kinsey Corruption: An Exposé On The Most Influential "Scientist" Of Our Time*. Ascension Press .

Britt, R. R. (2005, 10 10). *Dark Matter: Invisible, Mysterious and Perhaps Nonexistent*. Retrieved from Space.com: http://www.space.com/1662-dark-matter-invisible-mysterious-nonexistent.html

Brown, L. (2015, 01 23). *Adults Raised by Gay Couples Speak Out Against Gay 'Marriage' in Federal Court*. Retrieved from Cnsnews.com: http://cnsnews.com/news/article/lauretta-brown/adults-raised-gay-couples-speak-out-against-gay-marriage-federal-court

Brzezinski, Z. (1971). *Between Two Ages: America's Role in the Technetronic Era*. Penguin Books.

Bukhari, I. A. (2012). *Complete Sahih Bukhari.English Translation Complete 9 Volumes*.

Came, D. (2011, 10 22). *Richard Dawkins's refusal to debate is cynical and anti-intellectualist.* Retrieved from Thegaurdian.com: http://www.theguardian.com/commentisfree/belief/2011/oct/22/richard-dawkins-refusal-debate-william-lane-craig

Camenker, B. (2012, June). *What Same Sex Marriage Has Done to Massachusetts.* Retrieved from Massresistance.org: http://www.massresistance.org/docs/marriage/effects_of_ssm_2012/SSM_Mass_2012.pdf

Camp, J. B. (2009). *Odyssey of a Derelict Gunslinger: A Saga of Exposing TV Preachers, Corrupt Politicians, Right-Wing Lunatics...and Me.* BookSurge Publishing.

Carson, B., & Carson, A. (2013). *America the Beautiful: Rediscovering What Made This Nation Great.* Zondervan.

Charles, J. (2013, 07 12). *8 Points that Will Destroy the 'Homosexual' Agenda and Debate in America.* Retrieved from Wakethechurch.org: http://wakethechurch.org/Articles/tabid/410/ID/10524/8-Points-that-Will-Destroy-the-Homosexual-Agenda-and-Debate-in-America.aspx

Choi, C. Q. (2014, 01 30). *To Date, Particle Supercollider Detects No Evidence Of Dark Matter.* Retrieved from Insidescience.org: https://www.insidescience.org/content/date-particle-supercollider-detects-no-evidence-dark-matter/1545

Christian Comedy Channel. (2015, 02 13). *Satan's Top 10 Favourite Robert Tilton Insanely Crazy Moments.* Retrieved from Youtube.com: https://www.youtube.com/watch?v=De8qahr3Rtc

Clark, C. (2015, 10 07). The Truth About Teal Swan. (J. Schab, Interviewer)

Cohen, R. (2005). *Coming Out Straight: Understanding and Healing Homosexuality.* Oakhill Press.

Coleman, J. (1992). *The Conspirator's Hierarchy: The Committee of 300.* Amer West Pub & Dist.

Crothers, S. J. (2015, 11 28). *The Black Hole, the Big Bang, and Modern Physics.* Retrieved from Sjcrothers.plasmaresources.com: http://www.sjcrothers.plasmaresources.com/

Crowley, A. (1985). *The World's Tragedy.* Falcon Press.

Dalton, R. (2008, 04 16). *Archaeology: Bones, isles and videotape.* Retrieved from Nature.com: http://www.nature.com/news/2008/160408/full/452806a.html

Dangerfield, A. (2011, 10 18). *Church HIV prayer cure claims 'cause three deaths'.* Retrieved from Bbc.com: http://www.bbc.com/news/uk-england-london-14406818

Derrickson, S. (Director). (2005). *The Exorcism of Emily Rose* [Motion Picture].

Dhejne, C., Lichtenstein, P., Boman, M., Johansson, A. L., Långström, N., & Landén, M. (2011). Long-Term Follow-Up of Transsexual Persons Undergoing Sex Reassignment Surgery: Cohort Study in Sweden. *PLoS ONE.*

Diller, R. (2012, 06 20). *School Uses Planned Parenthood Curriculum to Teach Kids Oral Sex.* Retrieved from lifenews.com: http://www.lifenews.com/2012/06/20/school-uses-planned-parenthood-curriculum-to-teach-kids-oral-sex/

Diop, C. A. (1989). *The African Origin of Civilization: Myth or Reality.* Chicago Review Press.

Doran, C. F., Faux, M. G., Gates, S. J., Hubsch, T., Iga, K. M., & Landweber, G. D. (2008). Relating Doubly-Even Error-Correcting Codes, Graphs, and Irreducible Representations of N-Extended Supersymmetry. *http://arxiv.org/abs/0806.0051.*

Drain, L., & Pulitzer, L. (2013). *Banished: Surviving My Years in the Westboro Baptist Church*. Grand Central Publishing .

Edlund , L., & Pande, R. (2002). Why Have Women Become Left-Wing? The Political Gender Gap and the Decline in Marriage. *Quarterly Journal of Economics*.

Ehrman, B. D. (2007). *Misquoting Jesus: The Story Behind Who Changed the Bible and Why.* HarperOne.

Ehrman, B. D. (2010). *Jesus Interrupted: Revealing the Hidden Contradictions in the Bible (And Why We Don't Know About Them).* HarperOne.

Ehrman, B. D. (2011). *The Orthodox Corruption of Scripture: The Effect of Early Christological Controversies on the Text of the New Testament.* Oxford University Press.

ENCA. (2013, 06 05). *KZN man claims to be Jesus Christ*. Retrieved from Enca.com: http://www.enca.com/south-africa/eshowe-man-claims-be-jesus-christ-reincarnation

Ferrell, V. (2001). *The Evolution Cruncher.* Evolution Facts, Inc.

Ferrell, V. (2006). *Science Vs. Evolution.* Evolution Facts, inc.

Fischer, J. M. (2015). *Debunking Evolution: Problems between the theory and reality*. Retrieved from Newgeology.us: http://www.newgeology.us/presentation32.html

Fitzpatrick, S. M., Nelson, G. C., & Clark, G. (2008). Small Scattered Fragments Do Not a Dwarf Make: Biological and Archaeological Data Indicate that Prehistoric Inhabitants of Palau Were Normal Sized. *PLoS ONE.*

Fleischer, A. V. (2014). *The Black Hebrews and the Black Christ.*

Frankowski, N. (Director). (2008). *Expelled: No Intelligence Allowed* [Motion Picture].

Freeman, J. (2012, 02 05). *Joel Freeman on Fox News Channel: Black History Collection & the UN (2011 & 2012)* . Retrieved from Youtube.com: https://www.youtube.com/watch?v=ufM5Oig05u4

Freeman, J. A., & Griffin, D. B. (2003). *Return to Glory: The Powerful Stirring of the Black Race.* Destiny Image Pub.

Frend, W. H. (1982). *The Early Church.* Augsburg Fortress Publishers.

Freund, K., & Watson, R. J. (1992). The proportions of heterosexual and homosexual pedophiles among sex offenders against children: an exploratory study. *Journal of sex & marital therapy.*

GBPPR2. (2011, 02 22). *Yuri Bezmenov: Psychological Warfare Subversion & Control of Western Society (Complete).* Retrieved from Youtube.com: https://www.youtube.com/watch?v=5gnpCqsXE8g

Geller, P. (2011). *Stop the Islamization of America: A Practical Guide to the Resistance.* WND Books.

Germain, S. (1990). *Prophesy To The Nations Book II.* Summit University Press.

Gillings, R. J. (1982). *Mathematics in the Time of the Pharaohs.* Dover Publications.

Gould, S. J. (1981). *The Mismeasure of Man.* W. W. Norton.

Greer, S. M. (2006). *Hidden Truth: Forbidden Knowledge.* Crossing Point.

Griffin, G. E. (1998). *The Creature from Jekyll Island : A Second Look at the Federal Reserve.* Amer Media.

GUI News Media. (2013, 03 14). *(Full Length) Stephen J. Crothers on Non-existence of Black Holes,The Failure of General Relativity.* Retrieved from Youtube.com: https://www.youtube.com/watch?v=jlNHHXaPrWA

Hagelin, R. (2014, 01 30). *Do You Know What They're Teaching Your Kids?* Retrieved from townhall.com: http://townhall.com/columnists/rebeccahagelin/2014/01/30/do-you-know-what-theyre-teaching-your-kids-n1786796/page/full

Hamann, B. (2010). *Hitler's Vienna: A Portrait of the Tyrant as a Young Man.*

Harrub, B. (Director). (2012). *What Does Science Reveal about Homosexuality* [Motion Picture].

Harrub, B., Thompson, B., & Miller, D. (2003). "This is the Way God Made Me": A Scientific Examination of Homosexuality and the "Gay Gene". *Apologetics press.*

Harshananda, S. (1982). *Hindu Gods and Goddesses.*

Hawes, J. (2011). *Ghost Files: The Collected Cases from Ghost Hunting and Seeking Spirits.*

Hazlewood, N. (2005). *The Queen's Slave Trader: John Hawkyns, Elizabeth I, and the Trafficking in Human Souls.*

Hills, S. (2012, 02 24). *'I can't be sure God DOES NOT exist': World's most notorious atheist Richard Dawkins admits he is in fact agnostic.* Retrieved from Dailymail.co.uk: http://www.dailymail.co.uk/news/article-2105834/Career-atheist-Richard-Dawkins-admits-fact-agnostic.html

Hilton-Barber , B., & Berger, L. R. (2002). Robbing the Cradle: The Official Field Guide to the Crade of Humankind. *South African Journal of Science.*

Hitler, A. (1939). *Mein Kampf: Complete and Unabridged.*

Hochschild, A. (King Leopold's Ghost: A Story of Greed, Terror, and Heroism in Colonial Africa). *1998.*

Incredible Find, Credibility Questioned. (2010, 02 22). Retrieved from abc.net.au: http://www.abc.net.au/mediawatch/transcripts/s2827115.htm

INSIDE EDITION Investigates TV Ministers' Lifestyles. (2011, 05 24). Retrieved from Insideedition.com: http://www.insideedition.com/investigative/2502-inside-edition-investigates-tv-ministers-lifestyles

Iserbyt, C. (1999). *The Deliberate Dumbing Down of America.*

Ishaq, I., & Guillaume, A. (2002). *The Life of Muhammad.* Oxford University Press.

James, G. G. (2013). *Stolen Legacy.* CreateSpace.

Jay, K. (1979). *The gay report: Lesbians and gay men speak out about sexual experiences and lifestyles.* Summit Books.

Jones, A. (Director). (2009). *Fall of the Republic* [Motion Picture].

Jones, O. (2015). *The Establishment: And how they get away with it.* Penguin .

Jungers, W. (2010, 02 22). *RE: Query from ABC TV (Australia) in relation to Lee Berger/Palau documentary.* Retrieved from abc.net.au: http://www.abc.net.au/mediawatch/transcripts/1003_jungers.pdf

Kaku, M. (2006). *Parallel Worlds: A Journey Through Creation, Higher Dimensions, and the Future of the Cosmos.* Anchor.

Kamrani, K. (2008, 04 16). *Palau, Lee Berger, and the junction between entertainment and science*. Retrieved from Anthropology.net: http://anthropology.net/2008/04/16/palau-lee-berger-and-the-junction-between-entertainment-and-science/

Kanal von BrickOutOfTheWall. (2013, 02 05). *Yusuf al-Qaradawi: Killing Of Apostates Is Essential For Islam To Survive*. Retrieved from Youtube.com: https://www.youtube.com/watch?v=huMu8ihDlVA

Kathir, I. (2006). *The Life of the Prophet Muhammad Volume 1 to 4.* GARNET PUBLISHING .

Kelsey, H. (2003). *Sir John Hawkins: Queen Elizabeth's Slave Trader.* Yale University Press.

Khan, M. M. (1995). *The Translation of the Meanings of Summarized Sahih Al-Bukhari: Arabic-English.* Kazi Pubns Inc.

Kinsey, A. C., Pomeroy, W. B., Martin, C. E., & Gebhard, P. H. (1948). *Sexual Behavior in the Human Male and Sexual Behavior in the Human Female (2 Volume Set).* W. B. Saunders.

Kirk, M., & Madsen, H. (1985). The Gay Agenda. *Christopher Street.*

Kirk, M., & Madsen, h. (1987). The Overhauling of Straight America. *Guide.*

Kirk, M., & Madsen, H. (1989). *After the Ball: How America Will Conquer Its Fear and Hatred of Gays in the 90's.* Doubleday.

Layton, D. (1999). *Seductive Poison: A Jonestown Survivor's Story of Life and Death in the People's Temple.* Anchor.

Leslie, K. (2015). Ontario's new sex ed curriculum will teach consent in Grade 2. *The Canadian Press.*

Lifton, R. J. (2000). *Destroying the World to Save It: Aum Shinrikyo, Apocalyptic Violence, and the New Global Terrorism.* Picador.

Lopez, D. S. (2001). *The Story of Buddhism: A Concise Guide to Its History & Teachings.* Harper San Francisco.

Lowe, J. B. (2002). *The American Directory Of Certified: Uncle Toms.* Lushena Books.

Lubenow, M. (2010, 08 11). *The Problem with Australopithecus sediba*. Retrieved from answersingenesis.org: https://answersingenesis.org/human-evolution/australopithecus-sediba/the-problem-with-australopithecus-sediba/

Machon, A. (2005). *Spies, Lies and Whistleblowers: MI5, MI6 And the Shayler Affair.* Book Guild Ltd.

Marsh, I. (Director). (2008, 02 02). *Mystery Skulls of Palau* [Motion Picture].

McBrien, R. P. (2008). *The Church: The Evolution of Catholicism.* HarperOne.

McHugh, P. (2014, 06 12). *Transgender Surgery Isn't the Solution*. Retrieved from Wsj.com: http://www.wsj.com/articles/paul-mchugh-transgender-surgery-isnt-the-solution-1402615120

McKie, R. (2015, 10 26). *Scientist who found new human species accused of playing fast and loose with the truth*. Retrieved from Theguardian.com: https://www.theguardian.com/science/2015/oct/25/discovery-human-species-accused-of-rushing-errors

Merali, Z. (2014, 01 24). *Stephen Hawking: 'There are no black holes': Notion of an 'event horizon', from which nothing can escape, is incompatible with quantum theory, physicist claims.* Retrieved from Nature.com: http://www.nature.com/news/stephen-hawking-there-are-no-black-holes-1.14583?wafflebotCursorId=1390650685363202:0:0

Mersini-Houghton, L. (2014). Backreaction of Hawking radiation on a gravitationally collapsing star I: Black holes? *Physics Letters B.*

Meyer, S. C. (2013). *Darwin's Doubt: The Explosive Origin of Animal Life and the Case for Intelligent Design.* HarperOne.

Miller, R. (1987). *Bare-Faced Messiah: The True Story of L. Ron Hubbard.* Michael Joseph Ltd.

Moody, R. (1975). *Life After Life.* Mockingbird Books.

mrbigfun. (2012, 02 26). *Crazy Christians 7 - The amazing Mike Murdock .* Retrieved from Youtube.com: https://www.youtube.com/watch?v=kWVITd4_d0M

Muehlenberg, B. (2013, 10 04). *The consequences of homosexual marriage.* Retrieved from Youtube.com: https://www.youtube.com/watch?v=afDZPivGIo4

Muhammad, S. I. (2000). *Men of Madina: Kitab at-Tabaqat al-Kabir Volume 2.* Ta-Ha Publishers Ltd.

Muslim, A.-H., & Al-Khattab, N. (2007). *Sahih Muslim Volume 1 to 7.* Dar-us-Salam Publications Inc.

Nelson, R. W. (2009). *Darwin, Then and Now: The Most Amazing Story in the History of Science.* iUniverse.

Nicolosi, J. (1997). *Reparative Therapy of Male Homosexuality: A New Clinical Approach.* Jason Aronson, Inc.

Nicolosi, J., & Nicolosi, L. A. (2002). *A Parent's Guide to Preventing Homosexuality.* IVP Books.

noradicalgayagenda. (2013, 04 03). *Gay science is all fake, how gays control psychology.* Retrieved from Youtube.com: https://www.youtube.com/watch?v=7NyX5CxGraE

O'Leary, D. (2014). The syndemic of AIDS and STDS among MSM. *The Linacre Quarterly.*

Ontario's Radical Sex Ed Curriculum. (n.d.). Retrieved from Campaignlifecoalition.com: http://www.campaignlifecoalition.com/index.php?p=Sex_Ed_Curriculum

Owen, I., & Sparrow, M. (1977). *Conjuring Up Philip: An Adventure in Psychokinesis.* Pocket.

Parnia, S., Spearpoint, k., de Vos, G., Fenwick, P., Goldberg, D., Yang, J., . . . Schoenfeld, E. R. (2014). AWARE —AWAreness during REsuscitation—A prospective study. *Resuscitation.*

Pearce, S. (2015, 11 09). *New Age Bullshit Generator.* Retrieved from sebpearce.com: http://sebpearce.com/bullshit/

Perkins, J. (2005). *Confessions of an Economic Hit Man.* Plume.

Perkins, R., & Jackson, F. (1997). *Cosmic Suicide: The Tragedy and Transcendence of Heaven's gate.* Pentaradial Press.

Pitjeng, R. (2014, 09 18). *TB Joshua hit by bribery claims: The preacher has been accused of trying to bribe an entire television crew.* Retrieved from Ewn.co.za: http://ewn.co.za/2014/09/18/TB-Joshua-hit-by-bribery-claims#comment-1594690706

Poonawala, I. K. (1990). *The History of al-Tabari Vol. 9: The Last Years of the Prophet: The Formation of the State A.D. 630-632/A.H. 8-11 (SUNY series in Near Eastern Studies).* State University of New York Press.

Proud , L., Wilson , C., & Hufford, D. (2009). *Dark Intrusions: An Investigation into the Paranormal Nature of Sleep Paralysis Experiences.* Anomalist Books.

Prove All Things..... (2014, 03 20). *Kenneth Copeland "God is the Biggest Failure in the Bible".* Retrieved from Youtube.com: https://www.youtube.com/watch?v=sBzgbanAVVs

Puri, B. K., & Sigh, I. (1996). The successful treatment of a gender dysphoric patient with pimozide. *The Australian and New Zealand Journal of Psychiatry.*

Qadhi, H. A. (2008). *Sunan Abu Dawud Arabic - English Volume 1 to 5.* Darussalam.

Randles, J., & Hough, P. (2001). *Psychic Detectives: The Mysterious Use of Paranormal Phenomena in Solving True Crimes.* Reader's Digest Association .

Regnerus, M. (2012). How different are the adult children of parents who have same-sex relationships? Findings from the New Family Structures Study. *Social Science Research.*

Reilly, R. R. (2014). *Making Gay Okay: How Rationalizing Homosexual Behavior Is Changing Everything.* Ignatius Press.

Reisman, J. (2010). *Sexual Sabotage: How One Mad Scientist Unleashed a Plague of Corruption and Contagion on America.* WND Books.

Reisman, J. (2012). *Stolen Honor Stolen Innocence: How America was Betrayed by the Lies and Sexual Crimes of a Mad "Scientist".* New Revolution Publishers.

Rockefeller, D. (2003). *Memoirs.* Random House Trade Paperbacks.

Rosewood, J., & Walker, D. (2015). *The Waco Siege: An American Tragedy.*

rudolph323. (2015, 07 24). *Brainwashed young kid twerking at homosexual pride - disgusting.* Retrieved from Liveleak.com: http://www.liveleak.com/view?i=4fb_1437753990&comments=1

Russo, A. (Director). (2006). *America: Freedom to Fascism* [Motion Picture].

Sandford, T. G., de Graaf, R., Bijil, R. V., & Schnabel, P. (2001). Same-sex sexual behavior and psychiatric disorders: findings from the Netherlands Mental Health Survey and Incidence Study (NEMESIS). *Archives of general psychiatry.*

Savin-Williams, R. C., & Joyner, K. (2014). The dubious assessment of gay, lesbian, and heterosexual adolescents of add health. *Archives of Sexual Behavior.*

Schlafly, R. (2011). *How Einstein Ruined Physics: Motion, Symmetry, and Revolution in Science.* CreateSpace.

Schweitzer, M. H., Wittmeyer, J. L., Horner, J. R., & Toporski, J. K. (2005). Soft-Tissue Vessels and Cellular Preservation in Tyrannosaurus rex. *Journal Science.*

Schweitzer, M. H., Z. S., Avinci, R., Asara, J. M., Allen, M. A., Arce, F. T., & Horner, J. R. (2007). Analyses of Soft Tissue from Tyrannosaurus rex Suggest the Presence of Protein. *Journal Science.*

Sheldon , L. P. (2005). *The Agenda: The homosexual plan to change America.* Charisma House.

Shook, C. (1950). *The True Origin of the Book of Mormon.* COLLEGE PRESS.

Singh, D. S. (Director). (2005). *Feeding on the Dead* [Motion Picture].

Smith, T. (2011). *Thieves: One Dirty TV Pastor and the Man Who Robbed Him.* Trey Smith Books.

Smolin, L. (2006). *The Trouble With Physics: The Rise of String Theory, The Fall of a Science, and What Comes Next.* Houghton Mifflin Harcourt.

Son, H. S. (2015). *The So Called Same-Sex Marriage, Sweet But The Most Horrific Enemy: America in Crisis.* First Edition Design Publishing.

Sorba, R. (2007, 05 07). *The Studies: Debunked.* Retrieved from RyanSorba.wordpress.com: https://ryansorba.wordpress.com/2007/05/07/the-born-gay-hoax-america/

Sorba, R. (2014, 12 31). *Ryan Sorba Disucusses The Born Gay Hoax Part 1 of 2.* Retrieved from Youtube.com: https://www.youtube.com/watch?v=G2S4qM5gu_o

Sorba, R. (2014, 12 31). *Ryan Sorba Disucusses The Born Gay Hoax Part 2.* Retrieved from Youtube.com: https://www.youtube.com/watch?v=DdKjqxDnA9w

Sorba, R. (2015, 07 14). *Gay Child Molesters Caught on Tape! Hidden Cam. Explicit Content!* . Retrieved from Youtube.com: https://www.youtube.com/watch?v=gXGlawiibK8

South Africa police investigate 'snake pastor' church raid. (2015, 08 10). Retrieved from Bbc.com: http://www.bbc.com/news/world-africa-33846897

Stone, N. (Director). (1983). *Martin Luther, Heretic* [Motion Picture].

Strobel, L. (2004). *The Case for a Creator: A Journalist Investigates Scientific Evidence That Points Toward God.* Zondervan.

Stuart, W. (2012). *The Invisible College: 9.11 to Armageddon.* New Generation Publishing.

Sullins, P. (2015). Bias in Recruited Sample Research on Children with Same-Sex Parents Using the Strength and Difficulties Questionnaire (SDQ). *Journal of Scientific Research and Reports.*

Suzar. (1999). *Blacked Out Through Whitewash.* A-Kar Productions.

Tarpley, W. G. (2005). *9/11 Synthetic Terror: Made in USA.* Progressive Press.

Tarpley, W. G. (2008). *Barack H. Obama: The Unauthorized Biography.* Progressive Press.

Tarpley, W. G., & Chaitkin, A. (2004). *George Bush: The Unauthorized Biography.* Progressive Press.

tbjoshuawatch. (2013, 03 26). *Fake claims of healing HIV at SCOAN.* Retrieved from Tbjoshuawatch.wordpress.com: https://tbjoshuawatch.wordpress.com/2013/03/26/fake-claims-of-healing-hiv-at-scoan/

Thomas, A. (Director). (2001). *A Question of Miracles* [Motion Picture].

Thomas, H. (2010, 04 10). *Fossil warriors won't call a truce for Sediba.* Retrieved from theaustralian.com.au: http://www.theaustralian.com.au/news/inquirer/fossil-warriors-wont-call-a-truce-for-sediba/story-e6frg6z6-1225852020068

Tim Hayes. (2014, 12 17). *Yuri Bezmenov - KGB Defector on "Useful Idiots" and the True Face of Communism.* Retrieved from Youtube.com: https://www.youtube.com/watch?v=K4kHiUAjTvQ

Timmons, S. (1990). *The Trouble with Harry Hay: Founder of the Modern Gay Movement.* Reed Business Information, Inc.

Tomeo , M. E., Templer, D. I., Anderson , S., & Kotler , D. (2001). Comparative data of childhood and adolescence molestation in heterosexual and homosexual persons. *Archives of sexual behavior*.

TruthIsLife7. (2011, 09 12). *Scientific evidence can't justify soft tissue in fossils being millions of years old (NOVA 1 2).flv* . Retrieved from Youtube.com: https://www.youtube.com/watch?v=cVVZ-H4Xk9I

Unwin, J. D. (1934). *SEX AND CULTURE.* OXFORD UNIVERSITY PRESS.

VICE. (2012, 05 16). *Cult Leader Thinks He's Jesus (Documentary Exclusive)*. Retrieved from Youtube.com: https://www.youtube.com/watch?v=W2Cv5hZfOmk

Vltchek, A. (2015). *Exposing Lies of the Empire.* PT Badak Merah Semesta.

Warraq, I. (2015, 07 27). *Islam: Fastest Shrinking Religion in the World*. Retrieved from Jihadwatch.org: http://www.jihadwatch.org/2015/07/islam-fastest-shrinking-religion-in-the-world

Werner, C. (Director). (2009). *Evolution: The Grand Experiment Episode 1* [Motion Picture].

Werner, C. (Director). (2011). *Living Fossils Evolution: The Grand Experiment, Episode 2* [Motion Picture].

Werner, C. (2014). *Evolution: The Grand Experiment.* New Leaf Publishing Group.

Wilson, D. (2008). *Out of the Storm: The Life and Legacy of Martin Luther.* St. Martin's Press .

Windsor, R. R., & Hagahn, E. (1988). *From Babylon to Timbuktu: A History of the Ancient Black Races Including the Black Hebrews.* Windsor Golden Series.

Woodmorappe, J. (1999). *Mythology of Modern Dating Methods.* Inst for Creation Research.

Wright, P. (1987, 05 02). Smallpox vaccine 'triggered Aids virus'. *The London Times*.

ZAMMIT, V. J. (2010). *Psychic Detectives: IRREFUTABLE EVIDENCE AMOUNTING TO 'PROOF'.* Retrieved from Victorzammit.com: http://www.victorzammit.com/articles/psychicdetectives.html

Zaslavsky, C. (1999). *Africa Counts: Number and Pattern in African Cultures.* Chicago Review Press.

Zemeckis, R. (Director). (2007). *Beowulf* [Motion Picture].

Zimbabwean, Z. (2014, 09 22). *Prophet TB Joshua exposed after bribing Nigerian Journalists to 'panel beat' the church disaster story*. Retrieved from Iharare.co.zw: http://iharare.co.zw/prophet-tb-joshua-exposed-after-bribing-nigerian-journalists-to-panel-beat-the-church-disaster-story/

Printed in Great
Britain
by Amazon